Don't Let Engineering Ruin Your Life:

A Non-Technical Memoir Guide for Men of Color

in the Technical Arena

GOD BLESS! by

Dusty R. Walker, Jr.

Don't Let Engineering Ruin Your Life:
A Non-Technical Memoir Guide for Men of Color
in the Technical Arena

Copyright, 2016 by Dusty R. Walker, Jr.

Cover Art by: Keith Young

Book Design by: John Garrett

Copyediting by: K. Ceres Wright

ISBN: 978-1-4951-7200-7

Published by Conscious Systems Engineering, LLC

314 Forrest Valley Drive

Nashville, TN USA 37209

Email: info@consyseng.com

Voice: 1-314-495-2293

Printed in the United States of America

DEDICATION

As with anything, I have to give thanks and honor to God, first and foremost, because without Him, I wouldn't be here to write this manuscript. His love, guidance, and patience have brought me to this reality. I can honestly say that He is Real and He does perform miracles.

I want to give recognition and thanks to my parents, Dusty R. Walker, Sr., and Dr. Sadie H. Walker-Charlton (a published author). Your love and teachings have kept me on the path to success. Without you, I would not be the man I am today.

I cannot name everyone in this short amount of space, but to my friends, family, and acquaintances who encouraged me to keep working on this project when I didn't feel like it, I appreciate your help. I have to give a special shout-out to my Fraternity Brothers, Alan Holman and Jarvis Sheffield, because you provided the pep talks and the examples that it could be done. I want to thank Dr. Decatur B. Rogers, former Dean of the Tennessee State University College of Engineering & Technology, for his instruction and motivation to make me and my classmates the "Best and the Brightest" in this harsh corporate world. "Doc" Rogers, you pushed me hard, but prepared me for the rigors of real-world engineering. God bless you.

I wish to acknowledge and thank my children, Malcolm, Dusty III, Olivia, and Charlotte. It is because of you I work hard, and press you to do your best in everything you do. Daddy loves you.

Lastly, but definitely not least, heaps and heaps of acknowledgement, thanks, and love go to my wife, Shautel Marie Walker. She is the one who pushed me the hardest and "the mostest" to get this thing done. She believed in the topic and my ability to do it. Even in my periods of <u>massive</u> procrastination, she did not let it die on the vine. Thank you, Shautel Marie, for your love and encouragement, and for all you've done and continue to do for me and the "Fam." I love you always.

Dusty R. Walker, Jr.

31 July 2015

PREFACE

This book is part autobiographical and part self-help. I am telling my personal story while giving what I hope to be good, sound advice to those of you who may be considering engineering as a profession (having less than five years' experience in a technical field and are still fairly flexible in your career or choice of area of study), or those of you with more than 10 years' experience and need a good laugh and/or shot glass of bitterness to get your career and zest for life jumpstarted again.

I will be forthright and admit that my viewpoints are limited and somewhat biased. After all, I'm only a Black, Negro, African American male who has lived mostly in the southeastern United States. Therefore, my writings and experiences come from that perspective. I do not wish to appear chauvinistic or misogynistic, but this book is very limited in scope and would be of minimal benefit to women of color. I would also add that, unfortunately, there have been times when I have witnessed and experienced working relationships with Black women that have been more adversarial than beneficial. When I recount those experiences, it may upset some, if not all, female readers of this text. I don't expect too many women to purchase this book, but I wanted to insert that caveat.

Plainly stated, this book is for young men of color—mainly African Americans—who endeavor to become engineers, scientists, or any other sort of technologist in order to provide guidelines for navigating the pitfalls and traps of corporate America. These are events and situations that can "make or break" your career. Unfortunately, like with almost anything else we do in life, engineering has as much to do with handling people as it does with handling materials and devices. The majority of engineers and scientists in this country are White American males and for the most part, they are used to dealing with other White males and a handful of White females. This is not always the case, depending upon the industry and the region in which you work. But more often than not, you may be the only person of African descent within a five-mile radius of your design group. I hope that I can help prepare you for some of the situations you may find yourself in, and avoid some of the blunders and frustrations that I have had to deal with.

TABLE OF CONTENTS

1.0 THE BEGINNING

1.1 CHILDHOOD

I was born on June 10, 1971, in Memphis, Tennessee, at 6:07 in the morning. Not only was I an early-morning baby, I was born three weeks premature. Mama said I just couldn't wait. That seemed to be my persona from day one: "What are we waiting for? Let's do it!" Of course, over the years, I've learned to season my aggressiveness with optimistic caution and patience. But I'll discuss that later on.

I was the first-born son of Dusty Ryemorsyl Walker and Sadie Hollowell Walker. Daddy was an only child from a small community called Little River, Alabama, situated about 50 miles north of Mobile. Mama was the third child and oldest daughter out of eight children, and was raised in a part of North Memphis known as Raleigh. My mother was an educator and administrator at the elementary school level for more than 40 years in the Memphis City Schools system. My father was a jack of all trades, but spent the past 25 years or so in law enforcement and security services. The part of his profession that I can relate to the most, however, stems from his military service. Daddy was an Avionics Technician, or AT, as they were commonly called in the United States Navy. He worked on the electrical and electronic systems of different naval aircraft. This was actually a "pretty big f**king deal" (Joe Biden quote), because back then, a Black man served in the Navy as either a steward ("Mo' tea, Suh?"), a cook, or some other menial laborer. He had a combat tour of duty in 1965, in Vietnam, aboard the aircraft carrier, USS Independence (CVA-62), and he finished his career by serving in several reserve squadrons at Naval Air Station (NAS) Memphis in Millington, Tennessee, before he got out around 1990.

Ever since I can remember, Daddy exposed me to airplanes and different aspects of aviation in one form or fashion. He would bring toy airplanes by the house when he visited (my parents divorced when I was about six years old). After I had a sizable collection from his gifts as well as my own purchases, we would stage mock dogfights and aerial attacks on our opposing airbases (most notably the coffee table and Mama's sewing machine desk). When I visited my father, I sometimes spent hours on end reading and looking at all of the pictures in his Navy cruise book (WESTPAC 1965). By the time I was seven, I could identify the basic aircraft that made up the air wing of the Navy's carrier battle group.

Yes, I had developed an insatiable appetite for airplanes. Mama did her part, too. She bought me toy airliners, gliders, a "Flying Aces" toy aircraft carrier with a catapult to launch the plastic/Styrofoam F4U Corsairs, and on occasion, took me and my younger brother, Philip, to the Memphis International Airport to watch the planes take off and land. (Pity folks can't do that now.) For my seventh birthday, she bought me my first model airplane set, a McDonnell Douglas A-4 Skyhawk Navy attack jet. The kit was recommended for ages 10–12 & up. I had that thing built, painted, and decaled in less than a week! (I also got in trouble. Because I was so excited, I asked relatives at my birthday party to leave early so I could get started that night.)

It didn't exactly match the picture on the box, but it wasn't bad for a novice craftsman at such an early age. Needless to say, my skills and collection grew over time. When I graduated from high school, my bedroom had several modern and vintage aircraft hanging from the ceiling. It was beautiful.

In the neighborhood where I grew up, we could see the airport from a hill behind our house and there I would sit and watch for hours. And more than once our house was buzzed by camouflage C-130 transports of the Tennessee Air National Guard. Notice a pattern, yet? When I wasn't watching aircraft in real life, I watched war movies or weekly programs about aviation. Whether it was *Black Sheep Squadron, Midway,* or *NOVA,* if it had airplanes, I was watching it. My childhood friends can tell you about how sometimes I would take off for home in the middle of playing because a war movie or show about airplanes was coming on at a certain time. I was quite obsessed with aviation and military programs.

I recall an incident when I was in first grade at Vollentine Elementary School that involved an airplane. After school one snowy day, I waited for my mother to finish up her work—she was a third-grade teacher there at the time. Someone had brought a toy airplane to school that could fly with the yank of a cord that would spin the propeller with enough power to send it flying for a few seconds. I don't remember whose it was, but the other kids were flying it and I asked, then begged, to fly it, too. They refused, which upset me very much. So much so that the other boys started teasing me, chanting, "Dusty can't fly it!" I set off after these kids with my metallic lunchbox trying my best to lay into them, but they were too quick and too many. Mama finally pulled up, got out of the car, and got me into the front seat. I don't remember what she said, but I know she pretty much told me that I shouldn't have been that upset about people not letting me play with their toy.

This passion for aircraft was further fueled by my father sometimes taking me on base when he had reserve duty weekend. I remember three distinct events on the Navy base that forged my lifelong dream. The first one happened on a Saturday, when the entire base was humming with activity. It seemed that all of the squadrons had to fly. Both A-4 Squadrons were on the flight line, wingtip to wingtip, canopies opened to the sky, and pilots climbing aboard. One by one, those attack aircraft came to life as their turbines coughed and spun up to full idling power, belching black smoke. Then the signature waves of hot air blasted from the exhaust pipes. Twenty or more jets screamed in symphony as their pilots and ground crews conducted pre-flight and safety routines: checking flaps, ailerons, running lights, and tail rudders. A crew member gave a thumbs-up signal, and all of the canopies closed while the maintenance crews removed wheel chocks and scampered from underneath these giant warbirds. And like a well-orchestrated Tchaikovsky ballet, in two-ship formation, the planes rolled from their parking spots and taxied toward the runway. In two- and three-ship tandems, the Navy and Marine Corps jets took off, regrouped overhead, and disappeared over the horizon. Where was I? I was seated in a tow tractor not fifty yards away, front and center. I don't know how Daddy pulled it off, but he got me this view, then disappeared. Doing his job duties, I guess. Ahhh, I love the smell of JP-5 jet fuel in the morning. I don't even remember if I had hearing protection or not. Did I care? Not in the least. A free air show without the hassles of crowded bleachers or slow-moving traffic—I loved it.

The second experience was less dramatic, but was very impressive, nonetheless. One drill weekend, Daddy took me on base and I was able to sit in the cockpit of an A-4 Skyhawk being serviced in the hangar. It was late afternoon and the lights weren't turned on yet, so it was dim as my eyes scanned the instrument panel. My father was able to point out some of the more obvious buttons, switches, and levers that a young boy could comprehend. My lifelong dream was becoming more crystallized.

The third experience was when Daddy took me to my first of many Blue Angels air shows. The Blue Angels are the U.S. Navy's Flight Demonstration Team, performing at bases and airports across the country and at international air shows. At the time of my youth, they were flying A-4 Skyhawks. They currently fly the Boeing (McDonnell Douglas) F-18 Hornet. I discovered my dream: To become the first African-American Blue Angel in naval aviation history. It would keep me focused on my studies through high school.

Fortunately, the Navy didn't have to wait that long, and Commander Donnie Cochran, a graduate of Savannah State University, earned the honor. Sadly though, I don't think another aviator of color has been part of the primary flight team since Commander Cochran.

1.2 JUNIOR HIGH SCHOOL: FACE IT, YOU'RE A NERD!

I left the comforts of Alcy Elementary School after sixth grade and enrolled at Bellevue Junior High School. At the time, Bellevue was termed an "optional" school, and some of the best and brightest kids attended. Our academic rival was Snowden Junior High, and there was always a competitive spirit during athletic as well as academic events across the city to see who would win more trophies and titles for the year. Sadly, after Principal Dr. Barbara Branch left, from eighth grade on, Bellevue began busing in students from other areas and the halls were flooded with undisciplined inner-city kids. This influx led to fights, hints of gang activity, and other unsavory occurrences; on the positive side, there were more attractive girls (heh-heh), but the school was still "ghetto" as hell. The middle- to upper-middle-class bourgeois oasis was gone, and I was having a tough time adjusting. A new school, new classroom format—no more one-on-one attention from teachers—and harder courses were partly to blame. There were some other external issues going on, including a poor relationship with the man my mother married when I was eleven. But my difficulties were mostly due to the "growing pains" of teenage life.

Like most young men, I happened to "stumble" upon my father's, uh, "red light district" reading and viewing material. (Sorry, Pop, but did you really think your boys wouldn't find them?) I got a lot of reading and television time in, so by the time I was 12, I was horny as a toad. Suffice it to say, I had become distracted by the desire for girls and trying to fit in. I guess it's what most kids want to do. Peer pressure wasn't really an issue as it was just being able to have some folks to hang out with.

Well, by the end of eighth grade, my grades had taken a downturn, my attitude had gotten worse, and I think I may have even suffered a little bout of depression. When you wear glasses and have braces, you don't exactly command a photo shoot on the cover of some glamour or style magazine, nor do you have throngs of girls clamoring for your attention. Who knew? To make matters worse, at the time, a lot of kids were heavy into certain clothing and hair styles. If you were not a part of this following, you got singled out quickly. Being a single parent, my mother didn't have the money to spend on the latest and greatest polo shirts or name brand jeans. (Anybody remember "Toughs-kins?") But it wouldn't have mattered. I was teased and taunted regardless, because I was "four-eyed" and "metal-mouthed," so I don't think a pair of Jordache jeans or Nikes could've saved me. I hate to admit it, but I even contemplated suicide for a moment because I didn't have a girlfriend. It caused me to question my sexuality and even my stock value as a "man." ("Hey, you're only 13!" That doesn't matter to a teenager at the moment.) I even remember crying myself to sleep a few nights. In hindsight, it's sad to know that most of the girls I "liked" (lusted after is a more accurate term): a) Weren't on my level in terms of intel-ligence or academic proficiency, b) were not always the best-looking (Darwinism is in full effect when you're a social outcast) and I STILL got rejected, and c) If I saw some of them today, I'd most likely say, "My God! What was I thinking?"

Well, obviously, I didn't jump off the Memphis River Bridge over the Mississippi or hang myself. I was able to keep going through my love of fishing and football. I tried out for track but didn't make it. I should've tried out for football, but I didn't have the support or inspiration to attempt it. Fishing helped keep me inspired; it was an escape. (What happened to the airplanes? I'm getting to that part.)

In 1984, the popular movie, "Revenge of the Nerds," came out. It was a box office hit. It also created a social paradigm shift toward the unpopular and academically gifted. Needless to say, I was the Official Nerd of the School. Heard it every damn day. Sad part is that I was so worried about having friends or getting some pussy that I didn't even have the f**king grades to be labeled a nerd. My sixth grade teacher, Mrs. Geraldine Hunt, would've killed me! I hate the word "nerd" as much as Freedom Riders hate the word "nigger."

The lasting impact was at an awards ceremony in the school gymnasium during my ninth grade year. I do not remember the award, but we were seated on the gym floor and the seventh and eighth graders were up in the bleachers. The program droned on and on until the *pièce de résistance*: "For whatever-whatever and so-on-and-so-forth…Dusty Walker." I stood up to be recognized. Oh, I got "recognized" all right. As you can guess, it felt like I was receiving an Oscar for Best Actor, except in this case, all eyes were on me and a different kind of cheer went out. It started slowly and quietly at first, but quickly picked up steam like a fully fueled dragster. A single jeer at first…"Nerd!" Then the repetitions kicked in. "Nerd! Nerd! Nerd! Nerd! Neeeerrdd!!" Raucous laughter blended in with these chants to produce a perfect cacophony of painful insults. You quickly figure out who your true friends are when you're a social outcast. Now don't worry, I wasn't hanging with the Goth kids and smoking cigarettes, or plotting how to perform a Columbine-type attack (no disrespect to the victims of that terrible tragedy). But it made me realize to a certain degree that outside of one or two friends and immediate family, I was on my own.

That awards ceremony was one of my Moments in Life You Never Forget. I got so sick of being called a nerd that I have never used it maliciously toward anyone else. It was a moniker that would follow me to college. Them were some tough times…relatively speaking, of course. I didn't have to pick cotton, share my bed with rats and roaches, or have to walk to school "bare-footed, uphill both ways, at night, in the snow." But it was a tough, psychologically testing, character-building time. My self-image almost hit rock bottom. Before the end of the second (Spring) semester, something helped me to get my head back on straight and re-focus on doing well in school. What was it, you ask? It was the sound of thunderous waves crashing against a steel hull. The vision of the rise and fall of a gently pitching flight deck at sea. The sounds of steel-toed combat boots clacking on deck amid the growing whine of jet turbines starting up. And finally, the deafening roar and near-blinding light of afterburner plumes from an F-14 Tomcat fighter plane during a night launch. The dream of naval aviation was rekindled. On a side note, it was reassuring to know that in the Memphis City Schools system, only your high school grades are recorded on your transcript for admission to college.

I think my mother's desire for me to go to the high school up the street rather than the one whose district we lived in helped me limp out of ninth grade, also. So somehow, I was able to maintain my grades at an acceptable level to make it in. Thank God.

1.3 HIGH SCHOOL: YOU'RE STILL A NERD!

It was the summer of 1986. I had just turned 15, my mother had gotten rid of my no-account stepfather, and things looked like they were headed in the right direction. It was also the summer that the blockbuster movie, *Top Gun,* was released. The Cold War was at its height, and American patriotism was running with a full head of steam. I view these events as a blessing. Why? Because the very premise of the movie, based around the actual US Naval Fighter Weapons School—now called the Naval Strike and Air Warfare Center—was about the best fleet pilots learning how to become even better. "The best of the best." This movie helped me to develop a new-found attitude. In other words, I pulled my head out of my ass, stopped feeling sorry for myself [slowly], and started working toward my potential.

I think it should be fair to mention that it had been fewer than thirty years since the assassination of Dr. Martin Luther King, Jr., in my city of birth. The Civil Rights Movement had ended with desegregation and voting rights, but it was still fresh in the minds of Black elders. With the new economy looming, yuppie-ism (a good corporate job, home with a two-car garage, working spouse, a pet, and 2.6 kids) on the rise, and foreign and American companies growing in the country, African-Americans began earnestly slicing—and teaching my generation to slice—the American Pie. In the mid-to-late 80s, there was a surge in Black Pride, as well as the desire to succeed academically and professionally, while demanding equal treatment in all phases of American Society. I was about to enroll at Memphis Central High School, "The High School." If my memory serves me well, Central was the first high school in Memphis, and thus earned the nickname, "The High School." It was the best, or at least one of the best, school in the city for academics. Just like junior high, most of the kids from the Bellevue and Snowden schools wound up at either Central or White Station High Schools. And the competitive cycle started all over again. Amazing that you could actually come to HATE the math or debate club at another school, isn't it? But it was cool in the fact that most of my classmates were top-tier performers and it helped us all stay sharp. Our teachers were very demanding as well, and expected nothing short of our best. I am saddened at how much the present-day school systems have "dumbed down" the curricula and classroom environments.

I decided to go the math/science route because I wanted to become a fighter pilot and I also wanted to enroll in the US Naval Academy in Annapolis, Maryland. So I began the journey of selecting classes that would get me ready. As a backup, I took three years of Latin in case I decided to go to either law or medical school. All of my teachers were tough, but the toughest and my favorite was my math instructor, Mr. Richard "Rick" Yates. While most students avoided his classes like the bubonic plague, those of us who were "up to the task" and also wanted college credits had to go through him. Clean shaven and straight-laced, you'd have thought he had served in the military. Even his desk was immaculate, and from day one he would say his trademark sentence, "Notes ready!" and the lecture began. Anything less than a B would get you shamed. He would literally throw your test paper down on your desk and continue walking without so much as a look or even customary glare. And during drills or inter-classroom competitions, if you were called to the board and couldn't perform the math problem, he would threaten to fail you for the semester. It was good times, I tell ya.

As part of my competitive nature, I labeled myself "Top Gun," and would strive to make the best grades in the class. Of course, you can't be a hero without an arch nemesis, and I had several. I don't mean this in a bad way, I just mean that the title of Top Student was a tug-of-war between myself and a few folks in particular: Dana Vaughn, Hi Tao Liu (Chinese exchange student. That guy was TOUGH!), and Elizabeth Low, among several others whom I can't remember off hand. But it was a good experience and the ongoing competition kept me sharp and focused on my goal of becoming a fighter pilot.

Although I was at a premier academic high school, it was still high school, and yes, I was still a nerd. A neighborhood friend had a cousin that was a year ahead of me who relished talking bad about me. There were times when I would ride the city bus home and if he was on there, he would yell out, "Look at that nerd!" Kids would start laughing. You try to develop a tough skin at times like these. After all, I wasn't a big kid, and I knew that a physical fight wasn't going to make him or any-damn-body else like or respect me. So I just tried to ignore the taunting as best I could. Every now and then, I'd try to respond with a snippet or insult of my own, but they were usually not very successful and only garnered more abuse. I learned to just take it. Plus, I didn't want any discipline or legal issues to prevent me from making it to Annapolis.

By this time, my bedroom was filled with Navy posters, pictures, stickers, artwork, and model airplanes dogfighting from my ceiling. You could've used it as a recruiting station. My goal was set and the objectives were crystal clear. I wasn't going to let anything get in my way.

My tenure at Central wasn't all bad. I wasn't the ladies' man of my class, but I was a nice guy and well-respected and liked by my teachers and close classmates for the most part. I didn't really have a girlfriend who attended school with me. Not to say that I didn't try. I was a bit aggressive in spite of my glasses, big feet, unpopular clothing, average haircuts, and braces through most of tenth grade. But I was the Nerd of the Class of '89 and even the "ugly" girls wanted me "just as a friend." (Man, that was tight!) The few girls I did date, I met through mutual friends or cousins or at social functions, and they attended other schools in the city. I can attest that my desire to learn to drive was fueled by this distance. Because I was a good son, and didn't give my mother any trouble, I was able to drive her Cadillac from time to time to go visit and take my girlfriends to dinner or the movies. I was able to have some fun regardless of my nerdiness.

I participated in a few extracurricular activities—Latin club, math club, chess club, and the mock trial competition. Of these, mock trial was the most exciting because you actually had to try out as either an attorney or a witness and every year, a different case was presented. Mr. Yates was the coach and arranged for an attorney to visit the class to coach us or give us tips from time to time. My role was that of closing attorney. I had two or three minutes to present the closing argument and would have a baseline prepared, but depending on how the "trial" went, I would have to take notes and be able to adjust my argument as necessary. In the three years I was there, we won the city competition all three years. In my junior year, we won the state competition and won fourth place at the national competition in Dallas, Texas. From that experience, I thought I wanted to be an attorney for a while. It was one of three professions I was considering: lawyer, doctor, or engineer.

One of my regrets is that I did not try out for high school football. American football is, in my opinion, ONLY the greatest game in the world. Since elementary school, I've had a football mind. I drew football plays on my desk in third grade, and sketches of defensive formations in my notebook in Mrs. Fitzgerald's class in fifth grade. I cannot remember the exact reasons I didn't try out, but I will blame myself for letting too many people tell me I was too small or that because of my eyeglasses and braces, I shouldn't play. To this day, whether I'm coaching or not, I will tell kids that if they want to play football, they should at least try out. I've seen the biggest kids wash out and the smallest guys display the biggest heart on the field. It all comes down to desire. But I digress…

1.4 ACADEMICS

My decision to pursue engineering in college was solidified, believe it or not, at my paternal grandmother's funeral in Mobile, Alabama. I had turned 16 that summer and Grandma Sylvia had been ill the past few years I had seen her. During the last summer vacation I was with her, something told me it would be the last time I'd see her alive. Whenever Daddy brought us down to Little River, we'd spend most of the time fishing in the Alabama River. On occasion, he would arrange for us to spend a few days at the beach in Gulf Shores, Alabama, or Pensacola, Florida (where the US Naval Aviation Training Command is), fishing, swimming, and touring. We would make time to visit with old friends and relatives, but as a child after the initial greetings and small talk were done, I'd usually remove myself and find other kids to play with or a means of entertaining myself while the adults chatted. I have fond memories of chasing Grandma Sylvia's cats, chickens, and goats around the house, as well as shaking the small cherry plum tree beside the house to have fresh fruit in the mornings. This trip would be no different for me, even as a teenager. As we were getting ready to leave, I knelt beside her, took her hand in mine, and told her I loved her. She made her usual ebullient smile and responded, "I love you, too, Junior!" That Halloween weekend, she died of complications from lung and ovarian cancer. When Daddy called and told me she had passed, I was sad, but I didn't feel any type of shock or surprise. It was as if I was expecting it. My brother, Philip, however, took it pretty hard that night. As I reflect on it, my guess is that I felt that she wasn't suffering anymore. I was pretty glad about that.

My grandmother's viewing was held at a funeral home in Mobile the Saturday evening following her death. Many relatives and friends attended the funeral, some of whom I'd never met before. The funeral parlor was dimly lit, and there were maybe forty to fifty people in attendance. Her open casket was at the front of the room flanked by various floral arrangements. She wore a tan or cream-colored dress, and it appeared that she had a slight smile on her face. Even in death, she managed to not appear sad! Chairs were neatly placed in rows, with the first two reserved for family members. I sat with Philip and remember talking and joking with him. I never got emotional or shed a tear the entire evening. Not that I didn't care or wasn't saddened by her death, but it may have been attributed to the "big boys don't cry" mantra. I honestly don't know. The funeral director could've gotten her a better preacher to perform her eulogy, though. I think I could've found a "street prophet" that would've done a better job. Not only did my father have to correct him on my grandmother's name several times, but this man was jingling change in his coat pocket while he spoke, no, stammered rather, through a hastily drawn-up sermon.

When the ceremony was over, we filed into the main lobby area for a repast and visitation. After greeting a few distant relatives, I struck up a conversation with an older gentleman and I told him I wanted to be a pilot. He asked what I planned to major in and I said pre-law or something non-technical, because he immediately jumped in with, "Oh, no, you want to major in engineering! You need to study a lot of math and physics." He was very convincing. I don't know if he was an engineer himself, but he apparently knew what it took. I just remember this older white guy with glasses and balding hair at this Black woman's funeral telling me what I needed to do when I got to college. So from then on, I began searching for colleges with strong engineering programs, including the military academies and the Naval Reserve Officers Training Corps (ROTC).

At the end of my junior year, I had begun prepping for the college entrance exams, the ACT and the SAT. Between the two, the SAT was the Beast, and if you scored more than a 1000, you were in high cotton. A score of 1200 or better and you'd probably be on your way to the Ivy Leagues. I was able to score a 28 or 29 on the ACT and around an 1100 on the SAT. Either way, I was qualified for the Naval Academy in Annapolis, MD, and all of the other institutions in which I had expressed an interest. I had acquired a letter of recommendation from my local congressman, Representative Harold Ford of Memphis, for my application to Annapolis. I also took my physical activities and exercise exams for both the Army and Navy ROTC. I decided to cover all bases in case one or the other didn't work out. Finally, I went to the Naval Air Station in Millington, TN, to take my physical examination to get into the Academy.

All went well until I underwent the eye and ear exams. I had experienced problems with my Eustachian tubes since I was a child. I don't know if they were too small or always blocked, but I would always have fluid in my ears, which affected my hearing, as well as pressure equalization. I would have one-day surgeries where my ear doctor would insert these small plastic tubes into my ears to help ventilate and drain them. After junior high school, I grew tired of the surgeries and stopped having them, choosing just to pop my ears from time to time. Well, apparently your Eustachian tubes need to ventilate properly if you are going to be a pilot or a scuba diver. *I am convinced that God sometimes plays cruel jokes on his creations.* I can swim like a fish, yet I cannot go below five feet of water before the pressure on my eardrums becomes downright excruciating. As for my eyes, I have severe astigmatism and had been wearing glasses since I was eight years old. In fact, I'm legally blind without eyeglasses.

Anyway, the Navy flight surgeon came into the examination room, looked at my chart and test results, and told me in no uncertain terms, "I'm sorry. I don't think you're going to make it." Excuse me?! Do you know how long I've been training my mind and my body for this next phase of my life? I asked him a few questions and he explained to me the limits on my eyes and ears. I asked what options I had available and he told me I could ask my doctor to write the DODMERB (Department of Defense Medical Examination Review Board) and appeal for a waiver.

My regular ear doctor had been in the Navy before going into private practice and I figured if anyone would know how to get the military swayed, it would be him. Well, papers were filed, appeals sent, and when it was all said and done, DODMERB took a giant REJECT stamp and pressed it firmly against my forehead. To say that I was hurt and disappointed is an understatement. After getting the final letter, I went upstairs to my room and tore down all of my posters. I didn't tear down my model airplanes immediately, but I think I either gave them away or used them in a fireworks display the next Fourth of July weekend. I called my father to tell him what happened, then drove to his townhouse and ate butter pecan ice cream while watching television. I had no idea what I was going to do next. I had spent the past ten years dreaming of the day I'd go to flight school, earn my wings of gold, and get to fly with the best pilots (aviators) in the world. I was going to break through the glass ceiling and command my own fighter squadron. It was all laid out and carefully planned. And it all came down in a fiery heap. To this day, I have very little sympathy for young men who are perfect physical specimens and "ain't doing sh*t" with their lives. It is still a bitter pill for me to swallow. I still find myself questioning God on why I wasn't allowed to fly. Sorry, it was my vision.

1.5 REJECTED: NOW WHAT?

I was pretty down and depressed, but also realized that time was not waiting for me to keep feeling sorry for myself and that decisions had to be made on what I was going to do in the next phase of my life. During my senior year, I had applied to several universities with good engineering schools. Among them were University of Tennessee, Vanderbilt, Georgia Tech, Tuskegee, Prairie View A&M, and Tennessee State University (TSU). I also looked at Iowa State for their aeronautical engineering program, as well. I had the advantage of attending one of the premier high schools in the city (and the Mid-South, in my opinion), and the reputation helped in getting accepted. The issue I was facing was location, costs, and environment. I honestly had no idea how large a college classroom could be, but I knew I wanted to be in a supportive environment. Keep in mind I was also growing up in the days of "The Cosby Show" and "A Different World"—Positive television programming about African-Americans enjoying and enduring the Historically Black Colleges and Universities (HBCU) experience. My mother had attended LeMoyne-Owen College in Memphis, and my father spent a year or so at Tuskegee Institute (now University) in Tuskegee, AL, before joining the Navy. Some of my uncles, aunts, and neighbors had attended various HBCUs, as well, so I had a plethora of knowledge to lean on when making a decision. A key tipping point was the homecoming weekend at TSU during my senior year. One of our closest members of the church I grew up in, "Aunt" Shirley Mason, had a daughter, Sonji, who attended TSU. My cousin, Angela, (now a physician) and I traveled to Nashville to spend the weekend with Sonji. Two occurrences helped make up my mind that weekend about where to attend college.

The first occurrence happened at TSU's homecoming, when we attended the Friday night party of the Omega Psi Phi Fraternity (also known as the "Ques" or the "Bros") and the Delta Sigma Theta Sorority at the Nashville National Guard Armory. Sonji was a Delta, and was able to get us both in for free. The Omega working the door that night would later become one of my Prophytes when I pledged. In spite of the raucous events that night, including several fights and the DJ threatening to leave because the Bros hadn't paid him yet (damn Ques…), I enjoyed the atmosphere.

The second occurrence was a simple one. While we were driving to either breakfast or the homecoming football game, I asked Sonji about the engineering program at TSU. Sonji's response was pretty straightforward: "Oh! TSU got a 'hellified' engineering program!" Translation: "It's very good…" And because I trusted her as our "play cousin" and I knew she wouldn't steer me wrong, I decided to give TSU due diligence in my decision making.

Now that I had TSU and several other HBCUs on my radar screen, I started paying particular attention to what colleges showed up at Central for lunchtime and hallway visits. The recruiter from TSU gave a presentation in an open classroom. A very attractive African-American woman did an outstanding sales job for the University. I made it a point to meet her when I arrived as a freshman. But I digress.

I hadn't completely made up my mind about where to attend college yet, and going into my final semester of high school, the pressure started to mount. My mother had enrolled me in several summer and weekend pre-college programs, as well as a young black professionals preparatory Saturday program prior to senior year. Obviously, the coordinators of these programs wanted the participants to enroll at their respective institutions. Several choices to make, but which one?

With all due respect, Vanderbilt University made the best pitch with their Black Student Alliance (BSA) Weekend program. A group of minority students, myself included, were driven or flown to Nashville, TN, to spend a weekend on campus. I stayed with two engineering majors. One student was Black, the other White, both of whom were pretty cool. Another Brother on the visit bunked with us, as well. (He snored like a sonofabitch, though! Sinus problems, I'm guessing.) There were presentations, social activities, a "coming out" program for the pledgees of the Alpha Phi Alpha Fraternity chapter, and a campus step show and after-party. I also ran into several BSA members with whom I either went to junior high or high school, and in one case, a kid I played pee-wee football with. The Ques did not perform at the step show, but Bros from Fisk University and the surrounding area came that night with a neophyte that had recently crossed. And upon the Kappas making light fun of the Ques during their performance, the "Neo" made it a point to run into the midst of them and throw up the Omega sign. Needless to say, the Nupes (nickname for the Kappa Alpha Psi Fraternity members) weren't too happy with his antics. But the show was able to resume upon his exiting stage right. I met a lot of good people and pretty girls that weekend (heh heh heh). I felt pretty good with what I saw, and was confident that I could get a full scholarship to attend. Vandy ain't the cheapest school to attend, if you hadn't heard. But I still wrestled with the desire to attend a predominantly Black university. I think it was because deep down, I knew that after these next four or five years, that was it. I'd no longer be in the majority and would have to deal with being the minority on the job. I had no idea how correct I'd be, but I sensed it at 17 years old.

I'm great with faces most of the time. I can see a person one time and will remember him or her years afterward. During the BSA weekend, I was able to talk with one of the hosts, who happened to be from Memphis. I can't remember if I knew him from Bellevue or Central, or perhaps through a mutual friend or cousin. But during one of the presentations or open sessions, we had a few minutes alone and I told him about how I was grappling with making a decision. To this day, I can remember him pointing a finger toward my face and basically telling me that I needed to make a decision that was best for Dusty. Not him, not my parents, not Vanderbilt, but a decision that I could live with because I was the one going to college. After that chat, I was able to make up my mind by the time I got back home to Memphis Sunday night.

1.6 You're Going Where?!

As a person, you are going to make some decisions that are not popular or comfortable to people in your sphere of influence, namely, family members, friends, teachers, mentors, and mutual acquaintances who mean well by questioning your choices in life. They will even try to dissuade you from following through on that choice. But thank God we live in a country where, at least to a certain extent, we can act on our choices and be willing to accept the outcomes.

I made my decision to attend TSU in Nashville, TN. TSU is an HBCU that was founded in 1912 as the State Normal School for Negroes to produce teachers in the segregated South. With a student population of more than 5,000 at the time, it wasn't too small and yet wasn't too big for the type of classroom environment I was looking for. The engineering program was accredited and had introduced some quality engineers into the workforce, but because it was an HBCU, there was a stigma that the technical training was not up to par with predominately White institutions (PWI). I expected some pushback from my White instructors. After all, this was less than twenty-five years after the assassination of Dr. Martin Luther King, Jr., and de-segregation in Memphis, so why would non-Black people be expected to view anything outside of majority white schools as having a quality educational output? But I was shocked to receive pushback from people within my sphere of influence, i.e., "Colored Folk" who told me in a roundabout way, "Oh no! You don't want to go *there*!" One peer in one of the "get-ahead" programs told me that I needed to go to a large white institution so "I could grow..." I appreciated her candor, but I didn't feel like being the only spade in the deck at such an early age. Plus, I received numerous scholarships to attend TSU and felt it was as good an opportunity as any without having to come out of pocket for a four-year degree. The additional scholarships placed extra money in my pocket, as well, to buy needed supplies, sundries, and food. (Note: If you have the grades and the higher admission test scores, you can win more money to attend college! It pays to be smart!)

2.0 EDUCATION: FIVE TOUGH YEARS

2.1 FRESHMAN YEAR

I graduated from high school in May 1989, and my mother threw a nice graduation get-together for me. Several relatives, neighbors, and family friends were there, including the pretty girl I was dating at the time from North Memphis. (Hey, even nerds get lucky every now and then.) To this day I don't know how she did it, but my mother found out about a summer pre-engineering program at TSU and signed me up for it. The Engineering Concepts Institute (ECI) program was initiated at TSU by the new Dean of Engineering, Dr. Decatur B. Rogers. The purpose of the program was to prepare incoming freshmen for the rigors of the engineering courses by establishing good study habits early on, and laying the foundation for passing the advanced math and physics courses. I came to find out quickly that many African-American students were coming into college without a solid background in mathematics and science, whether or not they were technical majors. I also found out that because of this lack, many African-American college graduates were deemed unfit as technical workers in American corporate society, not having the ability to solve technical problems. Although this was widely not the case, it is a negative stereotype that had (and still has) to be overcome by African-Americans hoping to enter the workplace.

Dean Rogers spent time in the workplace (including a stint with the National Aeronautics and Space Administration), got his doctorate, and his Professional Engineer license. I also think

"Doc," as those of us in his inner circle began to call him, probably experienced his fair share of discrimination out in industry, which is why he initiated ECI, as well as several other summer and Saturday morning programs aimed at exposing minority students to engineering and science. Dr. Rogers had to deal with controversy because some of his programs were specifically tailored to African-American boys. The numbers told the story: On campus at TSU, the male to female ratio was about 1:14 when I attended. Compound that with the numbers of Black men not enrolling in two- or four-year colleges, or men being lost to mass incarcerations and violent deaths, and you've got a quiet genocide occurring. I think people understood what Dean Rogers was trying to do for the community, and they wanted him to give our young women the same amount of attention. To this end, I know that Doc was at times accused of being sexist in his tough treatment of the women in the college of engineering (CoE). But since I've been in industry for almost 20 years, I can see why he was at times harsh and unyielding on the girls as well as the guys. That will be shared in a bit.

On the Sunday Mama drove me to Nashville for ECI check-in and orientation, we arrived early (Mama was always a stickler for punctuality), and found ourselves wandering into the engineering building. We couldn't find anyone and were hovering outside the main office when Dr. Rogers came down the hall. I approached him and introduced myself, extending my hand.

"Hi. I'm Dusty Walker."

He shook my hand with both of his, "Decatur Rogers...Take

your hat off in the building, son." Talk about Old School. I think I was wearing either the TOP GUN or the NAS Willow Grove baseball cap that my father had brought me from one of his two-week-long Navy Reserve trips. Regardless, it was established then and there that the Dean had certain expectations of his students. I removed my hat. Mama told me a while later, "I knew you were in good hands when he said that to you." I was going to be part of the first ECI Class at TSU. I believe there were twenty to thirty students who participated that summer, a few more men than women, and from all over the country. Six weeks of living on campus, adjusting to dormitory life with the barracks-style showers and leaky toilets, not-so-great food in the cafeteria (The Caf, as it was affectionately called), going to classes and labs, mandatory study sessions, visiting lecturers, field trips, and learning the campus was both fun and harrowing for me. I met some cool and strange upperclassmen and campus dwellers in those few weeks, with whom I would have ongoing relationships with during the following years.

I can remember a lecture in orientation where the speaker asks you to look to your left and right, and see how many people are sitting with you. Then they stated that in a year, half of those persons would not be in school. It's a stark reality of college life, unfortunately. I also remember my father telling me, "Son, half of the people you meet in college are already crazy…And half of the other half have the POTENTIAL to be crazy. So what does that tell you?" Customary pause and blank stare from me. "Seventy-five percent of the people you meet in college are *already* crazy! Just make sure you ain't one of them!" Daddy could tell you some stories that you would never forget. And as he stated, we had a few incidents during my tenure where some folks had breakdowns and left school.

I treated ECI as my engineering Top Gun experience. Dean Rogers drilled into us a sense of pride and accountability. One of the things he taught us, which I have never forgotten, is the Five-Year Rule. During one of his first lectures to us in the engineering auditorium, he came strutting down the aisle up to the white board (which was the only one in the building at the time), and drew a timeline at the top. He gave it six hash marks, numbered them zero to five, and began speaking.

"Where you will be in five years will be determined by three things…One, the books you read." I began taking notes on this. BOOKS.

"You want to read at least one good book a month…a best-seller or a classic, or something that is constructive. A good reading habit increases your vocabulary as well as keeps you culturally aware. Two, the music you listen to. Believe it or not, the music you listen to can have an effect on your behavior and thought processes." MUSIC. Can anyone look at the advent of "gansta" rap in the 80s and what the music industry wants to label as "hip-hop" (I beg to differ) in the 90s, and not think that it has had devastating effects on the Black community? Why do you think they call it "programming"?

"Three, the People you associate with. You become what you associate with." PEOPLE. This is a known fact. That's one of the reasons Dean Rogers wanted us to room with each other and spend a lot of time together. Through group dynamics, he knew that our chances of success would be increased if we helped each other and fed off of our strengths and talents. I can't remember if he added this detail, but I always mention this to young people whom I mentor:

There are three types of people who will be in your circle of influence.

The people who can *help* you. These are people at your level and above. How does one get better at a skill or sport? By associating and working with or playing against more skilled opponents. Being around positive and ambitious peers can have long-lasting effects. Finding an older professional or classmate you respect who is willing and able to mentor you is a bonus. As I like to paraphrase a quote from the movie, Armageddon, "To be the best, you got to work with the best!"

The people who can *hurt* you. These are people who can exert negative influences on you. The old-time "peer pressure" is prevalent. The danger may not be physical, but mental. Negative attitudes, bad behavior, poor study skills, lack of work ethic—all of these things can rub off on you if you are not careful. You need to keep these types of people as far away from you as possible.

The people who don't matter. This is neither good or bad, but these are people who are in your circle of influence who are not necessarily doing anything for you—Casual acquaintances and passersby, people with whom you have the occasional conversation, but no mutual interests. You do not stand to benefit by associating with these people on a long-term basis. If you are on a path to a certain destination, spend the majority of your time with the people who can *help* you.

Obviously, you don't see this at age eighteen or nineteen, but looking back, I see what he was trying to do. Those of us in ECI were treated as the next "Best In Class" by Doc and some of the professors, not to create animosity with the other students, but to hold us to a higher standard, and hopefully inspire our classmates to rise to the occasion, as well. The graduation rate of engineers was a whopping 25 percent at TSU, and just like the real-life Top Gun school was established to train Navy fighter pilots to be better in combat in order to win and return home alive, ECI was created to increase the retention and graduation rates of TSU engineering students. Naturally, there was going to be some attrition. Some participants did not return to TSU at all, choosing to attend other schools, or citing various other reasons. Some of my classmates changed majors after the ECI program or the first or second year of school, deciding that engineering was not the right fit for them. Many have gone on to have great success in their chosen fields of endeavor. Those of us who remained made up a core group that would spend many hours together in and out of the classroom and the engineering building. We were "Doc's Kids" as he sometimes called us.

In the old cafeteria (before the new Student Union Building [SUB] was constructed), we had a particular table at which we sat, in the front. It was the Engineering Table, and with good reason was it selected. Our female compatriots would join us from time to time, but it was mostly the fellas. Engineering is still primarily a male-dominated major, and what women did enroll were not always the high-maintenance beauty queens. Not trying to be sexist, but I'm being honest. So anyhow, we sat at the front of the Caf because most of the cool folks wanted to sit at the back (it was one helluva walk from there to get refills and seconds, anyway), and we didn't mind because our objective was to get the bird's eye view of all the women coming in. Nothing with ovaries got past us without a visual scan unless we were engaged in deep conversation or focusing on our food. Shallow? Perhaps. But when you've been in a classroom full of geeky dudes since 8 a.m., you welcome the respite of smooth skin, wide hips, round backsides, and pretty faces walking by. And because I was the "Nerd" (Thank you, Big Sister Stephanie.), I didn't have to deal with Sistas beating down my door.

Freshman year was a big transition from the sheltered life of high school and living at home with parents and family around. The freshman men's dormitory was Watson Hall, a remnant from the late 50s and early 60s that rolled out the welcome mat, which included large cockroaches to help you with your luggage and singular air-conditioning units in each room that kicked out lukewarm air in the summer and sometimes hot air in the winter. The six weeks of ECI had prepared me for this, as we stayed in Boyd Hall, which housed the male athletes and they had it a little better than the regular students. An electric fan, microwave oven, small refrigerator (not allowed by the university), and a healthy supply of toilet paper were on order before I came back in late

August. We had barracks-style showers in Watson that were basically stalls with no shower curtains. Every now and then, someone would supply a curtain, but it would mysteriously disappear within two weeks' time. I found out quickly that TSU, although it was a university, was a small city within itself, and with this came a certain criminal element.

Most HBCUs don't have the luxury of a self-contained campus away from the local populace. They were usually built within the predominately Black part of town, which unfortunately meant being in or near the ghettoes, which could be pretty rough, to say the least. And because TSU was an open campus at the time, "anybody and they mama" could throw on a TSU shirt and go willy-nilly all over the place. And by open, I mean that Jefferson Street *literally* cut right through the center of campus, speeding cars and all. At Hale Hall, the upper class women's dormitory, at least one car was stolen every week from the parking lot because it was on a street that led to one of the largest housing projects in North Nashville.

Folks could get ahold of alcohol, which was not a big deal; it's college and we were young adults, right? And, of course, drugs were available if you knew whom to talk to. It's funny to me, because Mama at one time was worried that I'd "go up to Tennessee State and start drinkin' whiskey…" I guess it had a reputation for being a party school for Colored folks back in the day, and she was afraid I'd succumb to peer pressure. Well, that would not be a problem for me. Unfortunately, having several relatives on both sides who were chronic alcoholics growing up killed that curiosity at an early age. And as far as drugs were concerned, I knew not to mess with cocaine or any of the hard drugs because: a) I did my high school junior term paper on crack cocaine (Nasty stuff!), and b) My father did his share of "rolling up" when I was a child. He and his friends would "sprinkle down" on many a weekend and smoke, watch football or basketball, and play chess all day. But I can remember him looking at me one day and saying, "Now son, don't you do what you see your Daddy doing…" So to this day, I have never taken a hit off a joint. And in a twisted way, I think it was a blessing because by the time I did get to TSU, smoking weed was no big deal to me. There were plenty of days where you'd walk down the dormitory hall or go into the stairwell and you knew somebody was "blazin'" or "chiefin.'" You just went about your business and kept on moving. I wasn't one of those students who "lost they damn mind" being away from home for the first time and thinking freedom consisted of acting so wild as to get addicted to drugs, alcohol, or unsafe sex. Unfortunately, I remember one of my homeboys from Memphis a few doors down the hall had some sort of breakdown. Rumor was that he barricaded himself in his room and pretty much sat in there smoking weed all day. I was in the hallway when one of the dorm directors walked his parents to his room and forced the door open. Never saw him again or found out what became of him.

I think I got drunk in college a few times when I was up at the University of Michigan doing a summer research program, and during my junior year at TSU. The larger universities don't have the strict alcohol codes or opposite sex visitation rules around campus like most HBCUs do, so needless to say, I tried to make up for lost time in those six weeks at Ann Arbor, Michigan. My drink of choice for that summer was Boone's Farm "Wild Island" and "Country Kwencher" wines. Thank God I never got so inebriated that something terrible could've happened to me or I ended up doing something regrettable.

The criminal element was present from day one and, for the uninformed, it could hurt you in different ways. In the dormitories, they used to have the mailboxes next to the office and in plain view of the lounge area, if you want to call it that. There were always guys hanging out nearby and to the unobservant, it seemed like no big deal. But some of these cats were actually scoping to learn lock combinations so they could steal peoples' mail from home, especially if money was being sent. I fell victim myself to having my tax refund check stolen and CASHED at some local corner grocery, as well as someone stealing a post office money order my father sent me once. Them fools actually tried to cash it at the university post office and ran out when the lady working the counter recognized my name and knew they weren't me! After filing a complaint with the IRS, I began to have the ladies at the campus post office hold my mail and I would personally pick it up. When the new SUB was built, they built mailboxes in the post office itself with no area for loitering. I still wonder if someone within the dorm office lifted my letters, or if I was the victim of an external theft.

The other thing you had to watch out for was book theft, especially the first couple of weeks of school. Typically people sign up for classes and get their books in the first week of school. TSU at the time still had antiquated methods of registering people and there was always a fair share of class mix-ups, purges, incorrect classroom/building assignments, and whatnot. There would be a number of people changing classes and majors, so books would be returned to the bookstore for refunds. Now I don't know if people would get their full refunds, because you had plenty of cases where one person would buy a textbook for X amount of dollars, take it to Kinko's where a fellow classmate worked or someone had an account, get copies made for folks to buy at a fraction of the cost, and then return the book for a refund. The Middle Eastern students were notorious for this practice when I was in college. But the stealing of textbooks was a real problem at State. I knew of several people who paid part of their tuition by performing this thievery, unfortunately. So as soon as I purchased my $1,000 worth of books and supplies each semester, I employed permanent markers to mark my property. If someone did take my books, I wanted the bookstore staff to know whose book they were about to cash out. It also helped that most of the workers in the bookstore knew me by name before the end of the first month because I would always speak, intro-duce myself, and learned their names. TSU was not so big where you couldn't get to know folks in key positions. (More to come on that.) But it was a good habit not to leave your backpack or satchel unattended when it was full of valuables. Hell, that applies anywhere, but it should be emphasized to all incoming freshmen.

You also had to be careful walking on campus and to the lo-cal stores at night, especially if you decided to cut through Had-ley Park to Wendy's up the street. Very little lighting was around and sad to say, our campus security wasn't exactly "Top Flight" (reference to the "Friday" movies) back in those days. There were a few incidents of students being robbed when walking off campus, unfortunately. Coming from humble beginnings myself, I had average clothes and shoes. Because I looked at passing my courses as mental combat (taking a line from a Public Enemy song, it was the "Intellectual Vietnam"), I treated it as such by wearing my fair share of camouflage pants, headscarf or boonie hat, and an infantryman's jacket. I don't know if folks thought I was weird, crazy as a loon, or a covert Black militant, but in any case, I was never messed with. I firmly believe that an unassuming appearance will garner less attention rather than sporting the finest threads, especially when you're around a bunch of starving college students and low-income locals who may resent your appearance of wealth. Ask how many students down at Morehouse and the Atlanta University Center would agree with me on this after multiple incidents of armed robberies between their campuses. You had to travel with a certain measure of caution and street sense. I can say with absolute certainty that God was with me on those lonely nights when I was walking back and forth from the study rooms to the dormitory. Not a *single* incident, by His Grace.

The predators that lurked on campus were not just robbers, sexual aggressors, or deviants. Young women AND men had to beware of being taken unfair advantage of by older students or outsiders who were after an easy mark to either sexually dominate or add as a notch to their belts. That's a given. The other dangers I speak of concern matters of religion and spirituality.

I was raised Christian, Missionary Baptist to be specific. Mama had us in church every week for Sunday school and main worship service at Springhill M.B. Church in North Memphis (known as the "Raleigh" area.). I consider myself a good person and a spiritual person. Everyone around me was raised in the Christian religion in one form or fashion, so although I was aware of people having different religions, I never really encountered persons who believed differently until I travelled away from home.

TSU had a sizeable Muslim community, as well as varying denominations of Christianity and other faiths of Asian and African origin. Being on a college campus exposes you to differing thoughts, beliefs, and practices, which is not necessarily a bad thing. I think every young person who goes to an institution of higher learning should be exposed to things to educate and broaden their horizons. But I would caution that a newcomer know the difference between a person honestly proselytizing ("witnessing" as the Old Folks would say) and someone recruiting for headcount for their cult or religious order.

From my experience, I almost converted to Islam. It was the late 80s, Black Pride was at its azimuth, and Islam had been promoted as the "Black Man's True Religion." And why not? A predominately Black environment with a philosophy that taught pride, confidence, and righteous living for Black men? Sounds good. But the issue was that the Muslim men I met in the TSU library one evening took *one* obscure verse from the Holy Bible and used that as a means to state that Christianity was false and that I was meant to be a Muslim. Well, I had never had my spiri-

tual beliefs directly challenged before. I didn't know how to defend and respond to sincere or malicious inquiry from someone
who believed differently, so I was easily swayed into embracing
what was being offered. My conversion only lasted a few days
in that I didn't feel a peace within on what I was about to do,
and secondly, Mama called me up one night and in no uncertain
terms said, "BOY!! I didn't send you up there to become a Muslim!" I returned, so to speak, to my original beliefs.

The Muslims were not the only ones actively recruiting on
the Yard. There was a Pan-African group that appeared to be a
mix of Judaism, Rastafarianism, and God-knows-what, and I did
have a problem with them after they got a hold of a couple of
young guys I knew who enrolled at TSU after me. One Brother
had enrolled in architectural engineering, was riding something
like a 3.8 grade point average (GPA) after his freshman year, and
vanished. Then one day, I was up on Jefferson Street with somebody and spotted him. There he was, sitting in front of the closest
liquor store, sporting an Afro, selling incense and trinkets, and
reading about the Black Messiah or something. I didn't have a
problem with the reading material. I had a problem with the fact
that this Brother had a full scholarship in engineering and those
cats talked him clean into dropping out of school. I think he even
changed his name. I heard his parents finally rolled up from east
Tennessee to take him back home.

Another occurrence involved a non-denominational Christian group that was actively recruiting on TSU's campus, as well
as the other local colleges and young peoples' hangouts. One
day, I ran into a guy who attended my home church at one time

with his family. Naturally, it was good to see a familiar face and he invited me to go to church with him one Sunday. I was like, "Sure, no problem!" Well, he picked me up one Sunday morning in a van, and I didn't think anything of it. There were about four or five other people in the vehicle and I greeted them. We ended up somewhere in downtown Nashville at either an auditorium or gymnasium, but it was not a traditional church building. The people who were coming in for service were of different races, which I wasn't used to, but once again, I didn't think anything of it. There was music and singing, and "holy dancing," if you will, in the seats. Okay, no big deal, I thought. I was raised Baptist, so seeing folks "get the Holy Ghost" or speaking in tongues wasn't strange to me. However, when the minister began to give his message, I was getting strange vibes. Whenever he said "Jesus" or something, the audience would cheer wildly during the service. There was air of arrogance almost; that this church was the only way to Heaven. I'm not knocking people for being excited about their faith, but it felt like they were "expected" to behave as such; it didn't seem natural or genuine. And when they asked for all visitors to stand, I was bombarded with greetings, but also a sort of "you WILL be back here next week or else" feeling.

When my former church member was driving me back to campus, he mentioned wanting to get together soon for Bible Study, but he threw in an aside to the effect of, "If you're serious about God." I told him I'd give him a call.

The events that day had left me feeling a bit odd, but I thought, "Hey, this guy knows me, and knows my church upbringing, what could it hurt?" However, many days later, my former church member was supposed to come by my room for a visit or Bible study, I cannot remember which. But I do remember that when he did arrive, he had another dude with him, which I DID think was strange. We sat down around my desk, he took his Bible, and before he started looking over verses, he starting saying things to the effect that "We're going to help get **you** right with God…" And then he proceeded to quote certain verses of Scripture about becoming a Christian, which was fine, but I was puzzled at this because I had gotten baptized when I accepted Jesus Christ as my Savior when I was eight years old. But then he started painting a picture that if I didn't believe like they did and start coming to worship only with *their* congregation, I was hell bound on an express elevator with NO hope of ever getting into the Kingdom of Heaven.

Okay, well, first of all, whoever said I was *wrong* with God? Second, the fact that they were double-teaming me and trying to guilt me into thinking that my baptism at Springhill was "false and of the Devil," pretty much let me know this Brother that I thought I knew from back home now had more loose screws than Daddy's old '68 Chevrolet. His partner wasn't too far behind. I remember seeing him prowling around campus a lot. I don't think he was even enrolled, but what makes it even more evident that something was amiss with this whole situation was that after that day, I didn't go to any more worship services and kindly refused any more visits. He would pass me on campus and wouldn't speak. It was like, "You've refused our brand of Christianity so now we will have no dealings with you…" O-kay.

This group did do something that touched close to home, as

well. One of my female engineering classmates was involved with this group and apparently "invited" another female classmate to join them. The latter classmate was a mechanical engineering major from Michigan, beautiful and smart. I think I had a mild crush on her but, overall, had a genuine like for her, if you will, and we became good friends. Anyway, in summer 1993, we both were doing an internship at McDonnell Douglas Aerospace (MDA) Corporation (now Boeing) in St. Louis, Missouri. We all were housed in the same apartment complex by the MDA worksite, and her roommate was another student at TSU. I came by and visited with them once or twice, and then, she literally disappeared. Whenever I came by to visit, our classmate could only say that she hadn't seen her since she left work and didn't know where she was in the evenings. Maybe she has a new boyfriend, I thought. The summer came and went, and we rotated to our respective homes for the few days before the fall semester began. I did not see my friend until after the semester had started.

I ran into her in the SUB and inquired as to what happened to her. The usual bright smile she had quickly faded and she proceeded to tell me about her experiences with this church group in St. Louis. Apparently, they had branches across the country, and the classmate who was already a member must have made sure that she made contact with them. She would get off work and literally spend the rest of the evenings with these people. But what were supposed to be "Bible Studies or discussions" would end up being all-night hazing sessions where she would be sitting on a chair or the floor in the middle of a group of people, and they would read different verses and tell her that if she didn't follow the Bible to the letter, she was going to hell, and other such pleasantries. I'm no interrogation expert, but I know damn well that sleep deprivation and causing mental anguish are forms of torture. I don't think she mentioned any sort of physical altercations, and I don't remember how she left the group, but I could see the pain and hurt on her face as she uttered, "I don't know what to believe anymore..." as she walked away. It was the last time I had a full conversation with her, and I cannot remember if she remained at TSU or not. After that incident, I put those people in my official "cult category" and avoided most of them like the bubonic plague.

Now I want to be clear: this is by no means an act of disrespect to Islam or any other religious belief. I met a Brother from Texas who was a practicing Buddhist that I had a good relationship with during my tenure at TSU. I made friends with several other folks who had different spiritual systems, as I call them, from Islam to Christianity, and Akan to Ancient Kemetianism, I met and dialogued with a plethora of folks whose outlook on life, death, and the afterlife were as varied as snowflakes. But I wanted to mention these encounters for the aspiring engineer, or any other major, to caution them to beware the "wolves in sheep's clothing" that are coming to deceive, rob, and destroy innocent minds and souls for their own selfish motives. If you decide to change gods or spiritual practices, do it AFTER you've gotten your degree!

I am also in no means belittling my beloved TSU by discussing the issues of criminal activity that occurred there. I just want to impart to you, the Reader, some of the things that you have to watch out for, especially during your first year on campus if you've never been away from home. Regardless of where you attend college, you will have to "be harmless as doves, but wise as serpents," as Jesus said to his Disciples. I think he was saying, "Be nice, but don't be no fool!..." So the same teaching applies today in modern life.

ECI had prepped us for the rigors of college study. The basic rule for collegiate study was that for every one hour of class time, you needed to devote two hours of study time. I had established a routine of going to classes, setting aside time for group activities, eating in the Caf, and then heading off to the engineering building to study in the makeshift library/computer tutorial lab or one of the empty classrooms for the rest of the night. Sometimes I'd go to the main library to do some class-work, especially for courses outside of engineering, but all too often it was too noisy or distracting (womenfolk ever'whar, too!) if you couldn't get one of the study or conference rooms. But the engineering building was my domain; there was hardly anyone in there after the evening courses so it was nice and quiet. I'm not one of those persons who can study and concentrate with a lot of background noise. I prefer silence or, at best, classical or meditative music playing in the background. At one time, I had a copy of the master key, so I pretty much *owned* the building. And if the main doors were locked, the lower level was built in such a way that we would creep through one of the lower-level windows that never locked and climb down into one of the classrooms, run upstairs, and prop the door open for classmates coming to study later on. While friends would be off to parties or socializing in the evening, I'd be in Torrence Hall with my books and notes, even on the weekends. There was many a night that I'd be in there until midnight or 1 a.m., pack my bag, hustle back to the dormitory (more than once I'd catch glimpses of folks "creeping"—females coming out of rooms or the dorm after a conjugal visit. Hmmmm, ain't you so-and-so's girlfriend? Or, ooooweee, 'ol what's-her-name gon' be mad if she find out you runnin' round wit her! Heh heh heh.), grab a quick shower, sleep for about four hours, wake up between 4:30 and 5 a.m., prepare a cup of coffee, read the Bible for about thirty minutes, review my coursework for the day (especially on exam days), get dressed, show up at the cafeteria for breakfast when they opened, and be off to my 8 a.m. class to do it all over again. I've been an early morning person most of my life. I get more done when I'm by myself, and don't like to be around a bunch of people most of the time—less potential for trouble and confusion. Plus, I found out real quick that you got the hottest food and opportunities for seconds if you were at the Caf when it opened. After 7:30, droves of people started coming in with long lines, no guarantee of eating before your 8 or 9 a.m. class, and a definite guarantee of the Caf running out of something. I'd make up for lost sleep on Saturday and Sunday, or catch naps between classes if my schedule allowed it. There were a few classes that I was doing well in, and found myself zonking out during the lectures. Dr. Samuchin's graphics class was especially tough because he had a very nasally voice that droned on for minutes at a time. I sat directly in front of him and still would pass out from either coming off a caffeine high or a long night of studying. I had an A average, so he didn't seem to mind. There were other classes that I'd fall asleep in, the Instructors would wake me up with a question, I'd process it, give the correct answer, then give them an irritated look for waking me from a sound slumber, and drift right back off to sleep for a while longer.

Another issue was that my roommate freshman year was not a technical major, but a classmate from Central. He was a nice guy and all, but his course demands were NOTHING like what I had. So there were many days when I'd come to the room and he either had friends over playing Nintendo, hanging out, or female company that he snuck in for the night. I would encourage college students to seek roommates that share similar, if not the same, course of study. I think at one time, Doc had placed his cloud of influence over the student housing office. He tried to place the engineers with each other as much as possible. Only on a case-by-case basis were special requests for roommates approved. Things have gotten much better since then. They have off-campus apartment units with four-room suites, full kitchens, and living rooms. I can honestly say these kids have got it WAY better than when I was in school. I don't know if they have upgraded the rooms of the dormitories on the main campus, but they started allowing men and women in the same building, but on different floors, when I was leaving, thus relaxing the rules on visitation, as we called it back then. Only on the weekends and between certain hours could you have female company— "Visitation." It was an Old School rule, but the dorm directors and Top Flight Security tried to enforce it as best they could. But without security cameras at each door and 24-hour monitoring, people would creep into the dormitories with regularity.

Don't get me wrong, I took time to go to a few parties, especially if they were on campus, and I never missed a home football game, of course. I'd hang out in the SUB with friends or in somebody's room for a bit to talk and play spades (TSU is a MAJOR spades-playing school. Many a student flunked out from spending all hours cutting class to make their "books." That deck of cards could be very beguiling at times.). I didn't have a car, so it was through the kindness of someone with wheels that got me off-campus to the movies or a social event in those days. I was active with the Student Government Association (SGA) my freshman year as student class representative, and involved with several engineering organizations and the honors program, as well. That spring, the SGA staged a protest and a sit-in to change the conditions of the dorms and the cafeteria. One of my regrets is that I did not participate in the sit-ins. I was afraid that I'd lose my scholarship. Looking back, I would've given the organization my full support so long as my grades didn't suffer. But my focus was on being in the top 1 percent of my class, so all other activities (and people) were secondary to me at that time. This was both good and bad. Good in that I did excel my first three years, bad in that I wish I had taken a little more time out for me. I had established a rigorous class and study routine, but should've carved out a bit more for personal time. I was also very stringent in my dealings with people. I should've been a little more relaxed, follow the rules, but not to the idealistic extreme that I did back then. I will tell any college student nowadays to maintain a balance between work and play, which also includes physical fitness. Because I spent so much time hunched over a book, I developed a chronic condition in my lower back because the cartilage in one of my vertebrae was worn away, causing extreme back pain after I graduated and started working.

One of the things that I would emphasize to engineering departments and students is *teaching* the ability to manage time, develop good study habits, and minimize stress. The profession itself is stressful enough, but it doesn't help that at the undergraduate level, many potential engineers are turned away because they are thrown into a meat grinder on day one. It's the toughest undergraduate major, and not for the faint of heart. Because of this, I had developed a certain level of arrogance toward other majors. In my mind, if you weren't in engineering or one of the other science programs, you weren't sh*t. Sorry to say that, but that's how I felt at the time. I'm sure I missed out on having a girlfriend or two (or three!) because I wasn't actively pursuing female companionship at the time, either. I was all in as far as making good grades was concerned. This included an immeasurable level of selfishness, unfortunately. What do I mean? I remember one of the upper-classmen telling me the importance of helping others out. I didn't care about that at the time. I was concerned with Dusty being Number One. There were plenty of opportunities that I could've taken 10 to 20 minutes to help a fellow classmate out with a math or technical problem, but I didn't. As far as I was concerned, if you couldn't figure it out, tight on ya'. Only the Fellas of my inner circle got more than my allotted five minutes' worth of attention. This behavior would come back to haunt me my senior year. I was a nice guy and well known among my peers, but I could've been more helpful early on. Engineering demands that students be competent in their field, but it also requires teamwork. More to come on this.

Apparently, Dean Rogers shook up the whole engineering program by some of his unorthodox methods, including the creation of the engineering entrance exam (EEE) and requiring all engineering majors to take the needed physics courses from Professor Savoy. He definitely didn't win any friends with the EEE. Supposedly, students could not be declared as engineering majors or allowed to enroll in junior (Level 300) courses until they passed the EEE. The exam comprised math and physics questions that we, as future engineers, needed to have a grasp on before moving on. The physics questions were created by Professor Savoy.

2.2 Physics

Professor Savoy was basically the Gatekeeper of the Physics Program at TSU. Although he did not have a Ph.D. in physics, he had his master's degree from Ohio State University. Man, this motherf**ker was so eccentric and thorough when it came to physics, he put the other physics professors to shame, and they had their Ph.D.! But they didn't teach with the same passion and thoroughness that Savoy did. Needless to say, his courses were the toughest because he challenged you to learn the formulas, the concepts, and how to THINK the problems through to a solution. Thus, the reason why Dean Rogers wanted his students to go through him. I quickly found out why so many students avoided this man's courses like the plague. Because I had taken a good number of math and science courses at Central High School, I was better prepared than some of my classmates and my GPA was almost a 4.0 after my first semester of freshman year. Second semester is when things started to get heavy, which included Physics I.

Physics I from Professor Donald Decorsey Savoy was the first true trial by fire of my college matriculation. He was from Columbus, Ohio. When we first saw him, we had trouble determining what his race was, because he was very fair-skinned. Not that it really mattered, but it was a point of curiosity for most of us. (He told us one day in his lab that he was "quite Black." Mystery solved.)

On the first day of class, he walked into the room, introduced himself, passed out a syllabus, looked at the first topic, opened the assigned textbook, briefly looked at the chapter title, closed the book, and started writing notes on the board while lecturing! Man, talk about a mad scramble to get paper and pencil/pen ready! Caught totally off guard, and hustling to catch up, I quickly learned his system. He had a box of colored chalk that he would employ in his example problems; different colors used to showcase the aspects of the formula or diagram for better acuity. I followed his example, purchasing colored pens and pencils to copy his notes on the board word-for-word and diagram-by-diagram. Professor Savoy would create the example problems literally off the top of his head and walk us through the problem-solving method to get the correct answer. What are the facts? What are the formulae needed? How do you set up the problem? Can other formulae be derived from the information given? What conversion factors are needed? It seemed overwhelming at first, but once you got the hang of it, it was tedious at times, but manageable.

The class started out with roughly 35 to 40 students, all clamoring for a seat. After 3 to 4 weeks, we had our first exam, and the results were not pretty. I had the "hot shot" attitude when I came into the class. Well, after he bled all over my paper, the Kid was a hell of a lot more humble. Professor Savoy would make the exam up the night before, usually 10 problems, make the copies for the class the morning of the exam, and then during the exam, he would sit and work the test out with us at the same time. To make matters worse, when we went over the exam, someone would ask a question about a problem and his response was usually, "It's simple, you take this, this, and this…you've been given this, so you know to use this, and voilà! You have the answer." We would leave the class feeling more stupid than when we went in. I did anyway.

I knew that if I wanted to pass Professor Savoy's Physics course, I had to alter my methods. I was already a studious person, but I knew that the battle had taken on a tone of unconventional warfare, and something had to be done, lest I wash out like some others. I starting following the same example that I exercised during my tenure at Central. Before school, I'd arrive early because Mr. Yates would let students hang out in his class doing homework, reading, playing chess, or having intellectual conversations and/or tomfoolery. Professor Savoy's office comprised an office space as well as a portion of one of the physics labs, with a table, chairs, and some experiment counters with stools. I started coming to his office on a regular basis to get tutored and hang out with some of the other "techno-geeks." It was a small group, but the time spent with the Master was well worth it. And it wasn't always about physics or *Star Trek: The Next Generation;* there would be debates about world affairs or campus events and departmental politics. I developed a better study habit for physics. One of his corollaries was that if you practiced at least one physics problem a night, you would pass his class. I got to the point where I'd actually have dreams of solving physics problems, literally finding the solution to a problem from the day before. At the end of the spring semester my freshman year, when it was time to take the physics I final exam, 10 of us walked in. I heard that only eight of us passed. I earned a B in that course.

I spent the following summer at school taking four classes and working as a counselor for the next group of engineering summer program participants, which included ECI. Dean Rogers arranged for me and several of my other ECI classmates to attend summer school by working as counselors and chaperones for the incoming freshmen and local fourth- through twelfth-grade students. I was very hard on the ECI students, thinking that they had to have the drive and zest for success that I did. It was unnecessary stress that I created on both sides. I was also taking Physics II and the component laboratory course, so I needed to focus. The one thing no one prepped me for was that summer courses are more accelerated because of the shorter timeframe. By the time the mid-term grades were doled out, I had an A in my other courses, and a D in Physics II.

I was sick to my stomach to say the least. I had not seen a grade that low since junior high school, and my father used to tell me, "The only D on your report card better be in your name…" I was caught between dropping the class and taking it over in the fall, or plowing ahead and trying to bring my grade up to at least a C in order to pass. We had an adjunct professor by the name of Richard Griffin who was teaching some classes and taking some graduate courses, I believe. He was an Omega and we would talk from time to time about my interest in the fraternity, as well as his experiences in Corporate America. I went to him for advice on what to do about my physics grade situation. He was at the copy machine in the main office when I told him about the grade. He looked at me and quoted a portion of the poem, *If,* by Rudyard Kipling. It's a poem that Omegas, and most, if not all, of the Black fraternities' members had to learn while undergoing their "pledge" processes. The Question was, do I keep my composure and persevere through this difficulty, or do I drop the course and re-take it at the next available time slot?

I went to my dormitory room that evening and read some Scriptures, prayed hard about what to do, and went to sleep. I awoke the next morning and decided to roll the dice and ride it out. I applied myself to working several physics problems a night, checking the answer keys, and re-working the problems that I did not get correct the first time around. I continued to spend as much time as I could hanging out in the physics lab with Dr. Savoy. It was a juggling act because I was still responsible for the ECI '90 boys and their preparatory activities. I began to show marked improvement in my quizzes and exams prior to the final. I was even able to calculate my present grade point to know what I needed on my final examination to pass the course with at least a C. At the moment of truth, I went into the classroom with a relative calm about me. I think the exam lasted about an hour and a half. When it was over, I turned in my test sheets and walked out not knowing whether I passed, but I was confident in that I did my best. I can't remember if I contacted Dr. Savoy directly to ask what my score was, or if I had to wait for my grade report to arrive at home in Memphis, but I finished summer 1990 with three As and one B (Physics II), so I had to have aced it! That was my first true trial by fire in college and I was able to recover and succeed.

2.3 SOPHOMORE YEAR

I went into my sophomore year smoking, riding a 3.625 grade point average and things couldn't be better. At that time, the economy was still fairly healthy and large companies and government entities were recruiting and hiring like crazy. I had established a reputation of being a good student and a good leader on campus. I was involved in several engineering societies and CoE activities, the TSU Honors Program, and had maintained my "edge" as far as my studies were concerned.

My campus network reached most of the key offices in the university administration and the college of engineering. I made it a point to meet people in all areas where I might need help, and in some cases, I genuinely just wanted to get to know folks and obtain a better understanding of how things were done around TSU. I also figured it was a good idea to sit with some of these folks just to pick their brains for pieces of wisdom and advice;

after all, they had to do SOMETHING good to get to their respective level of responsibility and success, right? I was so bold that I even knew the university presidents (Drs. Floyd, Cox, and Hefner), several of the vice presidents (VPs), deans, directors, department heads, and their administrative assistants. As I stated earlier, the one thing I loved about TSU was that it was a large four-year institution, but small enough to where you weren't just a student ID number to the majority of the employees, and you could go all the way to the top if you wanted to. I used to sit with Dr. Floyd and Dr. Hefner, either in their office or over lunch in the faculty cafeteria at various times, discussing either a concern I had with the university or my future plans.

One of the key offices that helped me throughout my matriculation was the career development center (CDC). This was the primary gateway where students and prospective employers were exposed to each other. Mr. Inman Otey, Ms. Tonya Davis, and Dr. William Gittens were the people in charge of the office in their respective capacities. There were office assistants who played vital roles, as well, but unfortunately their names escape me.

I learned quickly about internships and the cooperative education programs (Co-Op as they are commonly called). These are opportunities for college students to spend time actually working for a company or sometimes government entity for a prescribed period of time. Internships were usually during the two- to three-month summer break between semesters. Co-Ops were much longer, as they were performed during a semester and over the summer, so they may range from six to nine months, depending upon the employer's needs and the student's course schedule. It came down to how long the student wanted to be away from campus, as well as the employer's desire to have the employee on board. I knew several students who went on work assignments, but took a course at a local college to keep their minds sharp.

The CDC was a good resource for professional development, as well. They had materials and information sessions about entering the workplace. They talked about appearance, dress, interviewing, resume writing, and so forth. But the main purpose for me visiting the office was to sign up for interviews. They had a blue binder on one of the counters that listed upcoming employers, what major(s) they were looking for, the date(s) of the interview, and a sign-up sheet for your contact information. Every week, I would stop by the CDC to see what companies were coming to town, and if one interested me, I'd sign up for a time slot. I don't think I got any of my internships from the CDC, but I did get valuable experience interviewing and I did receive more than my fair share of offers for summertime and Co-Op opportunities.

The CDC had relationships with several large companies and for a time every semester, there would be recruiters on campus to interview students for prospective jobs. Sometimes the recruiters were TSU alumni who became regular faces on campus, especially during homecoming and the career fairs. The spring career fair was the largest one held on campus every year. The floor of the Gentry Center would be converted into a convention hall with various booths and display tables, and for one or two days, graduate schools and companies would talk to the student attendees, collect resumes, give out trinkets, and sometimes perform onsite interviews. Speaking of trinkets, I can remember on more than one occasion seeing Doc walking from booth to booth loading up bags with pens, pencils, and writing pads to give to the Saturday academy students. I know one time we asked him, "Doc, what are you doing?" He said, "I'm getting supplies for my kids…they need supplies." And he finished with his trademark "heh-heh-heh" laugh, and kept right on down the line of booths. Because of TSU's reputation for producing good minority engineers, as well as Doc's propensity for hustlin' (He was ALWAYS hitting the corporations up for support, which was a good thing.), many companies visited the engineering building and gave presentations during the day or evening—which sometimes included pizzas—and collected resumes. I didn't realize the reach of Doc's influence across the country at the time, but the man had a network that would give the Central Intelligence Agency a run for its money. My two internships came from attending the evening information sessions that the company representatives gave from Exxon Corporation and MDA. I will discuss my experiences at each of these entities in a later section.

My advice from this section is that students should be aware of ALL the learning resources on their respective college campus. Your scholarship, parents, or student loan money is paying for these services. You should at least know what's available to you so that if you are having difficulties, or are just looking for additional opportunities to grow, you can get the help you need.

2.4 Internships and What They Didn't Teach Me

Being able to work in a real industrial environment is a key asset for anyone wanting to work in engineering before graduating. It gives a young person an opportunity to see how real world problems are addressed, as well as the cultural differences that come with working in Corporate America. There are good lessons that can be gleaned from these experiences. Unfortunately, some of these lessons I learned the hard way. I was not adequately prepared for the real world and I paid a heavy price.

Let's look at the facts: You are an intern, a college-enrolled *temporary* technical worker at a business entity that is evaluating you for *potential* long-term employment. You are a young Black man (or minority, whichever qualifies you) coming from the sheltered, free-thinking collegiate environment, and going into a large, sometimes harsh, predominately Caucasian environment. You may be there because they honestly need someone with your technical skill set and level of proficiency that will bring added value to the organization. But then again, you may be there only because their human resources (HR) department has been given a directive from their Equal Employment Opportunity Commission liaison to bring in a certain number of minorities to keep a discrimination lawsuit off their books. Hard to say, but something to be cognizant of. Regardless, you are on probation and you can best beware that "they watching yo' ass" to see if you are a good fit for their organization.

2.4.1 EXXON

Oh! How I wish I was old enough to drink before going out on my first internship! It was the summer of 1991 when I accepted an offer to work for Exxon, now ExxonMobil, in Houston, Texas. At the time, Exxon was one of TSU's largest financial contributors, and we even had several alumni who were working for them and came back regularly to visit and give sales pitches about the company. I was going to be working for Exxon Pipeline Company (EPC), a subsidiary of the main company, in downtown Houston. All of the Big Oil companies had buildings in Houston and Dallas, and I came to find out that they didn't have just one apiece. EPC just happened to be in one of the older Exxon buildings, and turned out to be the red-headed stepchild of the company. The work they did was an essential function, moving oil from well to storage or processing facility, but they didn't get the glory like Corporate or Exploration did. But overall, it wasn't a bad opportunity. The pay was great for a 40-hour work week for a broke college student. Energy industries can be one of the highest paying fields. I can even remember calling Derrick Broughton, one of my classmates, over the summer and him calling me "Daddy Warbucks" when answering the call.

Back to that drinking reference I mentioned earlier. I wish I had sat down over a drink with my father before departing for Texas. He tried to teach me a few things, but it didn't register with me because I was "at the top of my game" so to speak. I was a young Black man, single, no kids, in college with a 3.5+ GPA, with several "job suitors" pursuing me at the time. I had become overconfident and borderline arrogant with what

I thought I was bringing to the table. I remember that before going down there, I was irritated because the Exxon internship coordinator didn't get my flight information to me in what I thought was an acceptable timeframe. Daddy laughed at me over the phone saying, "What you gonna do? Go down there and straighten them out? You gonna go down there and straighten them out?!" And he laughed some more, knowing full well that a young Negro boy from Tennessee was not about to have any appreciable effect whatsoever on a monolithic entity like Exxon. An entity that kicked sand in the US federal government's face during the Exxon-Valdez oil spill in 1989. But I digress.

Daddy would tell me all the time to learn the culture of an organization when going into a new work environment. Learn who everyone is—everyone has a role—but also who the key players are. Who appears to be in charge, and who is *really* in charge? Who is the go-to guy? This is the person who has intimate knowledge on how things are done, and how problems get solved within the organization. Find out who the Minister of Information is. This is the person, good or bad, happy or sad, who knows all the truths and rumors flying around the office. You don't want to be too close to this person, but you want to have a pulse on what may be going on that could affect you.

Daddy would tell me to read my trade magazines. At the time, I didn't really know what he meant. The only magazines I knew of then were National Society of Black Engineers (NSBE) monthly publications or other minority-based readings. I had no clue about the energy or petroleum industry or which publications were key resources for that field. And I don't remember trying to find out, unfortunately.

Exxon flew me down to Houston where I was picked up by one of the senior engineers in my department. He was an older white guy, probably in his mid-forties, who had been with the company for more than 10 years. We had a nice lunch at one of the better restaurants in Houston, where we were joined by another coworker, a young white girl who had been with them for a little over a year. It was a nice outing, but I wish I had known the "game" better from the outset.

In my department, there were three other Black folks whom I can remember—the secretary, an older man who worked for another group down the hallway, and a young electrical engineer (EE) from Baton Rouge who had been in the group between two to three years named Darius. The young Brother was a graduate of Southern University, an HBCU in Baton Rouge, Louisiana, and was my unofficial mentor during my time there. The engineering group comprised mostly older white males (some were definite good 'ol boys), younger white and Hispanic men, a sprinkling of white females, and the aforementioned Colored folks.

Obviously, you're the new guy and everyone is going to smile and shake your hand and tell you, "Welcome aboard!" whether they mean it or not. You have to be the judge and decide who is and isn't really happy to see a new face in the group, especially one that doesn't look like them. You're excited to be there, as well, and nervous about wanting to make a good impression and "hit the ground running." Well, ain't nothing wrong with that. But one thing I wish I had been told was that, unless you are a Co-Op on a six- or nine-month assignment, you really aren't going to get that much done in a large corporate environment. Some companies have engineering projects that run anywhere from six months to three or more years to complete. Each person or group plays a small but key role in bringing the overall project to completion. Unfortunately, a lot of companies do a poor job of utilizing their interns. What do I mean? There is a greater than 75 percent chance that when an intern is brought aboard, the receiving department has *no clue* as to what they will have them doing for the next few weeks. They usually will spend the first week or two reading departmental manuals on engineering processes, procedures, and if they're lucky, product drawings to gain some idea on what the group really does. Sometimes the intern may be given a direct mentor who has been tasked with "showing them the ropes" by allowing them to shadow them on a daily basis, learning the exciting and mundane tasks that engineers have to deal with.

I mention all this so that you won't do what I did, and demand to take on all the department's technical issues within the first week from the department head. Big mistake. I'd say take an "I'm looking forward to whatever tasks you assign me" attitude and see what happens. Otherwise "they'll show you," and give you an assignment that Einstein himself couldn't solve in three years, much less three months. I quickly learned the technical side of the house with a new block valve installation project, but the entire drawing and design release process took longer than I was aware of and I almost missed my deadline. There was a situation where a design change had come into play and I had gotten stressed out about it. I was too flustered to notice that the engineers I was doing this for were none the bit worried, because it was business as usual. Thus, learning the culture of the organization—when to scramble and when to coast—are key ingredients to having a successful internship.

I was put up in a hotel for my first week and had the responsibility of finding my own housing while working over the summer. I can't remember if they gave me an advance so I would have money to get an apartment, but Darius was cool enough to take me apartment hunting after work. I looked at two or three complexes and ended up choosing one that was on a major bus line and not too far in walking distance from grocery stores. It also happened to be in an area that was more "seedy" than I anticipated. I love my people, but being a young guy from out of town with no real support system in an apartment complex that turned out to be more on the ghetto side than the refined side left me a bit unnerved. I also made the mistake of letting the apartment salesman, and I do mean salesman, talk me into renting furniture from them instead of a credible furniture rental place in the area. But I was at a disadvantage in that I didn't have much time in the hotel without coming out of my own pocket, and this was not a cheap hotel in downtown Houston. I also didn't have any contact with other interns at Exxon in the beginning of my work program, so I didn't have the option of finding a roommate. And to be honest, at that time, I wasn't thinking about cost savings. I was thinking about the luxury of having my own place, sleeping with beautiful women, and possibly having a few folks over for get-togethers. So here I was, paying for rent, utilities, a king-sized bed, couch, coffee table, and a big-ass dining table for four with chairs, by myself. I could afford it because of the great salary I was making from EPC, but I was the only intern in that subsidiary, and didn't get to meet other Black interns or young professionals until later on.

I didn't have a car and caught the bus around 6:30 in the morning to be in downtown Houston by 8:00. It was roughly an hour to an hour-and-a-half commute each way, but by God's grace, I managed to get back and forth. I was in the 'hood and didn't know it. I should have known something was up when on my first day of moving in, I was with the Brother who sold me the apartment and I met the guy who stayed across from me. Soon after he went about his business, the leasing agent looked at me and whispered, "Whatever you do, don't lend that guy any money…" O-kay. Apparently this Brother had a track record for borrowing and not repaying. Red flag waving, but I didn't know any better. I should have looked at the lease agreement to find out if I had an early escape clause. Some rental agreements will let you cancel and get your rent money or deposit back without penalty if you decide not to stay there within the first few days or weeks. Something to keep in mind that, again, I learned the hard way. I was in the valley of the shadow of death like a lamb among wolves.

With all this going on, I should've exercised extreme frugality and focused on living moderately to save more money. I wasn't near anyone I knew, and with the exception of briefly dating one of the sisters of a young woman I met who worked for

Exxon, I never had any visitors save for Darius and his room-mate, Andrew. I didn't think to rent a television, but as usual, my ebullient personality won favor with the ladies in the apartment management office, and one of them was kind enough to drop off an old black-and-white television for me to use while I stayed there. As Daddy would say, "God takes care of babies and fools."

A major lesson I want to leave with the reader: Keep it professional, keep it professional, *keep it professional!* As the intern, you are not only the new guy (or the FNG depending on the attitude of the group; ask a military person what the "F" stands for if you don't already know), but more than likely the youngest person in the group so you have to learn the attitudes and be-haviors of the people, first of all. Second, you are no longer "on the yard" or hanging out in the Quad or SUB with your boys or homies or whatever the present-day slang is for best friends. It is a shame, but half of the carefree and fun things you could do or say back at school can be mistaken or taken as offensive or unac-ceptable. You have to make sure that you are meeting the dress code as well as their prescribed code of conduct. This includes pronunciation, joking, horseplay, flirting, work clothing, work ethic, tardiness, and any damn thing else that could be used as a strike against you. I'm not saying that you have to be a robot, but watch what you do or say to the degree that you err on the side of caution.

Don't make the mistake of discussing sensitive subjects at work, mainly sex, religion, and politics, with people you just met. You don't know their thoughts on these things. I made the fatal mistake of letting my hormones take precedence over my common sense and career aspirations. One day out at lunch, I made the observation of how most of the Hispanic women I saw while we were out were pregnant. That didn't go over too well with the Hispanic guy, Leo. Darius came by my apartment a day or so later and cautioned me on watching what I say when around the group. I really dug myself in a hole also by getting too friendly with the young white girl whom I had dinner with my first day in Houston.

One, I remember taking some pens and a drawing template from the supply room and I think I had made a comment to the effect that I could use them when I got back to school. Her immediate response was, "You'd take company property?!" I don't remember what I said, if I said anything, to answer her. But let's be real here. If I hadn't opened my mouth, she wouldn't have been none the f**king wiser whether those pens and template stayed in my desk drawer or wound up flying back to Tennessee. I was using them to accomplish my assignment and I should've left it at that.

Two, I made the *critical* error of *flirting* with her one day on the job. She was cute, no doubt, but if I had kept my ears open, I would've known in due time that she was dating some white guy down the hall, and that you don't flirt with coworkers, period. I'm lucky they didn't fire my ass for sexual harassment right there and then. I wouldn't have had any type of defense to save myself. Now after you've been with a company for a year or so and you know the lay of the land, *maybe* you can get away with some harmless jesting or a compliment or flirtation after you've been accepted. But make no mistakes, for those three months, you want to be all about the business, and get paid, too!

Well, sad to say, I received a phone call from the Black HR manager that fall to inform me that I would not be coming back to Exxon. I was sitting at my desk in my dorm room and slurping on a cup of coffee while listening to the man. I think I just accepted it and hung up without inquiring as to why I wasn't going to receive another offer. I may have been too busy focusing on the work I was doing at the time, or I may have still been in that arrogant, smart-black-man-in-college-you-can't-hold-me-down mode, so I didn't care. In either case, it wasn't until I did some deep reflections many moons later that I figured out that my personal behavior, not my technical performance, was probably the nail in the coffin as far as my Exxon experience was concerned.

2.4.2 MCDONNELL DOUGLAS AEROSPACE CORPORATION

From the previous chapters, you know that I have always had a love of aircraft, especially military aircraft. So when I had an opportunity to intern at MDA, it was a no-brainer. MDA was a premier manufacturer of tactical aircraft and weapons for the US military and international customers. Their bread and butter was Naval attack and fighter aircraft, so I was hoping for a chance to work on the F-18 Hornet, AV-8 Harrier, or T-45 Goshawk programs. Obviously, I had no clue what I was stepping into when I accepted a position with the Avionics Integration Center (AIC) in building 105 for summer of 1993. I thought I was going to be either in the hangar, out on the flight line, or in the production facility working on the planes themselves. Wrong! The AIC was basically a four-level building that was an enclosed laboratory for the testing, repair, and upgrade for all the avionics systems that the MDA aircraft used. There was very little action on the outside, and for someone who wanted to actually be around the aircraft, this was a huge mistake. But who knew? Not I. Didn't think to ask many questions, if any, about what the group did and how it supported the corporation. I was just glad to have another chance at a job.

When I interned at MDA, the average employee was age 57. What does that tell you? The company has been around for a long time, and a lot of these workers have been around for a long time. Thoughts and routines are pretty much established, and only the people at the top can cause things to change. The customer is the military and a lot of the managers and workers were former military, so it was a pretty rigid environment, to say the least. It was also the least diverse company I had ever been in. Nothing but older white guys, with a sprinkling of 20-some-things, women, Asians, and a *handful* of Negroes that included the guards, the flight controls laboratory technician, the director's secretary, somebody in purchasing, and the few engineers that included myself and one stand-offish, overly masculine Sister from Arizona or someplace. I can remember roughly twelve people of color in the building over the nearly two-year span that I would eventually spend there over my career, not including the cleaning and maintenance workers.

To say I had culture shock is an understatement. Not only was I a minority, I was non-existent. One thing you will find in the corporate world is that unless you are necessary, most folks, especially white folks, don't need you. They will walk right past you in a narrow hallway and either look down, away, or "through you" to avoid eye contact or having to speak. It can be very impersonal and downright baffling at times, but that is the culture and mindset I had stepped into. I hadn't learned how to shift gears to adapt to the cold, almost inhumane, environment that was "normal" to the majority.

I was assigned to the flight controls group in department 318, under the direction of a man who was pure authoritarian, at least from my perspective. My immediate supervisor was a very soft-spoken, mild-mannered gentleman who kind of scared me because of his extreme lack of personality. You could ask him a question and 90 percent of the time, the answer would be one word. The environment was very draconian. Each group had an open area with eight to twelve or more desks and either a shared telephone or a telephone on every other desk. I was given a desk that faced the wall, as did the others, with my supervisor sitting one desk back and over on the right side of the aisle. It took some getting used to, sitting in a row of people who are supposedly part of a team but hardly any of whom speak to each other on a daily basis, even though they are a stone's throw away from each other. And the whole thing with the supervisor sitting behind everyone to watch and make sure you are working was disconcerting, to be sure. But somehow, I guess I managed to read up on F-15 and F-18 flight control computers and their functionality. There were at least two labs in the basement where flight controls had work benches and testing stations, as well as on the third floor, where we resided.

The project I was assigned to had something to do with board-level electronics, designing a circuit (perhaps for testing?). I spent more days than not falling asleep with my head in a boring manual, which was unfortunate because I'm sure someone caught me asleep and may have said something to the people in charge. I tried befriending a few folks, but didn't realize quickly enough that you couldn't be too sociable or else you're perceived as "not working." I had a mentor assigned to me, but he was a manager over in another group in a faraway building. We would have to schedule meetings and what advice he gave me was actually pretty useless for the environment I was in. I did my best to keep a positive attitude and tough it out. If had known better, I would've gone straight to the summer intern personnel and requested a departmental transfer. But at age 21, you're under the impression that you shouldn't be moving around a company right away because it could look bad on your resume. Well, to this I say if you are in a work group as an intern and not happy with the situation, you should at least find out if you have options to move around. Better yet, ask as many questions as possible during the onsite or phone interview to determine if the opportunity would be a good fit. You can figure out how to politely ask about the demographics of the organization. (Translation: How many Negroes you got up in there? None, you say? *Hmmmmm, might have to rethink this.*) But the main thing is to learn as much about the job itself, what the company does, how your skill set can be used, what opportunities for advancement and training are available, how they treat their employees (especially how many minorities are in key positions), and whether or not the benefits are to your advantage while you are there.

The internship wasn't all bad, but it wasn't all great, either. MDA had a good internship and co-op program in place as far as bringing in students from all over the country and placing them in work departments that required their respective majors. They provided furnished housing for us in an apartment complex that was literally within view of the west side of the company complex on the other side of the I-270 highway overpass. Over the course of the summer, they would have social activities offsite, at the complex, or orientation/motivational meetings at some large auditorium at work. The HR representative responsible for you would call you from time to time to see how you were doing, as well. If you had any problems or concerns, you were supposed to contact them. The down side was that in several instances, they placed three students in two-bedroom apartments. So, like in my case, whomever was the last one to arrive on their work assignment (me) was at the mercy of the other roommates as far as sleeping arrangements. What made things worse was that these are complete strangers you suddenly have to share a bedroom and bathroom with, with no direct oversight or inclination as far as living habits or hygiene were concerned. Oh, and you had responsibility for paying the utilities, telephone, and cable.

I was rooming with two guys from Purdue, one Caucasian, the other a bi-racial Brother from Haiti, originally. The Brother was cool because he was a genuinely nice guy, devout Christian, and wanted to be a Navy pilot. Needless to say, we hit it off right away. The white guy was from a town called Hobart, Indiana, and one of my line Brothers from Gary pretty much told me it was a good chance he was prejudiced because that area had *no*

Black people near there. I had the unfortunate pleasure of bunking with him and it wasn't long before the differences in lifestyles became apparent.

I'm not trying to come off as racist, but facts are facts: *There are differences* between Black folks and White Folks, physiologically and psychologically. Something as simple as the smell of body odor and wet hair can help discern a person's racial profile. This guy would work out or do some physical activity with the other interns, come in, have dinner, and go to sleep. He would shower in the morning. The smell coming off him would make me nauseous at times, and of course, the room took on his scent because he rarely washed his sheets. I think one reason I put up with it was he had a car, and I asked him if he could give me a ride to my building, which was way over on the other side of the complex. This arrangement worked out okay until one morning I was running late getting dressed. I should've told him to go on without me, but he begrudgingly waited and dropped me off in the parking lot. He was visibly upset and as I was getting out of the car, he said that by making him late, I was ruining his credibility. I wasn't trying to discount his concerns, but I think I was trying to assure him that this one time wasn't going to get him in trouble. He responded without looking at me, "Well…I don't need your advice!" And sped off.

The arrangement was that he would call the phone I was sharing to let me know when he was coming to pick me up. This particular day, he called about 30 minutes later than usual to ask if I needed a ride to the apartment. He probably thought I would find another way home and wouldn't have to deal with me. Anyway, I went back with him that night. Over the weekend, I asked if I could get a ride either to work or somewhere, and this dude didn't even look up from the kitchen table. He said, "You can walk." Yeeeaahh. That's all I needed—an assault charge on my record for whooping some smart-assed white boy for mouthing off when it wasn't necessary. But you know what? They are good for that. Long as they don't feel threatened or find your existence necessary, they can be rude as hell, and will say whatever comes to mind because they don't think there will be any consequences.

I had to scramble, but was able to work out some arrangements with some other interns in the complex who had transportation. The Haitian Brother worked in Building 270, which was the first building on the other side of the expressway, so many a day, he would trek on the sidewalk or the median of the road to get back and forth. I finally implored the Haitian to let me share the room he was in. It turns out he had the master bedroom anyway, and it was a hell of a lot roomier. The white guy was a dick, to say the least, and I think it may have irritated him even more because the two of us got along just fine, and we were able to maneuver around him without having to interact with him unless absolutely necessary. I was upset with him to the point that I left without paying my final share of some bill that was in his name. I think I even left in the middle of the day without telling him or saying goodbye. I said to myself, "You screwed me, so I *screw* you…"

I'm not advocating this type of retaliation, but this is what I had decided to do. Fisticuffs would've only landed me in jail. And apparently our apartment wasn't the only one that had conflict. Another group of guys had some sort of disagreement and their telephone got cut off because one guy didn't see the need to pay his portion for one reason or another, so the other guy(s) either sent a partial payment or no payment at all, and the phone got turned off with only a few weeks left to go.

2.4.3 *Internship Caveats*

One of my pet peeves with intern programs is that the companies will want to bring a college student in to work for a prescribed period of time, but treat them like they are already established professionals. Nine times out of ten, the student doesn't have a car, much less a checking account, but they expect them to travel to a city that is not close to home and be able to get around with no problem.

Much has changed since my college days, especially with the advent of cellular telephones and other neat advances, but the broke college student shall be a staple of the American landscape for years to come unless the government suddenly subsidizes college education for all qualified citizens. So when you are considering a possible internship with a company away from your home or college town, make sure you inquire about transportation, such as whether there is help available from the company or public transportation nearby. Some companies even have relationships with local cab companies that provide low-cost rides to their employees or potential new hires. It's all in how you research the opportunity.

Another question to ask is if housing is provided, what are

the living arrangements? Will you have to share the unit? How many bedrooms? If you have a situation where you are sharing the actual bedroom, I'd strongly urge you to ask what other options are available. It's bad enough to have to share a shower or toilet, but to have to sleep in the same room with a complete stranger can be a challenge. Hopefully, things have advanced since 1993, but just in case, this and similar issues should be kept in mind. How are roommates assigned? Can you discreetly find out how you can be matched up with an intern of similar tastes/ demographics? Is there someone from your university going on the same work assignment you already know who you could request? Just because you're both technical students doesn't mean you're going to "just get along" like Rodney King once asked during the Los Angeles Riots of 1992.

Is the unit furnished? If so, what other amenities are provided? Television, bed and bath linens, cookware, soap/cleaning supplies, toilet paper, etc. You may have to provide many of these sundry items yourself, so it also wouldn't hurt to ask the HR representative where the nearest stores are. What will your expenses be? Sharing an apartment can be cool, but splitting a bill in half for something that you may not use is a waste of your hard-earned, money. (Example: Paying for cable but the only television is in your roommate's room.) You need to have an idea of how best to address such touchy subjects.

You're not spending the summer or six months away from home and college for free like you're on a missions project, so you need to know what and *how* you're going to be paid. Difficult to fathom, but you also need to calculate if the salary you receive will be affordable for you after taxes. Take away roughly 35 to 40 percent of your gross pay and that will be your estimated net or "take home" pay. Single folks without dependents get the hell taxed out of them. Unless you're going to be in a homeless shelter, cardboard box, or sleeping in your car, there will be upfront living costs when you start an internship. You need to be aware of the employer's pay cycle. Some companies pay monthly (once a month), but most are on a biweekly scale. That is, every two weeks, you will receive either a check or check stub for which you have the responsibility to cash at your bank or liquor/corner store, or have it direct deposited into your account. Others make payroll on the first and fifteenth day of the month regardless of calendar day. Two weeks is a long time to go without any income, especially if you have limited savings. When I was either at Exxon or MDA, I was able to ask for an advancement to be able to pay for some things that required payment up front. The second check wasn't as much because of this, but I was able to get by until I was on a regular work and pay schedule. I share this with you so you don't get caught with your pants down, many miles from home, and having to ask "Mama 'Nem" to Western Union you some loot to tide you over.

At social functions on or off the job, beware of potential snafus that could give you a bad reputation. You're a starving student, but don't make the hors d'oeuvres your main course or take the largest piece of cake at a coworker's retirement party. If the department is paying for lunch or dinner, a nice meal is acceptable, but don't order the $45 lamb chops and a $40 glass of wine, unless this has been okayed by the manager footing the bill. I made this mistake recently and got slightly chewed out by the man who hired me for some off-site freelance work. I didn't do much in the sense of lunch one day, but more than made up for it with a $50+ meal that included a $12 glass of wine. When I turned in the receipt, I got a phone call within minutes of the email. I thought that there was a daily allowance, and as long as I didn't surpass the total amount, I was okay. Apparently not. Make sure you know what the company meal allowance is, and don't give them jack-squat to complain about. If they are letting the white folks spend $40 on a meal, you spend $35, until somebody who approves the expenses is cool with you and asks why you aren't using the full amount.

Even taking a can of soda or juice mistakenly from another group's platter can have indirect repercussions, regardless if they were sitting on the table in the break room without a sign or label distinguishing them as such. You probably will already stick out like a sore thumb, so you don't want to do anything that will bring undue attention to yourself, because fortunately and *unfortunately,* people talk. When I was at Exxon, we had some treats for something and I apparently took what was deemed to be an extremely big piece of cake. Several of the white guys never let it go, making side comments at later events such as, "I think I'll grab me a Dusty-sized piece of pie," and other such things. As the Rho Psi Ques would say, you want to be "straight-laced, no chase'(er)" while around your coworkers.

Just like you've been cautioned on how much food you take at the company Christmas party, be aware of how you use the office supplies and copier/scanner. Yes, even the amount of folders, notepads, pens, and copies made of your summer school course-work can be a potential strike against you. During the first week on the job, unless they are just hurting as far as budget for supplies is concerned, you will normally get basic items like a stapler, staple remover, pens, highlighters, sticky notes, notebooks, paper clips, and whatnot. As you use these items up, there will be a supply room or closet there you can go to in order to replenish what you need. I've been some places where they actually had the room or cabinet *locked up* and you had to go to the secretary (office administrator is the new politically correct term now, I think.) for the key or they themselves went in with you to give you *exactly* what you told them you needed. Use sound judgment (you *will* see this phrase again) when getting, or pilfering, the company stockpile. I'm not saying myself or others haven't taken the extra highlighter or binder home for personal usage, but what I am saying is that you should be discreet in what you take, when you take, and how much you take. You don't want to be the one busted for taking half a pallet of copying paper out of the building because you wanted to make party flyers for your side DJ'ing gig on the weekends. In this case, *it is stealing* and a misuse of company resources. Sometimes, you have to resist the temptation of easy pickins' and buy your own stock to be on the safe side.

How you use your idle or down time can be a blessing or a curse. As I mentioned earlier, on most internships, you will spend most of your assignment just learning the ropes. Stuck behind a desk and a computer (hopefully) with a garbage assignment that a monkey could do with its eyes closed can be frustrating, to be

sure. But remember you are on their dime, and on their proba-
tionary period. So regardless of the task, unless it's dangerous or
flat out unethical or illegal, attack it with zeal. If you are reading
manuals, learn as much as you can take; find coworkers whom
you can approach and ask when would be a good time to meet
with them to have some questions answered, and don't bother
them again until the agreed-upon time. When you do meet, have
some direct and intelligent questions for them to show that you
are trying to learn their systems or products, even if you already
know damn well you have *no* intentions of coming back for a
second stint.

If you find yourself getting drowsy, especially after lunch, go
for a quick walk around the floor or outside if it's not a big deal,
or get a cup of coffee or a soda or water, or splash some cold
water on your face in the bathroom. You don't want to embarrass
yourself or your school by gaining a reputation for sleeping on
the job. If you choose to do some exploring on the job, run it past
whomever you work for—more of a courtesy than anything. And
when you do go roaming around, don't do it all in one big time
period. You don't want to be away from your work area for more
than 30 minutes just looking around or meeting new folks in
other departments; 10 or 15 minutes maximum is my suggestion.

Everyone pretty much has a cell phone nowadays, but find
out what the written and unwritten rules are as far as cellphone
usage goes. If you work for a defense agency or contractor that
produces extremely sensitive projects, sometimes cell phones
aren't even allowed, in order to protect the organization from
defense or industrial espionage. (If you are in one of these envi-

ronments, make sure you *always* follow the rules. The last thing
you need is a misunderstanding with somebody's security department!) The normal policy is to take personal calls away from
the work area. Go out into the hallway, foyer, break room, or
outside, so as not to disturb others around you. Plus, some phone
calls are personal in nature where you don't need folks knowing
your business anyway. If it's a quick business call, "Hey, this is
the cable guy, I'll be at your spot at 3:30," then you don't necessarily have to dash outside for a 30-second conversation. Just
exercise sound judgment and common sense. Let this carry over
to your usage of the desk telephone, as well. Gone may be the
days of the boot camp one-phone-shared-by-all philosophy, but
many an intern has had to give account for running up the job's
long-distance bill because they were bored and thought it a good
idea to start calling up all their boys around the country, talking
for hours at a time. If you do have a telephone with long-distance
privileges, make sure you use it for company business or in
moderation if you do call home or a classmate at a rival firm, and
so forth.

The final caveat I will share with this new generation of
engineers is that the use of company computer resources can be a
potential pitfall for an idle intern. The usage of email, web surf-
ing, social media postings, and webpage development on company time is a double-edged sword. When you arrive on the new
job, every company now has some sort of written technology or
internet policy. It will contain language that the usage of their
computer resources are for company business and there is no
privacy when it comes to being monitored while in use. As usual,

learn the do's and don'ts concerning the company's computer usage. The email address you receive should be used for company communications within and without their firewalls. Not saying that you can't send emails to family or friends, but for really personal stuff, stick with your personal email account on yahoo or gmail or whatever you have. Obviously with smartphones, you can send and receive emails and texts on your personal device, but if you are using the company wi-fi network, your information is still passing through their servers, so be mindful of this. If someone should happen to send you questionable or pornographic material, delete it immediately. Better to view such things, if you have a propensity toward such, on your own time away from your place of employment. You don't want to be fired from a $20–$30-an-hour job over a picture that you could see in a $10 magazine or *for free* on, once again, your own time in the privacy of your own room on the Internet!

I remember a few incidents when I was at MDA involving interns from an HBCU who were so bored and underutilized that they commenced to creating web pages while on the job. The problem is that I heard they were using or posting explicit or sexually related materials and that is definitely grounds for being terminated. Now I will say that they should have used better judgment and restraint when this temptation presented itself. But I also found fault with whomever their managers were, because obviously, they were not being challenged or kept engaged with work tasks that would've prevented such a waste of time and talent. I heard about another intern or new hire who got in trouble because he used a lot of bandwidth sending a *ton* of email back home to Michigan. Find out what the policy is regarding social media sites, as well. I've been at places where you couldn't get onto Yahoo, much less Facebook or MySpace (yes, I'm old), and I've been at others where they were so laid back that *everybody* seemed to have a Facebook or YouTube page up on their monitor all day long. It just depends on the culture of the company. But whether you are in a maximum security production facility or a hippie-owned applications development firm, tread cautiously when it comes to posting things on the web or sending emails from the job.

2.5 BURNOUT

In the fall of 1991, I began my junior year at Tennessee State. I was beginning to get into my major curriculum courses, 200- and 300-level classes. I was following the prescribed schedule for a four-year track, and I got into a conversation with our electrical engineering departmental secretary, Mrs. Romona Perry, about the number of classes I was taking. The normal progression chart for a bachelor's degree was to take four or more classes and one or more labs per semester to graduate "on time." Now this is an oxymoron, if there ever was one. Allow me to explain, as Mrs. Perry tried to explain to me. A true undergraduate engineering degree program is really a five-year track. They (whoever "they" are) say that a full-time student can do it in four if they really focus. But this is not taking into account the human factor, as Daddy would say. Enjoying a certain measure of life, working, eating, sleeping, and attending classes and having periods for successful study and learning must be accounted for. But no one in admissions or the engineering department ever 'fessed up to this fact.

The picture had been painted for me, my classmates, and I'm sure the previous generations that came out of TSU when Corporate America finally opened her doors to African-Americans and other minorities—that to be considered for a good job, you had to have a good GPA and have attained your degree in four years. Of course, I bought into this hook, line, and sinker. Until that semester, I was taking between six and eight classes per semester and carrying a 3.70 GPA. How hard could it be? I was still active as an officer in several engineering organizations, as well as other campus activities, including preparing to pledge for the Omega Psi Phi Fraternity, the "Mighty" Rho Psi Chapter. Mrs. Perry was trying to caution me on spreading myself too thin because she told me the 300- and 400-level courses were going to be much more time intensive than the freshman and sophomore classes I had taken previously. But by this time, I had developed a high level of confidence. Hubris was more like it.

Mrs. Perry had been the EE department secretary for some time now, so she had a pulse on the successes and failures of the enrolled students. Like a good Sergeant Major in someone's army, she knew how the CoE worked and what it took to get out in one piece and fairly sane. If I had kept my humility, I would've taken her advice to heart: take enough classes and labs to remain qualified as a full-time student to keep my Presidential Scholarship. Then I'd have enough time to effectively study and have some personal time to stay grounded. Instead, I took six classes that made up 16 attempted hours that fall. I ended up with two Cs that brought my semester GPA down to a 2.875. I hadn't earned a C since junior high school, so I was a bit taken aback, but not yet deterred from my prideful ways.

In the spring, once again, I was enrolled in six classes totaling 16 hours, operating as an officer in several organizations, preparing to be initiated into the Fraternity, and doing God-knows-what-else aside from studying effectively. I think I had an opportunity to do an internship with AT&T or Bellcore that semester as well, but because I wanted to be an Omega, I turned down the opportunity. I will now tell anyone at the junior and senior level to be involved in one, maybe two, activities besides physical fitness so they can maintain a good GPA. If you do decide to pledge a Fraternity or Sorority after your sophomore year, make sure your coursework is not so heavy that you risk a GPA nosedive. I finished spring 1992 with two As, two Cs, a D in linear systems, and a withdrawal in Electronics I. Not my best work, but I was focused on "Crossing the burning sands" and nothing would deter me.

The "Mighty" Rho Psi Chapter of the Omega Psi Phi Fraternity, Incorporated, was founded on April 30, 1930, at Tennessee Agricultural & Industrial State Teachers College. It had a long line of proud and illustrious members. And obviously, I wanted to be a part of its history. When my chance came in 1992, it was because a good group of guys, myself included, had been meeting in secret (at least we thought so) because we wanted to be Omegas and were preparing ourselves as such. The issue was that the Chapter had been on suspension since 1983, because of the death of an inductee, Van L. Watts. Most of the Fraternity members enrolled at the time had moved on, so rumblings had been stirring on the Yard since my freshman year about when the Ques would be back.

The University had gotten a new president in 1991, Dr. James A. Hefner, who happened to also be an Omega. Our secret group (We called ourselves the Positive Leadership Club, "PL Club" for short) already had a make on every professor or University employee who was a "Que." From Track and Field Coach Ed Temple, to Dr. Walter Vincent and Dean Rogers in Engineering, we knew who was a potential advocate on our behalf should the opportunity to petition arise. The PL Club was a registered organization on campus and we were doing social and service activities to emulate, if you will, the practices of what the Greek-lettered service fraternities were supposed to be about. This was kicked up a notch because traditionally, TSU was an HBCU where the Omegas were very visible and involved in almost all aspects of campus life. Talking with older alumni, when the subject of the Chapter being on suspension came up, you'd hear comments like: "What?! The Ques are on suspension? When we were in school, Rho Psi *ran* the Yard!" This is no disrespect to the other Fraternities that had chapters at TSU, but the mindset was that Rho Psi set the bar pretty high when it came to academics, leadership, and social and community involvement. (Omegas also had the reputation for being the "bad boys" among the Black Fraternities, the "Que Dogs.")

So we had motivational speakers come in, threw a party or two, and did some community service. This was well-documented, because we had begun to poke and prod the administration about the possibility of bringing the Chapter back. We were met with many a roadblock. But in true Omega fashion (perseverance is one of our cardinal principles), we "stayed on mission" like a platoon of Marines. One fateful day, I told the leaders of the PL Club that Dr. Vincent was an Omega and suggested that he talk to Dr. Hefner on our behalf. It was like a light bulb appeared over everyone's head, and we figured, well, why not? So early in the 1992 spring semester, several PL Club members and I marched to the engineering building and had a sit-down meeting with Dr. Vincent. We expressed our interest in the Fraternity, but also presented our case, highlighting the type of students we comprised (high GPAs, leadership positions, service activities, etc.), and asked if he could speak with President Hefner about the possibility of bringing the Chapter back. Dr. Vincent sat for about 30 seconds, picked up his telephone, and called Dr. Hefner's office directly. Dr. Hefner wasn't in, but he left a message with his secretary. It was more than direct.

"Yes, I have some young men here in my office that are interested in becoming members of Omega Psi Phi Fraternity, and I'd like to speak with Dr. Hefner about reinstating the Chapter here…"

After he left his message, we shook hands, thanked him for his support, and quickly left his office. The racing pulses and wide smiles could not be concealed as we grew excited with the possibility that maybe, just maybe, we were about to do something great. We still had to exercise a large amount of discretion, but secrets are sometimes leaked as rumors, and rumors spread like wildfire. It would be several months of legal and administrative wrangling before the final approval was given, but that visit to Dr. Vincent was the catalyst that started the process; the planets couldn't have lined up any straighter. Nevertheless, under the watchful eye of the national office and local graduate chapter, out of several dozen interested men, 28 of us were initiated into the "Mighty" Rho Psi on June 7, 1992. By the way, my Exxon internship money paid all of my expenses (both expected and a *whole lot* of unexpected) to pledge and officially join the Fraternity.

We called ourselves the "Mystic 28" and set about doing Omega's work. I was elected as the Keeper of Records & Seal, basically the secretary, as well as the Chaplain for the upcoming school year. I was still floating around campus in early June when Dean Rogers saw me and asked what I was still doing on campus. You see, I had turned down my internship with AT&T, but didn't give a clear reason to them, and I hadn't told Doc that I wasn't going, either. I should've asked for a later start date, but as a neophyte, I was focused on learning as much about Omega's venerated secrets, signs, and observances while I had the chance before school started. Although visibly upset, Doc arranged for me to go up to the University of Michigan for a six-week research program where I would work for one of the EE professors and receive a nice stipend from late June to early August. I hadn't gotten the grasp of how my not going to AT&T could've affected the relationship between them and Dean Rogers.

Going to Ann Arbor, Michigan, was a great experience for me, as far as being in a true college town goes. The University is *huge*. I was part of a large group of visiting minority students and experienced some things that I hadn't yet encountered being away from my small HBCU and the Southeastern United States. When they gave us maps, they weren't kidding. The University of Michigan campus was so large, the engineering school and several other schools had their own mini-campuses and you had to take a university bus from the dormitory to get there. If you had a car or a bike, maybe you could get there in a timely fashion, but walking was out of the question. I mentioned earlier in the book about how relaxed the liquor laws are on and around large majority (a nice substitution for "white") institutions. I had just turned 21, so when I went into one of the local bars for the first time with some of my program participants and some frat Brothers I had just met, it was quite a shock to see so many young people sitting around casually drinking. I could order a drink and take it on campus with no fear of retribution? For real? Shouldn't have told me that. Mama was worried about me getting drunk at TSU; she should've cautioned me about being around a bunch of drinking Caucasians and others.

When you have the opportunity to make some money, learn some new things, and represent your family and school, don't take it for granted! In a nutshell, I was focused on being "a mean, nasty Que Dog" (Omegas embrace the bulldog as their mascot, although not officially) and not on the opportunity I had before me. I was busy "hanging with the bros," drinking, and trying to chase women instead of focusing on the tasks that my host professor, Dr. McAfee, had given me. I was able to throw together a presentation for the end of the summer awards program of what I had supposedly done, but it was a sham and definitely not reflective of what I was capable of. I left U of M with a somewhat tainted reputation. Not bad, but not great, either.

I returned to TSU that fall and spent a lot of time working on Fraternity business, keeping records of activities and monies spent and received. I was still involved in my other officer duties, including being president of the Institute of Electrical and Electronics Engineers chapter and several honor societies. And I was still trying to live up to the fraternity bad boy image: carousing, drinking, and hanging out. Did I mention that I was taking 17 hours that semester? I earned my first F, dropped a course, and *still* managed to get a 3.3 GPA. You'd think that I would've learned my lesson, as well as noticed the signs that I was spread too thin and was getting burned out.

Burnout is defined by Webster's Dictionary as "a state of emotional exhaustion from mental stress." I was *there*. In the spring 1993 semester, I was attempting 13 hours in five classes, but these were all 300- and 400-level classes, including my honors senior thesis and capstone design (senior project) courses. Still trying to do it all, my mindset had withered to the degree that I was unfocused, my personality had taken on a rough edge, and I had no joy in my studies, to say the least. Still trying to be a womanizer, I ended up hurting some good girls' feelings, and at one point, had a near miss when the condom came off while having intercourse with one of these young ladies. I was in no position to become a father, and thank God that didn't happen. But for the record, I was engaged in behavior that I was not really comfortable with, and I'm truly sorry for the close friendships and special relationships that I had and damaged. I hadn't reached a level of maturity where I could be myself and still be a part of the fraternity, as well as student life, without compromising my values or my studies. It was a tough lesson I would soon learn. I finished the semester with two Cs and a D after dropping my senior project and honors thesis classes. My GPA was a whopping 1.500! WHAT??? A 1.5?! That's not even a "good" D average. But at the time, I was too emotionally tired to care.

With the exception of the 1990 summer term, I had been taking 15-plus hours per semester for four years straight with no real break except for the summers. That spring, I had the chance to go with a couple of my classmates on a Co-Op at General Dynamics Electric Boat Division and work on US Navy Trident submarines. Being caught up in this "graduate on time" foolishness and my own arrogance, I turned it down. One of my good friends who was going up there, Keith Nolen, implored me to go with them—take some time off and unplug. I think he saw what was happening to me. But I was also worried about my Presidential Scholarship and thought I would lose it if I skipped a semester. I didn't do any research or ask the folks in financial aid what my options were. Well, the Bible reads that like a good father, the Lord corrects those He loves. And believe me, I was about to be *corrected*.

Daddy had come up to drive me home for the break, and I had packed all of my belongings in my dorm room. On the ride home, I was telling him about how badly the semester had turned out. Now this is *before* I got my grades. But he basically told me that I needed to figure out a way to regroup and get myself ready for the next semester. No kidding. I think I had about two weeks before my internship at MDA in St. Louis was to begin. So what to do? I had my answer soon enough.

The Thursday or Friday before I went home, I helped one of my very best friends, Reverend Joe L. Jordan, Jr., move some things to his family's new home. It was raining that day and I got soaked and exposed to the elements. Even though it was Nashville, it was still fairly cool for early May and although I had a coat on, it wasn't built for rainy weather and I got wet over time. Joe's stepson, Brandon, was a toddler at the time, and was attending a preschool. He was there at the apartment when we were moving things, so I didn't think anything of it. The Sunday after I got home, I woke up several times the previous night feeling feverish and sweaty. No big deal, I thought, probably just a slight illness from the rain. I went to church with my family and later that afternoon, I noticed a bump above my lip. I thought it was a pimple and popped it with no hesitation. A little while later, it had reappeared, along with a couple more in varying places. I had one on my right bicep that I popped and I noticed it was filled with clear pus. Obviously, this was something different, but what? My Aunt Roz was visiting at the time, and during the course of conversation, I mentioned my consternation with these pimples popping up all over me. She took pause and asked me to raise the back of shirt. I turned around and raised my shirt for her to observe.

"Dusty, you have chicken pox!"

My entire back with covered with pus bumps, and began to itch like a *mother*! I had never had chicken pox, and Mama had never had them, either. She apparently had a natural immunity to the virus and passed it down to me and Philip because I don't think we had been given a vaccine for it as kids. My suspicion is that when I was helping Joe move, the stress from the school year and my getting wet lowered my immune system to the point that my being around Brandon exposed me to the virus because of him being around a bunch of little kids all day at his preschool.

For those of you who have read stories in the Bible about how God gets folks' attention by exposing them to adverse conditions and situations, I can tell you He *will* get your attention when He wants it. They say that if you are going to get the chicken pox, you should get it while you are young. Apparently, it is much worse when you are grown. I have found this statement to be true. Upon the realization that I was infected, I was quarantined to my bedroom, only to leave for the bathroom or to get something to eat or drink if it wasn't delivered to me. For the next 10 days, I would have to suffer until the virus ran its course. We tried Caladryl lotion, among other products, including "corn silk" tea my Uncle E.T. recommended. Nothing really cleared up the bumps, but the fever broke after the first day or so. It was extremely difficult to sleep and being cooped up in a bedroom, you have a lot of time to yourself. While I was in quarantine, I received my grade report and it was then and there I realized I had hit rock bottom. I took this time to really reflect on what had happened to me and how. I picked my Bible up and started reading it again, as well as praying for forgiveness and guidance. I also read the *Autobiography of Malcolm X*, among other books.

I wanted to get my mind and soul back in fighting shape. My body was broken, but my mind and spirit were in need of serious repair. I made a commitment to get my grades back on track that fall semester.

After completing my internship at MDA, I returned to TSU with a vengeance. I dropped most of my extracurricular positions, except for Rho Psi Chaplain, and tried to focus strictly on coursework. I can't remember if my Presidential Scholarship had been exhausted, but I was still following the prescribed course load. I had 15 attempted credits and was enrolled in seven 300- and 400-level courses. I ended up dropping two of those courses and earning three As, a B, and a C. Not my best work, but a hell of an improvement from the previous semester. I wish I had slowed down and taken fewer high-level classes but hindsight is 20/20, as they say. I came back in the spring for more punishment, enrolling in six classes and attempting 14 hours. I dropped my Capstone Design II (Senior Project) course and finished with two As, two Bs, and a C in one of my engineering electives.

My GPA by then was a cumulative 3.396, and I was seeing the light at the end of the tunnel. Mama paid for my last two or three semesters, which included summer of 1994. (To earn extra money, I tutored people in math and physics.) For my senior project, I was doing research for the EE department in renewable energy sources—wind turbines, to be specific. This was through a grant from the National Renewable Energy Laboratory in Boulder, Colorado. So I was coming up with a design for a small, rural community using both hybrid and wind-only concepts. I did this research for Dr. Devgan, our department head, and received a small stipend over the summer. This was also part of my course completion for Capstone II, but I would not present for my final senior project until the fall. Maybe things have changed now, but when I was in school, the seniors nearing graduation presented their work either in the spring or fall semesters. There weren't enough students enrolled in the summer to have a presentation. The project would be judged by members of industry invited by the various departments. These were professionals who were alumni or had a close relationship with the CoE. I completed my research for the summer and received an A, but the final piece of the graduation puzzle included the dean signing off on your senior project. This would not occur until after I presented my work in the fall.

During the summer, I was able to attend the Fraternity Conclave (convention) in Cleveland, Ohio, by road-tripping with my chapter Brothers. It wasn't a bad trip and I met Brothers from other schools saw some I had met during my neophyte year in '92 and '93. The Lord was merciful to me and even allowed me to meet and date a young lady who was in graduate school at TSU before the summer semester ended. The companionship was a welcome respite from the stress of doing a research paper at a high level for meager wages.

My final semester at TSU was a beast once again. I was enrolled in six classes and attempting 16 hours, including rewriting my senior project. What's that? Yes, I do believe I did "lose my damn mind." The ultimate goal was to graduate, period. So between classes, trying to study, write my senior project, and have a relationship with my girlfriend at the time, it was tough sledding. I had still spread myself too thin even though I had cut out all of my distractions. I withdrew from my Africana Studies course to focus squarely on engineering. I can remember that the last few weeks were some of the most stressful I had ever had in my life. I remember having to study for finals AND write my senior project over from the summer. It didn't have enough design content or something that Doc wanted to see. Dr. Devgan said in such a matter-of-fact way to "just add 50 more pages." Uh, yeah, sure thing.

During the last few weeks, I was averaging three hours of sleep a night. Drank so much coffee that a crack addict would raise an eyebrow. I slept on the desk in the EE lab I was doing my research in sometimes. Never did a flat surface feel so good. I had already done my senior project presentation in November, so I didn't have to worry about putting on a suit and tie. I was just trying to graduate and I spent almost every waking moment either reading, writing, or studying. I was so strung out that I went those last four days without shaving or showering; I slept in my clothes, woke up, brushed my teeth (maybe), and went back to the engineering building or the Caf to get something to eat. I finished with one A, two Cs, and two Ds.

The engineering program allowed you to graduate with two Ds on your transcript. I had a 2.000 GPA for the semester and a cumulative 3.277. Rounded up, that's a 3.3...*I'LL TAKE IT!* I just wanted to get out and move on. But wait, I wasn't out of the woods yet. For whatever reason, Dean Rogers hadn't signed my senior project, and Dr. Devgan told me that I had to return the following Monday by a certain time for it to be signed. I cannot

remember if I had to add some more writing, make more copies to deliver, or if Doc needed time over the weekend to review
it. But regardless, early that Monday morning, I took Mama's
Toyota Camry, picked up Keith Nolen and his radar detector, and
hit I-40 East toward Nashville at a modest 90 miles per hour on
the cruise control. I believe we had to be there by 10:00, and we
had no time to spare. Everything else is a blur, but I was seated
in the EE office, talking with Mrs. Perry, when Dr. Devgan came
in with signed copies of my senior project. He gave me my
copy and congratulated me. I was done. It was almost a letdown
to be honest. That's it? No balloons falling from the ceiling or
sirens going off? I turned to the signature page to make sure he
was telling the truth, and sure enough, there was Doc's John
Hancock. When you completed your senior project, you had to
make at least three or four copies: one for yourself, the Dean's
Office, and the Departmental Office. I can't remember if a fourth
copy was required. But I was done, Son. The inevitable question
flooded my mind: Now what?

3.0 ENTERING CORPORATE AMERICA —FROM COLLEGE TO INDUSTRY

When I packed up for my final stay at Epps Hall, I was unsure of what I was going to do next, aside from coming back to complete my senior project requirements the following Monday. I had several options at the time: A job offer (believe it or not) from MDA in St. Louis, graduate school at TSU, graduate school at Prairie View A&M (PVAM) down in Texas, or take some time off in Memphis and wait for other opportunities. I was uncertain about what to do. On one hand, I wanted to stay in Nashville and spend more time with my girlfriend and continue with my graduate studies, but I felt I was too burned out. On the other hand, I wanted to get out of academia, at least for a while, and get some work experience, but MDA wasn't my first choice and I was having issues with that. I expressed my thoughts to my father as we were loading up the truck.

Daddy and I were back in the dorm room, and he had sat down on one of the desk chairs while smoking a cigarette. This was before all of the non-smoking bans had taken effect (or maybe he just didn't care) and smoking was allowed inside. He took a drag, stared up at the ceiling for a while, slowly exhaled, looked at me, and said the following words:

"If a turkey…goes outside while it's raining, and looks up… he'll drown." He nodded a couple of times with the complementary "Huhs" as if subconsciously asking me if I agreed. *WHAT?!* I think I asked him to repeat that.

"If a TURKEY goes outside, while it's raining…and looks UP, he'll drown!" he stated, this time with more emphasis. He took another drag from his cigarette as I looked at him blankly. I'm wondering if I should've responded with the customary, "Okay, sure, *everybody* knows *that*…" because I sure as hell didn't. After inhaling, Daddy took his right hand, with the cigarette clutched expertly between his index and middle finger, and quickly pointed at me.

"Now!…that same rain, that'll kill that turkey…will produce crops!…Huh?…Huh?" Longer, more agonizing, blank stare from me this time, and I think he got the fact that I was completely lost as to what life decision to make, and what the *heck* drowning turkeys and growing crops had to do with *any* of this. As if I had done something wrong, he appeared to become agitated at my lack of understanding.

"*Can't cha' see?!…* One man's curse, is another man's blessing. You need to count yo' blessings…" O-kay.

I guess he was trying to tell me that things were not really as bad as they appeared. I had options. And I had plenty of time to go home and ponder what to do. So we packed up the truck and rolled west back to Memphis.

In either mid-December or early January, I contacted the Dean of the Engineering School down at PVAM. I had been accepted there for graduate school, so now there was the question of how to get there, what curriculum to enroll in, and most importantly, how I was going to *pay* for all of this. For whatever reason, the Dean didn't seem to remember talking to me on previous phone calls I had made down there over the course of the fall semester. And he didn't seem too hard pressed to get me any information on starting grad school that spring, or summer, for that matter. It was very strange, to say the least. I didn't feel too bad, because my roommate, a civil engineering major from St. Louis, had had the same experience with this gentleman. So I promptly scratched PVAM off my What to Do List.

I had had enough of the meat grinder at TSU, and wanted a change. I was still mentally exhausted from my final semester of school, but was itching to do something. That's something else that I'm hoping has improved at State, as well as other colleges and universities: helping students make the transition to life after college. Mama offered to pay for me to take a trip somewhere for some R&R, including Jamaica. I turned it down, because in truth, I was flat-out scared. I didn't feel a sense of adventure or desire to see the world at that time, and wasn't hyped on traveling to a foreign country by myself. Another one of my regrets was that I didn't do any real traveling while I had the chance as a young man. I had been so programmed and institutionalized by the past five years of following the engineering game plan, that I was completely flustered by the notion that I had to suddenly grow up and make my own life-changing decisions. I wasn't ready to get out there, research, and hustle for my own piece of the pie. I equate it to the three little pigs leaving home to seek their fortunes. I wanted to leave home, but I didn't know how.

Another reason for my mental frustration was because I had completed my Bachelor of Science Degree in Electrical Engineering, with honors, cum laude, and a GPA of 3.277, and had only *one* job offer. This can be attributed to several factors. The first one being my graduating in the fall/winter part of the year. I didn't know that this was a potential problem at the time, but something you, the Reader, should take into consideration. Most companies have their new-hire budgets for recent college grads apportioned for the late spring and early summer timeframes. This includes attending career fairs in the spring, as well. So if you want to increase your chances of having several job offers upon graduation, I would recommend shooting for a May/ June graduation if it's not an extreme burden. In today's volatile economy, there are no guarantees, but I want to give you as many tidbits of information that will hopefully make life a little easier as you complete your undergrad tenure. This leads to my second factor that caused me to be nearly jobless. Because the economy had started turning in 1994, a lot of companies that were normal supporters and recruiters at TSU starting pulling out and stopped coming on campus altogether. I had the fortunate occurrence of one of the Exxon recruiters telling me in confidence over the telephone that they were shifting their focus strictly to the Southwestern States: Texas, Louisiana, Oklahoma, New Mexico, etc. It was disappointing, but I guess he thought enough of me to disclose it, although he made me swear to secrecy. I don't know if they were waiting until the last minute to tell TSU they weren't coming back, or if they just didn't tell them. But regardless, a lot of the major players that were steady supporters of the school dropped us like a bad habit. Several of my classmates finished up with no job prospects at the time. It was a trying time for us all.

I finally made the decision to pursue the MDA job, and I think I called the department head to tell him I accepted the job, all for the low, low price of $38,000 a year. That was a lot of money back in those days. No, not really, but it wasn't a bad starting salary. Arrangements were made for relocation assistance, which included me staying at the St. Louis Airport Renaissance Hotel for a week or two, and a moving company to move what meager belongings I had from Tennessee to Missouri. That was a big thing with taking on a direct-hire or permanent position. What does the benefit package consist of? I'll talk more about this a little later.

Because I was about to take a job, my first job (Anybody remember Calvin and his new job on the old McDonald's commercials?), out of town, my own transportation was needed. My father used to sell cars for a while, so he went with me to look at several vehicles and walk me through the whole registration and insurance processes. I looked at small trucks and finally settled on a 1995 Chevy S-10, stick shift. I used some money from the savings account my mother had created for me when I was born. I was hoping for a vehicle after I graduated, but Daddy told me, "I didn't have a car when I was in college and had to get my own when I got out of the Navy…Besides, you wouldn't appreciate it as much if someone else bought it for you." I'll say that most of that was true, but this was also the same father who sent me some money my freshman year and thought it was enough to get me by: a whopping $7. To this day, several of my classmates and I still laugh about that. Daddy called and told me he was sending me some money, and I was looking forward to the mail. When

I received the letter, I opened it and pulled out a five-dollar bill and two well-used ones. My roommate, Keith, and maybe another one of our boys just happened to be in the room. My mother actually called me that same day not too long afterwards and as the conversation went on, she inquired if my father had sent me some money. He had flat-out told Mama he sent me some money and she didn't need to worry about sending me something for a while! I told her yes.

"Okay, how much?"

"Seven dollars," in a muffled voice I said.

"How much?"

"Seven dollars," this time a little louder.

"SEVEN DOLLARS?! Boy, that ain't nothing!" My friends, by this time, were rolling on the bed trying not to laugh out loud as I stood there holding the phone in my dorm room. She sent me some more later in the week, but this was a "Moment in Black History" that will not soon be forgotten. Anyway, I got the truck, packed up my clothes, and rolled up to Missouri to the hotel to prepare for my first week on the job and go apartment hunting.

I reported to MDA in Berkeley, Missouri, in late January. I first had to go to the human resources building for employee orientation and processing. Before showing up, I had to pass a drug test. This is usually a trip to an assigned testing facility where you will give either a blood or urine sample, or in some cases, both. Once it's determined you're not a user of illegal substances, then you will usually receive a start date to arrive. You will be given a stack of forms to fill out that will include insurance, company savings plans, emergency contacts, company policies on behavior/sexual harassment, and so forth. Some you have to fill out that day, others can be turned in by a deadline. These days, I'm sure a lot of these forms are online. I was about to become employee number M254433, and aside from my immediate family and close friends, nobody else gave a damn. I had signed on to one of the largest corporations and Department of Defense contractors in the country. A small speck in the soup. There was no welcome wagon or band playing when I showed up. If I wanted to be an "impact player," I picked the wrong place.

I was assigned to the Inertial Navigation Systems (INS) Group, which was a part of the AIC where I worked during my internship. Sounds awesome, doesn't it? This was in Building 105, the three-story structure with additional labs in the basement. Our lab was in the basement with a wide-open area that jutted out into the open area between B105 and Building 106 (B106), with two domed windows that faced the sky. Skylights we called them. Beneath the skylights were three-axis platforms that would simulate the six directions of movement for the avionics units we tested, in this case, inertia navigation units (INUs), which gave the pilots information on their approximate position as they flew above the curvature of the earth. This was before the global positioning system (GPS) satellites were fully integrated into the battlespace and commercial airspace.

The lab was given the nickname, "the dungeon," because the skylights were the only source of external light we had. If we wanted to see if the rest of the world still existed, we had to go back up to level 2 and up. We had desks on the third floor, which had overhead walkways that connected B105 to B106, B107, and B101, where the cafeteria was. But we spent the majority of our time downstairs and everyone at least had a computer and a seat. The senior engineers had a desk telephone, and I think there was a telephone that was for general usage and receiving calls from the outside.

The INS group was sub-divided among aircraft types that MDA built at the time: T-45, AV-8, F-15, and F-18. I was in the F-18 group. INS was a small group within AIC, and the members had been together for quite a while. It was mostly older white men, with one white woman, one white guy in his mid-thirties, and one Brother in his mid-to-late thirties named Eugene. The day I hired in, another new hire from Michigan Tech came aboard. He was actually pretty cool for a technocrat, but I never got around to really getting to know him outside of work. The INS F-18 manager was a short, Sicilian guy who had been with the company for a good while. He wasn't a bad person, but his leadership skills were a bit lacking. I had the sorry pleasure of being paired with the senior engineer of the group, a 30-plus-year employee who was eyeballing retirement right around the corner. My first few weeks, I was trying to learn about inertial navigation and how they all tied in with the avionics (aviation electronics) on the aircraft. I hadn't been given a specific as-signment yet, there was no formal training program, and I was getting bored out of my mind. As much as I tried reading manu-als and looking at handouts to try to learn the business, it wasn't sparking any real interest. From time to time, we would sit in the conference room to watch a training film on inertial navigation or required company training, and I would fall asleep. I fell asleep at my desk several times as well. After I had moved to another group, a Brother I knew from TSU who worked in a different building told me he saw a picture circulating of me somebody had taken with my head down, hands on the keyboard, completely knocked out. That wasn't too cool, was it? You'd think they'd have the courtesy to wake me up.

Although I was assigned to work under the senior engineer's wing, so to speak, he wasn't trying to teach me anything. As Eugene, or "Gene" as they called him, put it to me, "He's in cruise mode. His retirement is coming up soon, so he's not hard pressed about anything." When he wasn't doing any real work, he was usually checking the company stock prices, looking over his investment portfolios, or on the phone with his financial advisor. The few times I did go to him for something to do, he would blow me off with a curt, "I don't have anything right now, I'm busy…" or something to that effect. I remember the last time I asked him about having something to do, I guess I must've caught him at a really bad time because he cursed at me, and I left him alone ever since that day. I even went to my manager about the situation and told him, "Look, I *earned* my degree, give me something to do!" He gave me some lip service and said he was going to give me some substantial tasks, but nothing had come up yet, blah-blah-blah.

Every day, it was the same thing: I had to wear a shirt and tie to work because at the time, the director expected his engineers to look professional. This was a tough but manageable transition for me because I was leaving the relaxed college atmosphere for a very military-like corporation that enforced a strict business dress code. I've never been comfortable in business or "church" attire, as I prefer to call it. This was compounded by the fact that our lab was always dirty, and at the time, I took my suits to the cleaners, so I was trying to keep my pants as clean as possible for as long as possible. I finally started investing in some khakis and other less expensive, but acceptable, shirts and pants after I tore one of my white shirts on an equipment cabinet. I had to drive to work from a small apartment I found in the township of St. Ann up Lindbergh Boulevard to McDonnell Boulevard, and jockey for a decent parking space in the B105 parking lot. There were plenty of parking spaces all over the work complex, but each building had its own lot that was much closer to the entrance. It was a real circus because they were still operating under the same rules from the heady days of Vietnam and the early Cold War. The spots closest to the building were actually roped off in the evening by security, and at 6:50 a.m., the guard would show up to take the ropes down right before 7:00. People would already be lined up on the side of the entrance lane to get the best spots. Those who were early risers would park at the bottom of the hill and walk up to the entrance. I would muster enough strength to get there by 6:45 sometimes and wait it out, but usually I'd get there right at 7:30.

The typical day was an eight-hour shift from either 7:00 to 3:30 p.m. or 7:30 to 4:00 p.m., with a 30-minute lunch break. The manufacturing and skilled labor workers, all unionized, worked on an earlier shift and would leave the plant between 2:30 and 3:00. During those times, you stayed off the parking lot and out of the hallways, because at "quittin' time," you had dozens of people flying to their cars and trying to get as far away from the Hazelwood and Berkeley townships as fast as possible. I heard one guy got hit while walking to his car. Even going to the cafeteria could be risky business as most folks in our building ate promptly at 11:30, so there would be a mass exodus at noon of people going back to work.

Day in and day out, it was the same monotonous routine. To say that I was missing my college days is an extreme understatement.

3.1 THE COLOR LINE (YEP, IT'S STILL THERE)

I stated earlier that during my internship, I was one of a handful of people of color in my building. It became a glaring fact to me that the aviation and defense industries were devoid of significant numbers of minorities. Throw in the fact that a lot of these companies are run by Caucasian people who are consciously or subconsciously racist, and you can see why our numbers are so low. Needless to say, there were very few minorities in management or executive positions. Most of the folk were either in the factory as laborers, part of the cooking and cleaning crews, or non-technical areas like human resources, supply chain management, finance, and transportation. We had a few folks I knew of at MDA/Boeing who had achieved a relatively modest amount of success; this included some managers in areas like human resources, business & community development, and supply chain/supplier diversity, along with one male VP and two female VPs. One of the Sisters was VP of Lean Manufacturing—she had an engineering background, was brought in from the outside, and knew her stuff. But that was it. As far as having a group of "home grown" black managers who worked their way up through the ranks, the numbers were few and far between. Now I'm sure there are other industries where the numbers are way better, but from my travels and talking with my peers, the problem is across the board at present.

I had to adjust to the fact that I wasn't at TSU and her friendly confines anymore and learn not to take the avoidance of eye contact or speaking personally. But it would be a lie to say it didn't irritate me and cause me to wonder, why people didn't speak on the job It is even more frustrating when you have other people of color walk right past you and give you the same treatment. I told myself that I would not lose my soul like some of these other Brothers and Sisters had. I think living in the Midwest had a good deal to do with this unfriendliness, as well. I found the people in St. Louis were not as friendly and open as what I was accustomed to Down South.

Don't get me wrong, I tried to make the most of what I had to work with at the time. I met other young black professionals within and without MDA, and was able to hang out a little bit and even got invited to a few parties and social events. To pass the time away, I would walk around and talk to folks. I would even sit with the director from time to time to ask for advice on career advancement. He shared with me some of his success stories and techniques that he learned from reading self-help books like the Dale Carnegie series. But at the end of the day, I was alone, on my own, and miserable.

Let's face it, people are usually comfortable with what they are used to and can relate to. Having someone of a different ethnicity around, especially a Black person, can have a traumatic effect on, or result in xenophobic reactions from White folks who have been among their own for so long. This is especially true when it comes to African-American males. We are already stereotyped by the mainstream media as mindless animals that are only capable of procreating out of wedlock, being lazy, and behaving like a criminal. That damn rap music doesn't always help our cause, either. (I'm closer to 50, so I can say that now.) I didn't have a mentor to guide me along, and wasn't about to get one, even though the HR people knew I was uncomfortable. It's funny to see how people in a work group have been together for so long that they get accustomed to each other to the point that they feel that the group is theirs. It's their private country club, and you and I are the intruders. I quickly found out how much I was wanted around there. When people talk about going to lunch but don't invite you to roll with them, it's a sure sign. Don't forget to look for the situation where you're engaged in conversation with a co-worker and either another co-worker or a manager will come up to you guys and just start talking to your co-worker as if you are not there. Also, take quick notice if things are happening within the group, department, or company that everybody else seems to always know about, but you are constantly left out of the loop.

Another incident involved me leaving work early for a dentist appointment. Now there were several people who would leave work 5 to 10, sometimes 15 minutes early to avoid the mad rush at the end of the day. As far as I know, they made it a regular routine. I told my supervisor that I had a dental appointment at whatever time, and had to leave early. I remember going down the steps and the department head was coming up at the same time. He had his head down, and I politely bid him good night. He said good night, and as I continued down the steps, I saw him stop and look at his watch out of the corner of my eye. It didn't register with me what was going on until the next day. The following morning, my supervisor pulls me into the hallway to "have a little chat". He said, "Well, ———— wanted me to talk you about your leaving work early yesterday."

"What? I told you I had a dentist appointment."

"Yeah I know, I told him. But he wanted me to make sure you understood what our working hours were…" Really? That was deep. I don't know what upset me more, the fact that the department head was under the impression that I was skipping out or the fact that my supervisor clearly didn't take up for me, because if he did, the conversation would've been more of a friendly, "Hey, try to schedule your appointments around a different time or take time off…", etc. I remember afterward walking down the hallway one day and the department head just looked at me, but didn't say anything as he passed by. Damn, what did I do? On a side note, this was 1995, the year of the OJ Simpson trial, when a Black man was being tried for the gruesome murder of his white ex-wife and her lover. I'm not leaning either way as to whether or not he did it, but I mention this because during that time, incidents of racial turmoil occurred across the country.

One day, I had walked into the labs and several of the managers and co-workers were standing together, talking. When I walked in, everyone grew eerily silent. I told Daddy about that one night on the phone, and he responded, "They was probably talking about stringin' OJ up by his nuts…" So I'm just speculating on one of the many possibilities as to why I was not "shown any love," so to speak.

Refrain from engaging in conversation about racial matters with White people over 45, unless you have concrete proof that they are hippies from a liberal state like Washington, Oregon, or California. I made that mistake with one of the people in INS, and no matter how much logic I threw at him, he couldn't or wouldn't see my point. Gene schooled me on that after this particular incident. He was cool, and gave me a few tidbits of advice, but at the end of the day, I had to fend for myself. He told me on several occasions that the labs, as the AIC was commonly called, was a bad place for Brothers and Sisters as far as career advancement was concerned. If I was trying to move ahead, I needed to get out, plain and simple. The labs were rife with good ol' boys who took care of their own, and treated the women and minorities like crap, unless it was a fairly attractive female, then she stood a chance. I remember that the salaried workers didn't get Martin Luther King, Jr.'s birthday off, but the union workers did. I thought it strange, seeing how most of the union boys I had interactions with were clearly, if not slightly, biased against Blacks.

One day, as I walked through the plant, some union guys stopped to chat. One asked the other why he didn't take the day off, and the other responded to the effect, "Why should I take the day off? I don't care nothing 'bout that man!" To show you how bad it was, we overheard one of the managers in the flight controls group tell the HR person that he would take an intern but he "didn't want a Black one." Wow. And this guy actually came off to me as one of the nice ones! The intern he wound up with was a very attractive young lady of Asian or Middle Eastern descent. During her internship, she *always* had some white guy at her desk talking to her. I'm sure they were more than willing to teach her whatever she needed to know about what they were doing. Like my Daddy once told me, after his years of growing up in South Alabama in the 50s and 60s, "Son, there are some good white folks out here…but don't you *EV-ER* make the *mistake* of thinking that the *average* white person *gives a damn* about you!" Daddy wasn't telling me to hate white folks, but he was teaching me not to be too trusting of them. I give the same advice to you, Dear Reader.

My first performance review said it all. I sat down with my supervisor and his immediate boss (our group manager), an old guy who reported to the department head, to go over my performance of the previous year. The group manager said I was "doing a good job" and I had some areas of improvement. The one statement they put forth was "needs to work on his (my) technical skills." Okay. What the hell does that mean? Vague, to say it best. After a year, you were promoted to engineer. I was promoted to associate engineer and given a 2.5 percent pay raise.

I remember the look on his face when he handed me the little card that had my new title and rank (it read something like 1/2 or 2/3 because titles had a numbering system that went along with them) on it. It was almost a look like, "Gee, I hope he doesn't get mad," but none of this registered with me at the time. I was a "newbie", the rookie, the novice, the newcomer, the FNG, and all the other wonderful terms that describe a person fresh on the job. I had no *clue* what to make of all this. No clue as to how a performance review should go, or how I should respond. I read over the form, meekly signed the paper, thanked them both, took the little card with my new title and pay raise on it, and went back downstairs. I came into the lab and Gene was sitting at his computer. I stopped and spoke to him about my review and showed him my card. He looked at it, took a pause, and then proceeded to tell me that I had basically been given the title of a technician, not an engineer, and the pay raise said a whole lot as well. Anything less than 3 or 4 percent means that you're not really that valuable to them. I figured he was right because one young white guy in another group in the AIC I had befriended told me later in the week how he had gotten a 6 or 7 percent raise, and he was going on some trip some f**king where in the not-too-distant future. I was happy for him, but didn't really care at that moment.

Well, didn't I get myself into a fine mess? I guess it didn't help that I didn't really socialize with my group too much outside of normal working hours. I'd sit at lunch on occasion, and Thursdays was Chinese food day where everyone inter-ested would order from this local restaurant that delivered. They would take an hour for lunch on those days, and so I'd make it a point to eat with them. But anything offsite, with the exception of the time we all went to lunch for St. Patrick's Day, I generally avoided. I hadn't yet grasped the social and political side of engineering.

We got some Swiss gentlemen who came aboard to work for a period of time in an exchange program. Switzerland was an F-18 Hornet customer, and one of them was assigned to our group. His name was René. A real nice guy, he was a pilot as well as an engineer, and I got to know him well. We went to lunch on several occasions and while he was in the US, he worked on one of his flying certifications because he was taking lessons at the tiny airport in St. Charles, Missouri. He invited me to go with him on a solo flight and it was a very exciting experience. To be able to shadow someone who was training as a pilot—performing the walk-around and pre-flight checks, watching him submit his flight plan at the airport office, and then getting into the cockpit of a single-engine Cessna and taking off—was a memorable time. He even let me take the controls for a couple of minutes. I didn't do any fighter pilot maneuvers, but it was very gratifying for me. We were able to stay in touch for a while after we both left the AIC.

The one cool thing about being in the INS Group was that as they released new software loads for INUs, they had to be tested on the three-axis pedestals, as well as in real flight. The AIC had access to two test-bed aircraft at the hangars where they housed the tactical aircraft for final delivery. These were twin-engine turboprops, a King Air 90 and a larger King Air 250 or 350. The

INS group would load the INUs, usually the line replaceable units (LRUs) that were used on both the F-15 and F-18, onto a specially designed tray assembly that was bolted to the floor of the aircraft along with several racks of test equipment, which included a computer that would run the tests and record data of the INUs' performance. At the conclusion of the flights, the equipment would be offloaded and the data would be analyzed to see if the units were performing within a specified tolerance. Basically, the equipment recorded the position and movement of the aircraft accurately. Some of these flights required aggressive maneuvering, which included climbs and dives to prescribed altitudes in rapid succession, and the infamous spiral of death, which required the aircraft to fly level at a certain height, about 15,000 feet. Then the pilot would bank the aircraft into a hard turn and dive down to about 5,000 feet before leveling out again.

I think some of my coworkers got sick on previous flights, so when I was physically cleared to participate, I jumped at every chance I got, even though I learned to sometimes act like I really didn't want to go. The time I spent in the air was considered hazard pay, so I got a little extra on my paychecks when I did get to fly. Plus, I wanted to spend as much time away from that go-dawful lab as possible. Part of this effort finally afforded me the opportunity to do some real design work in my mind. René and I had designed some new cable harnesses and a switch box that was to be used with a new INU coming on line. I think it was an LRU that was being design by Litton, and it combined the laser ring gyroscopes from the existing INUs with a new GPS receiver that was supposed to be more accurate than the INUs in use.

It was called an EGI unit, embedded GPS/inertial navigation, and was much smaller and lighter than its predecessors. One day, René and I took the test equipment to the hangar and got to talking about the work environment and my role in it. Out of the blue, René said to me in his Swiss-German accent, "You know the only reason you're there is because you're Black, right?" Uh, say whaaaaaaatt?! So, the truth finally revealed its ugly head, although I wasn't in complete shock about it. That's the one thing I will say about the European cats, in their broken English, they can be up front and honest like a muthaf**ka'! We didn't have too much time to discuss this matter in detail, because we were already close to the hangar when he dropped that on me, but I had had my fill of subtle harassment and bullsh*t from these people. I knew that I wasn't going to progress any further than where I was and how far they decided to let me go. I was finally privy to how to make moves within the company and found an opportunity in the building next door, B106, which was the training systems organization.

3.2 A Move in the Right Direction

After 18 miserable months in the AIC, I transferred over to McDonnell Douglas Training Systems (MDTS), and worked in Department K321 in Building 106. The "K" represented training, and 321 was electrical engineering. The guy who hired me in was pretty cool and helped me get acclimated as quickly as possible. With any large organization, there were multiple layers of bureaucracy and, for those of you going into multibillion dollar corporations, you will have several managers whom you may report to. I had a project manager, a group manager who reported to the EE manager, and the EE manager who reported to the department head, and an electrical lead (direct supervisor). I had a fairly steep learning curve, but as long as I stayed focused, I was doing okay.

My first project was on the Apache crew training suite that was already in progress. It was called the APS, Apache player suite. It was a very simple mock-up with basic helicopter flight controls and three television monitors patched into a computer system and graphics generator that produced a crude video of a first-person view of a selected landscape. The AH-64 Apache is the US Army's premier attack helicopter that earned its reputation blasting tanks from up to seven miles away during Operation Desert Storm in 1991. There were always improvements and modifications coming from the airframe manufacturing side. Our organization was responsible for keeping up with these changes and providing them in our training and simulation products on all of the airframes that MDTS was marketing toward military customers.

Needless to say, I was still a minority, but the differences between AIC and MDTS were like night and day. MDTS was its own "company within the company," and was fairly young compared to the tactical aircraft (TACAIR) side of MDA. We had our own VP, who reported to the Senior VP of what soon became Boeing Support Services after the company merger in 1997. It was a little more diverse, as well. Still a handful of Black folks, but more women and not as many old white guys. There was an older African-American gentleman in my department, and a few contract employees of color who came and went over time. It wasn't ideal, but it was heaven compared to where I had been. The dress code was a lot more relaxed than over at AIC. I can't remember if we could only wear jeans on Fridays, but the shirt-and-tie look was definitely out the window. By the time I left MDA (now Boeing), we were wearing blue jeans every day.

The training and support systems (TSS) group was more fast-paced than INS. I wasn't dealing with boring LRUs trying to figure out why a printed circuit board didn't work. We were actually building trainers, or simulators, from the ground up. We designed and built large video games for pilots to practice their craft of flying and deploying various weapons in a simulated environment. We had simple one-screen desktop units; multiple-monitored cockpit mock-ups; and fully-enclosed, six-axis full-motion simulators (FMS) that provided very realistic combat training for US and foreign customers; and various systems in between those aspects. When a contract was signed and a statement of work was handed down to the engineers, we had so many months to meet certain project milestones (deadlines) to get payments, and some contracts had penalty clauses in the event that our deliveries were late, so when it was time to get to work, it was time to get to work!

The electrical engineers did their designs from a top-level system point of view, or as my group manager schooled me: "We are integrators." What this meant was that we didn't do detailed, board-level design, but rather complete systems design where we started with a blank sheet of paper, an idea of what the customer wanted, and began the process of different ideas and design constraints. I wasn't on anybody's flight line, but I was finally getting the chance to do what I considered real engineering work.

After the introduction to TSS on the APS project, I was able to be on the Apache program and worked on several major projects from start to finish. We had two major projects going on, the US Army mobile trainer and the United Kingdom (UK) Ministry of Defense Army Apache FMS and mobile trainers. The US Army program consisted of building cockpit mock-ups with a motion seat and a set of five or six flat screens that could fit inside air-conditioned trailers and could be pulled by truck into theaters of operation. The British program had mobile trainers with the same concept but had domed screens that would enclose the cockpit to give a wider field-of-view instead of the fixed screens. The FMS had two cockpits inside large domed screens that sat atop platforms on six hydraulic legs that would move up and down to represent the various ranges of motions that a helicopter encounters during flight. For 4½ years, TSS in B106 would be my home.

I still wasn't privy to all of the politics of Corporate America, but I was a bit more social with the members of my project group and department. I made a few friends along the way, some of whom I still keep in contact with to this day. But I still had plenty of learning to do. In a fast-paced or high-pressure environment, the potential for mistakes is greater than in a slow-paced one. You have to ensure that your work is accurate, and then hope to God that the senior engineer who checks your work is pretty good and will catch any mistakes you may make. TSS had a drawing check group, the Checkers we called them, who would review our drawings to ensure they met TSS drawing standards, and were also grammatically and visually correct. There were more than a few occasions where you hated them because you'd get your drawings back with red-inked comments and corrections on every page. They "bled all over it," as we used to say. But in hindsight, I will say this, "A good checker makes for a good engineer." You will begin to apply the same principles and techniques on your designs, drawings, and reports, and your mistakes will become fewer and fewer.

I became more knowledgeable about how things were done at TSS and became fairly good at doing electrical design work, from top-level block diagrams down to detailed cable assembly drawings and power system layouts. I learned how to use the computer-aided design (CAD) package for electrical engineers called L-Cable. It was a schematic, wiring diagram, and wire harness design program that helped create documents for the manufacturing of the electrical hardware on the simulators. From power distribution, lighting, audio communications, to ethernet signals, this CAD program could produce reports that consisted of the detailed piece parts needed for our interconnections and intricate circuits. Another good thing about these programs was that the devices were manufactured in-house. In other words, all parts and major components were ordered for delivery to, or made at, the facility, and the systems were built at the MDA plant. We had allotted space in B101, which was a major manufacturing plant there. Various parts for the C-17 transports and fighter aircraft were built there, and then shipped over to final assembly in California or across the road (TACAIR). TSS was given the back corner to build the training devices and store all of the parts needed. Our engineering group was eventually moved from B106 to a section in B101, where we had closer access to where the trainers were being built. Once the manufacturing started, it was here that I was able to really "cut my teeth" as an engineer, because now I had to learn the function of liaison engineering. The workers who worked in the shop (workshop or factory floor) were blue-collared and unionized. I learned quickly that at MDA, there was a sort of love-hate relationship between salaried and hourly workers. It could be even more precarious because these were skilled craftsmen who disdained young, hotshot, know-it-all, "Hey, you have to listen to me because I have a college degree" engineers who set foot on their turf and tried to tell them what to do. You had to give them their respect, to a certain degree, and let them know you were there to help, not fight. You couldn't be pushed around, either. There were times that I had to respectfully disagree with the union lead man over a drawing change or requirement. He didn't like it too much, but I was able to get past the "Oh no, he's mad at me" phase, and take care of business.

At TSS, I even got a pay raise my first few weeks there because my hiring manager looked at my rank and inquired as to what was going on. I can't remember exactly why I told him, but I do remember him saying that that needed to be fixed. I wasn't rolling in the money, but the rate increase was enough to be appreciated. The guy who was my electrical lead at the time eventually moved on and his replacement was a quiet guy from Massachusetts. He was amiable enough, but standoffish to a certain degree. When I got my annual review from him, I didn't accept everything on there this time. It was something to the effect that I was "doing a good job, but…" and the pay raise was around 3-4%. An average raise, to be sure, but I had a problem with his comments. They weren't negative per se, but they weren't glowing, either. For a time, I experienced a small victory because he amended his comments on my review.

The one thing I can say about my time at TSS on the Apache Program is that I got a real respect for the "tool pushers." I already had some respect because in either '95 or '96 before I left AIC, the International Association of Machinists and Aerospace Workers Union went on a three-month strike. To keep the company going, they "drafted" white-collared workers to perform factory floor jobs while they were getting replacement workers (called scabs by the unions) from across the country. You ain't never lived 'til you have to go to work and cross picket lines on a daily basis. And unfortunately, I got "drafted" out of my department and ended up working the sheet metal line of the F/A-18 Hornet wing stub section. If I was smart, I would've volunteered and been one of the security monitors who got to ride around the plant on bikes and watch for any acts of sabotage or vandalism. But because I was trying to avoid getting involved altogether, I didn't volunteer and my supervisor and group manager in INS came up to me one dreary sunny day and asked me to volunteer to work in the plant. I spent a week going to an evening class for a crash course on sheet metal work, learning how to drill holes and drive and buck rivets.

When I ended up on the factory floor, I got a real taste of

what the blue-collar work environment was like. The supervisors were very pushy and rude; it didn't help that a lot of the scab workers looked and acted like they had been kidnapped from truck stops or prison work release programs. Some of these individuals were either strange, or weren't the brightest stars in the sky, and their work ethic and technical skills showed it. We had one wing section for the Swiss F/A-18 program that we misdrilled and butchered so badly that it had at least three bright orange non-conformity (noncoms) tags hanging off of it by the time we moved it on down the assembly line. I stood there thinking, "I sure hope to God they don't try to fly with that thing." The one guy I had to work with on rivets one week just started riveting one day before I could properly put the bucking bar in place, and it damaged my right hand. To this day, I still have the scars on the fingertips of my three primary fingers. But I did learn a lot in those three months and had a greater appreciation for the skill and experience that the union craftsmen had to employ.

Over the course of the initial manufacturing of the Apache training systems, which included the building of support equipment cabinets for instructors/operators, computers, and graphics processors, there were numerous drawing changes and design upgrades. Some of these were attributed to design errors, and others were due to improvements for ease of manufacturing and maintenance.

One day, the shop lead man (the senior craftsman on the job) called me over to an equipment cabinet to question a facet of the design that consisted of placing a piece of equipment in a very tight space. I wasn't a mechanical design engineer and didn't feel qualified to address his concern, but he wanted me to see what they had to deal with when following a design on paper. He said to me, "Dusty, try to fit your hand in here with a screwdriver…" He handed me a tool and I proceeded to try to screw an LRU to a dzus rail within the tight confines of the lower cabinet. I have fairly skinny fingers and arms, so slipping my hand and screwdriver into the space was no problem…The *problem* was actually turning the screwdriver and fitting a screw into the confined space. There was no room to turn the tool to the proper angle, as well as fit your second hand into the space while holding a screw, *and* being able to see this orchestrated chaos take place simultaneously. I gave up after the third try and handed the tool back to him as he stood there with this *huge* grin on his face. I told him I saw the point he was making. Since that day, I've always tried to tailor my design with the manufacturer and maintainer in mind, while meeting the customer's design requirements. They are the ones who ultimately have to build it, install it, or remove and repair it. Having to liaise between manufacturing and engineering was one of the best things that could've happened for me as far as my technical career was concerned. I can remember both the union workers and my father occasionally saying, "They didn't teach you this in school, did they?" I learned to see a product from both the engineer's and manufacturer's point of view. Because of this hands-on experience, I even learned how to fix a few things around my house that I finally purchased in 1999, instead of paying someone $80 just to show up in my driveway before even looking at a problem.

Meanwhile, I was working, trying to build up my savings in my company 401(k) program, and taking the occasional self-improvement classes the MDA had to offer. They called them VIP classes, which was the acronym for Voluntary Improvement Program. At the time, it was actually a pretty top-notch program for the employees across a wide range of subjects, both technical and nontechnical. I readily admit that I didn't take complete advantage of the learning that was available to me, but I'll get into that later on.

One thing that I will expound on was my behavior while at MDA/Boeing. I have always been an outgoing and friendly person, for the most part. I am not your typical engineer: quiet and introverted. I don't think most African-Americans are, regardless of profession, but that's not my field of expertise, just my opinion. I still made it a point to get around and meet people, shake hands, find out who did what, who the major players in the organization were, and so forth. My coworkers began to call me Senator Walker, because it appeared that I was out trying to win votes. I had also gained ambitions to become a lead or manager in the organization. And why not? I was the older Brother in my immediate family and I have always enjoyed the responsibility of leadership. And there lies the rub: I wanted a managerial position, but I wanted to be a leader. Unfortunately, in a huge multi-bazillion-dollar corporation with enough employees to create a small city, it's hard to effectuate change from the bottom up. Plus, I was still in an old, conservative, white-male-dominated environment that didn't have too many Colored folk in key positions, save for a few in visible positions but with very little power. But I was still green on corporate culture and politics and figured in this age of equal opportunity, I had just as much a chance as anyone else to move up. I would set up appointments with upper management to pick their brains and ask for advice on how to advance. I'd get some useful advice that sounded good and was textbook material based upon the corporate environment of the 80s and 90s. I was also hoping that if they knew me well enough, maybe they'd recommend me if an opportunity presented itself. *Silly Negro*.

I was friendly and outgoing enough, but I was probably too friendly. You see, the same rules that apply to certain populations, i.e., Negroes, Hispanics, Asians, and any other race of non-European origin, don't apply to White people, unless they really, really, really, screw up. The White boys can stand around and laugh and joke and talk about non-work-related stuff like golf for 20 minutes. But if I took 5 or 10 minutes to chat with people, I was being "unproductive" or a "distraction" to those trying to work, even though they were probably as engaged in the conversation as I was. It's cool to be able to talk about a wide range of topics or a major current event, but at the end of the day—don't nobody give a damn. I also made the mistake of thinking that because a White person was congenial at work, I could call them a friend. Wrong! I found out the hard way that most White folks at work are congenial because they have to be. You work with them in relatively close quarters and you may be on the same project together, so they really have no choice, especially if they need sh*t from you to get something done. When you're out and about and you happen to see them with their family or White friends, nine out of 10 times, they will walk right past you without seeing you or speaking to you. If you do happen to speak, they may give you that, "Oh wow! Hey! What's your name again?" look to play off the fact that they have some sort of relationship with you so they won't get kicked out of their social circle. There were more than enough instances of where I'd be playful, not in a harmful way, but playful nonetheless. This is a big corporate no-no. Whereas the White boys can be practical jokers all day, even to the point of damaging company property or typing things up on your company computer without your permission, you try to pull a prank or a joke on somebody and your ass might be called into the HR department for disciplinary action or worse, termination. So my advice is to be cordial at arm's length, get to know who is really cool, but maintain the appearance of being about the company's business.

3.3 LEARNING TO READ THE "SIGNS"

After 4½ years on the Apache Program, I had seen two training systems designed and built to completion for delivery to the military customer. It was a refreshing accomplishment for me. I even received a few certificates of appreciation and decent pay raises in the process, but I wasn't satisfied. I wasn't satisfied with my pay rate because I knew over time that I was being underpaid as compared to what my White contemporaries were making, and I still had aspirations to become a manager within TSS. So somewhere along the way, I thought it would be a good idea to pursue my Master's Degree in Business Administration (MBA). I looked around at the local colleges and settled in for the evening program at Saint Louis University (SLU), or "slew" as it was called. In hindsight, I wish I had enrolled at Washington University. It was more of the "Harvard of the Midwest" than SLU was; but regardless, I had never heard of either university before moving to Missouri. I was under the impression that an MBA would make me more marketable as a manager and that I'd learn valuable skills for running an organization or "business unit" as some companies like to call their divisions. So I started taking the requisite courses in a 3-year, part-time program.

While I was at TSS, MDA was bought out by, and merged with, the Boeing Company, which was headquartered in Seattle, Washington. This was both good and bad, in case you, the Reader, ever end up in a company that is bought by another one. Bad because there will be changes by the new owners. Good because there will be potentially *good* changes by the new owners. In a lot of cases, the old management is rarely left in place after a merger, the new owners want their own people in the business units running the show the way they want it run. I was too far down the totem pole or corporate ladder rungs to be worried about it. I mention the merger here because Boeing did implement some additional training programs, which included producing future managers from within rather than continually going outside the company. These were training courses set up like a college curriculum, where any potential or existing managers had to have certain courses completed before they could be considered for higher level positions and so forth. I signed up for the entry-level courses, and got initial approval from my Apache program manager at the time. He was an older gentleman, a former army pilot, a bit of a hard-ass in that he had a no-nonsense type of personality, but he was a pretty straight shooter and in my three years working for him, I never had the indication that he lied or "bullsh*tted" me on the things I talked to him about. So there I was, enrolled in an MBA course or two at SLU and also taking pre-management classes at now Boeing-St. Louis, and working on a major US/UK Army Aviation Simulator Program, all on Boeing's dime.

Speaking of dimes, apparently while all the paperwork and "legalese" were working their way through the Securities and Exchange Commission and US Congress, Boeing had a team come in and do a trade study on our salaries. They came to the conclusion that we at MDA had been grossly underpaid for forever and a day and we all got significant bonuses or pay raises that year. They even changed the job descriptions and ranking system to be more in line with how they operated. I was now an Engineer 2. Woo-hoo!

Meanwhile, back at the plantation, on the Apache Program, things were starting to go awry. I was in the hardware group and we pretty much had completed our designs and were now providing technical support as the program began the testing phase on the trainers. The big issue now was that the software programs had bugs in them and it was costing time and money to get them fixed. This caused some delays that the customers were not too happy about. One time, a customer came in and one of the managers flat out lied to them about something, either how the program was progressing or whether we were going to meet a milestone (deadline). I couldn't believe it, but I was a fly on the wall as I just happened to be passing by. A lot of people transferred out of the group and off the programs, "turnover" as it is commonly called in the business world. Webster's defines turnover as "the rate of replacement of workers."

One day, I noted that one of the rare, "good" smart White guys had flown the coop. I said to myself, "Man, if so-and-so left, what's really going on?" I called Daddy one night about it and he didn't hesitate to tell me to get the hell out of there. "Son, if the White boys is runnin,' you *KNOW* it's time to go!" This country and corporate system is designed by and for White males, so if they are "jumping ship," that's a surefire sign that something is wrong. I began to look around the company for an opportunity, and landed a design position within TSS, but it was on F-18 Maintenance Trainers (MTS – Maintenance Training System). Because it was a Hornet program, even though we were still part of Training Systems, the group was located over in Building 270, the "Hornet Building." So I packed up my belongings and rolled out. It would be another growth opportunity, but it would have its challenges, as well.

The Maintenance Training Group was responsible for building training devices that teach military personnel how to maintain and troubleshoot (eliminating the source of trouble in workflow or functionality) systems on aircraft. In my case, I was now on the program that had responsibility for the devices that represented the seven primary systems on the F-18E Super Hornet. The Super Hornet was a new version of the venerable F-18 and had entered service with the US Navy in 1999, so the maintenance crews had to be trained how to fix them while operating from land bases or underway in aircraft carrier battle groups. The devices we had were already built by another simulator company out of Florida as trainers for C & D versions, and they lost the contract for the E/F training program. Our jobs were to upgrade the trainers to match the Super Hornet configuration. Part of this mission entailed us getting all technical data from the drawings and designs of the existing devices, comparing their layouts to the actual aircraft systems, and then making the necessary changes to make the trainers match the aircraft. Upon completion of the hardware and software changes, the US Navy maintenance instructors would be able to conduct classes and then subject students to scenarios where they would have to determine the cause of system failure and fix it. The devices were housed at Naval Air Station Lemoore under the command of Naval Air Maintenance Training Group in Lemoore, California, and I'd eventually get to travel out there to see the devices firsthand.

In my group, there were two other EEs, one being the supervisor, and a group of mechanical engineers who sat in a row of desks on the other side of our cubicle walls. There were other Maintenance Programs going on in the building, and our small rabble was embedded with the Royal Australian Air Force and Royal Canadian Air Force F-18 Maintenance Training groups. The guys I sat with were more systems engineers than designers, doing risk assessments and project scheduling on their foreign military programs. One of them was a Brother from TSU who was in my freshman class. We had a decent relationship, but we weren't close at TSU and it wasn't about to change now. As I mentioned earlier, with any large organization, the executives find ways to create multiple layers of management and bureaucracy to keep the workers focused and organized on the tasks at hand (not always). I had a supervisor, a group supervisor, a program manager, a director, and then a VP of whatever he was, but my director reported to him. We also had a host of people in the organization who, to this day, I literally have no idea what they did. They would show up to work every day, and a lot of times it didn't look like they were doing much of anything. That's the one thing about huge companies, they have so many people that at some point, jobs are going to overlap and/or the job requirements will be so minute that people can be "lost in the shuffle" and will sit there collecting checks for years without doing any real work. That usually doesn't apply to Colored folk, mind you, but you get the idea. On a positive note, I did get my very first Black manager, the program manager for MTS.

My new program manager was a Brother from St. Louis who was cool, but also very hard-driving and ambitious. He let me know in no uncertain terms that "Yeah, we Brothers, *but* I still got a job to do and with you or without you, I'm getting it done." Those weren't the exact words, but you get my drift. Having an African-American manager is a double-edged sword. It can be cool because for the first time, you're reporting to someone who looks like you and, for once, you're not looking up to what I call "The Grand High (White) Benefactor." You can only hope that they know that they are Black and can relate to you on the social level, not necessarily in exact background and experience, but they still know that your upbringing, culture, and thoughts are *not* going to be that of mainstream America, i.e., the White majority.

If the manager is over a group that is predominately White, you have to tread lightly, especially if they have superiors above them who can have them easily replaced. More often than not, your coworkers secretly resent the fact that they have to take orders from a nigger, and depending on how much they like or hate him (or her), that will determine if they decide to conspire to have him or her removed. This can be done either by trumping up complaints that they will take to the next higher up, or they will slack off in their work production to the point that it's noticed by the upper management and the Black manager will have to give account. It's not their fault, but the coworkers have planted the seeds of doubt in the mind(s) of the executives and they will start looking for a replacement. So with all of this in mind, don't expect any preferential treatment because you have the same skin color. Matter of fact, you may have to work twice as hard just so they can continue to look good and keep their job and YOU in the group!

Unfortunately, I have seen Black managers be unnecessarily harsh with their fellow Black subordinates because they didn't want to appear that they were fraternizing with them because they were Black. It's a trip, but it's reality. If they have a choice between helping you along with job opportunities, greater responsibility and visibility, pay raises, glowing reviews, and whatnot, at a certain level of risk to their own position and status or remaining comfortable and keeping the status quo, you will LOSE every time. Every now and then, you will have a maverick who will help you out regardless of grumblings and naysayers and potential backlash from the workers or upper management, but it's very rare and you need to make damn sure that you perform to the level of expectation if you are given a chance to advance from them.

Now if it's a small company and the Brother or Sister owns the thing, they are the "HNIC" (Head Nigger in Charge) and can do whatever they please. But in a large, publicly traded company, it's difficult. On the other side of the coin, you may be given an opportunity to advance or "show what you can do" at the behest of the Black manager, but you need to make sure he or she is kept in the loop as to what you are doing. First of all, you need to make sure whatever tasks and assignments you are given are realistic and doable. When given the tasks, do them correctly and in whatever timeframe is allotted. Second of all, you need to make sure that the manager is still in the chain of command while you are doing this. Case in point: I met a Brother a few years ago who was working at some company, and the VP of this particular unit happened to be Black and I don't know if he hired him or took him under his wing shortly after he came aboard. But I do know the VP went to the workers in the group and basically told them that he wanted them to take care of this young man and he expected them to do this, this, and this for him and I guess it gave the impression that he was under his protection, so to speak. Well, boys and girls, them White folks got together and began to dump *loads* of work on this poor Brother. Meanwhile, his protection had moved on to doing other things to keep his job valid and I don't know if he left him stranded on purpose or if the young guy didn't know how to report to him about what was happening. But eventually, he either transferred out of that group or left the company altogether. So unless you are in a highly diverse environment with managers of both sexes and various ethnicities and backgrounds, you're going to be on your own.

While I was on the MTS Program, I did get some good advice from my program manager, as well as the VP of the organization. Of course, when I got there, I wanted to meet this guy and do the same thing I had done over in B106 in TSS. I found his office and promptly introduced myself to his secretary and why I wanted to meet with him. Well, different group, larger group, different philosophies. I guess this guy didn't have as "open" an open door policy as my previous managers. For whatever reason, she called my program manager about my visit and I guess she scolded him and told him he needed to keep his birds in the cage or something to that effect, because he took me off to the side and told me I shouldn't have done that and that I just got here and needed to get my feet wet before approaching folks. I understood what he was saying, but I was still ambitious and hadn't gotten completely institutionalized by the corporate machine yet.

I finally got a few minutes one-on-one with the VP after a huge organizational meeting in the building cafeteria. I approached him and asked if I could walk back with him toward his office. I asked the same thing I had asked of my previous managers, "How do I get ahead?" He told me that I needed to do as good a job as possible, but I also needed to learn as much about my job and the workings of my organization so that I could become the "Go-To Guy." This is the person who can be relied upon or is regularly sought out to resolve a difficult problem or situation. So that was a valuable piece of advice I have carried with me ever since. My program manager told me one day in the relative privacy of his office that I had a difficult uphill climb as far as advancing within Boeing. It was a defense contractor, so a lot of its workers and executives were former military, composed mostly of White males with extremely conservative views. Being an African-American male, I had to overcome the stereotype of being "angry all of the time" and shiftless, as well as avoid using slang when communicating with them. I would have to prove myself to them with very little room for error. While I did not think this was a fair shake, I appreciated him talking straight to me. The time for "baby talk" was indeed over.

During my time with MTS, I got a taste of reality of working with a group of different, and sometimes strange, White people. I was still the effervescent, happy-go-lucky individual in the group. Talking too much about football and how I hated the Rams or loved fishing or whatever, not knowing that I was presenting an "image," or my favorite term, "perspective," that I wasn't doing any work. I also learned the hard way that you can't joke with White folks the same way you can with your boys back in the dorm or at the bar. One day, I thought I was harmlessly joking with this systems engineer who sat in the cubicle with the MEs, and he straight gave me the middle finger, flipping me off, and then turned right back to his computer monitor as if nothing happened. You had people who would fall asleep at their desks almost daily because they didn't do jack sh*t; everybody knew it, but nothing was ever done or said to them apparently. Like

I mentioned earlier, keep everything professional and at arm's length. Every now and then, you'll befriend a cool White person whom you can relax a little bit with, but do so cautiously. And, of course, beware of your conversation when women are around. You never know what could be construed as offensive or sexist. There were some nice people in the group, and I'd go to lunch with them from time to time, but I was still not completely comfortable with them.

3.4 IMAGE IS EVERYTHING

Although I look back on my early career and see things that I wish I had done differently in hindsight, I know that I was a hard worker as far as meeting deadlines and providing technically correct designs. I was with MTS right at two years when I decided to go back over to TSS in Building 106. This time, I'd be working aircrew trainers for fixed-wing fighters, primarily Air Force platforms like the F-15, F-16, and T-38C. The last piece of advice my MTS program manager gave me was to go into this new group and hit the ground running, work really hard the first eight to twelve weeks to establish a good reputation. Well, try as I might, this didn't work too well for me.

I had an EE supervisor, a systems engineer who could provide me direction, a project manager, a program manager, and another director who reported to the TSS VP. When I arrived at my new spot, I had an overview of what I was going to be working on and I pretty much knew the layout of the area and I thought, "Piece of cake." Well, apparently the project manager liked to have an eye on his minions at all times, and the systems engineer I sat next to was telling me how this guy was already talking bad about me because I wasn't at my desk when he stood up one particular time and made a comment, "Well, he certainly isn't in a hurry to get to work, is he?" *What? Damn. For real?* I just got here.

Remember how I told you that I had developed a back condition that got exacerbated when I started working? There were times when I was over in AIC in my dress shoes with my flat feet, that the pain in my back would be so excruciating, I could barely walk to my truck. I would hardly make it to my apartment, and once there, would lie on my stomach for a few hours before the pain dissipated. I finally saw a chiropractor who showed me an X-ray of my lower back. The vertebra was slightly angled and the cartilage around it had worn away, so it was pinching the nerve. The first doctor I saw was okay, but he wasn't the best. I saw him once or twice a week and the treatments were only advancing a little at a time. I finally figured out that he was milking my company's insurance because we had a limited number of doctor visits per year. I went to an African-American doctor who looked at my X-ray and pretty much told me that I was too young for him to be cutting me open to perform surgery on. I needed to get on an aggressive workout program to build up my lower back muscles, and because I sat at a computer all day, I needed to take time every 30–45 minutes and move around for a bit.

Anyway, I got heat from the project manager several times more for being away from my desk too long or him not knowing where I was, and I had become fed up with it. So I said to myself, "OK, he wants to know where I am at all times? Fine, so be it." So I started playing a little game of my own. Whenever I got up from my desk, I would tape a sheet of paper either on the computer monitor or the back of my desk that would read something like, "RESTROOM," "CAFETERIA," "GONE to SEE FRANK," or "COFFEE ROOM," and any other conceivable place I could be if they really wanted to keep tabs on me.

After a week or so of this, I was called into the program manager's office and my project manager was in there, as well. The program manager said that all that wasn't necessary, and to this I replied that I had been reprimanded for being away from my desk too long according to the project manager, and so I wanted to allay his concerns by letting him and anyone else know where I was and at what time I had departed my desk. I think he understood my take on the matter and why I resorted to doing what I did. I even gave him a copy of a doctor's statement about my back condition and how I needed to get up to stretch and move around for a few minutes every hour. He then proceeded to explain to me that they weren't trying to harass me, but I needed to avoid a certain perception. *Perception?* I inquired as to what they meant and they danced around the answer with a "Well, you just don't want to appear to be gone from your desk too long…" Translation: You're a Black guy in our group and we don't want anyone thinking that we're giving you too much freedom, because to be 'working,' you have to be seated at your desk. OK, whatever. I was one of the fastest and most thorough electrical engineers in the group. When the folks on the shop floor had a question, they would either give me a call or come upstairs to speak to me directly. And I was cranking out my electrical schematics and wire harness diagrams for the trainers on time or ahead of schedule.

I was still the social butterfly, but I was doing my work and still taking MBA classes at SLU and progressing through the Boeing pre-management and leadership courses. For the executive track, I had to take three courses before I could apply for classes that my department head had to approve. I applied for, attended, and tested out of all three in less than six months. Whatever the timeframe, it was a relatively short period compared to the "average" attendee because several people marveled at how quickly I had completed them. I didn't think it was that big a deal, to be honest. But you tend to think that way when you've been trained to excel at whatever it is you do. Because I still had aspirations to be a leader within the company, I was taking the classes and I was still trying to get one-on-one meetings with executive-level managers within the company.

I was able to have a few minutes with the senior VP of Boeing Aerospace Operations, which TSS fell under. He was an older gentleman of British descent, and he was very friendly and open, which I found surprising for a man at his level. Most executives I've met are arrogant cutthroats who would sell their firstborn child if it meant getting ahead. I remember the one lesson he taught me on how business is sometimes really done. He gave me an example of what he meant.

"Let's say I have an open position, and I have two candidates. Both are experienced and well-qualified for it. But as I begin to look at their work histories, I notice that one of them has worked in a company or a division for somebody that I know and have a good relationship with. I will immediately call that person up and say, 'Hey, what can you tell me about this guy? Is he a good person to hire?' And if they give me a favorable report, he will be the one hired. The other one will be relegated to a category I term, 'Necessary, but not sufficient.'"

I was being taught the value of working relationships and having a good reputation in the corporate world. Some people call it networking, others call it "greasing the skids (or the wheels)," but ultimately, it comes down to who you know; more specifically, who you know who *has power*. I have found this to be true, and will expound on this in a little bit.

I was working on designs for new fighter simulators as well as retrofits for existing trainers. I was still in the MBA program, but I had come to the end of the prerequisite management classes I could take without department head approval. I was also looking at advancing my career as an engineer. I reviewed the job descriptions for the engineering ranks, which went all the way up to Engineer 6. Based upon what I saw on paper, it looked like I was already doing Level 3 work. I visited my HR representative to discuss this matter as well as a few others over time.

HR departments give the impression that they are there to serve the needs of the employees. Well, I can say without hesitation that that is a big, fat lie. HR is there to take care of the company by screening job candidates based upon some long-ass, verbose job description (and they themselves *have no clue* as to what it is we engineers do); handling payroll, savings plans, health insurance benefits, and employee issues ranging from drug and gambling addiction to mental health; and finding ways to fire people without bringing a lawsuit upon the company. They are not there to look after your needs even though they have people who are supposedly in positions to do so. And unless you have a definite grievance that can be corroborated by "credible" witnesses (i.e., White people who aren't afraid to speak up on your behalf), you're wasting your time. They are the biggest waste of oxygen in the company, in my opinion, save for a handful of people whom I'm good friends with and who actually did what they were supposed to do. They know who they are, and I hope I don't upset them too much by writing about this.

I went to my HR representative repeatedly for two things: 1) I wanted to get promoted to Engineer 3, and 2) I wanted a better pay raise. My HR representative was an older African-American gentleman who had been with the company for more than twenty years and was nearing retirement. Sad to say, but he was on the downhill stretch and was just holding on until he could retire and get the hell out of there. He wasn't about to cause any waves with my department managers, especially over a young Negro who was trying to take over. I talked to him about what jobs I had been doing and how they aligned with what the Level 3 job description required. He responded to me by saying that I had to have 15 years in before I could be considered for promotion. Okay, check one off. As far as pay increases went, I was getting 3 to 4 percent increases for the past two or three years and I felt like I was losing money due to cost-of-living increases, as well as watching my White male counterparts get larger increases. He looked at my rate card (Remember the little white card?) and responded, "Well, that's about average. So you're doing good." Okay, check two off. I thanked him for his time and went back to my desk. I sat there for a while and pondered on what had happened.

I took notice of the people who had been at the company for at least 15 years. What were they doing? What kind of money were they making? What type of lifestyles did they have? Remember that when I hired into MDA, the average employee age was already 57. I kept hearing about how the company was going to be in a crunch for subject matter experts (SME) as more and more of their experienced employees were nearing retirement age. I was naive enough to think that if I kept buzzing my superiors about how I wanted to get into lead and management roles, and the "impending doom" of 30 to 50 percent of the workforce leaving or dying off, *surely* someone above me would take me under his or her wing and begin grooming me for such a spot. I remember my HR rep giving me that "average" crap, and I thought, "Wait a minute! I'm doing above-average work and I don't consider myself an *average* employee or person!"

I had gotten to the point where I just wanted to achieve the rank (and money) of Level 3 before I started looking outside the company for other opportunities. I began to systematically talk to my group manager and department head about my ambitions to become a Level 3, almost to the point of sheer harassment. It was done professionally, of course, but I became a thorn in their side,

I'm sure. On my annual reviews, I would put my "goals" down, and among them was to become some sort of lead or management within the business unit. When the usual promotion cycle came around, I either received an email or another white card that showed me as an Engineer 3, and with it came an 8 percent pay raise. I had accomplished my mission. I also remember that my department head sent me a message that pretty much translated to: "Okay, here's your promotion and pay raise you been harassing us for…now go away!" Hey, I had the title and the money, so I was good for the moment. I kept my head down for a while and tried to be inconspicuous, but you know us ambitious Negroes can be troublemakers without much effort.

My desk was adjacent to a table and a file cabinet that stood next to the system engineer's cubicle wall. Because I was at the corner, I didn't have a wall to my left and sat exposed to the walkway that ran out to the main aisle and to the other workgroups in the opposite direction. One of the ways that I kept track of all my projects and drawings was to use a large notepad or a whiteboard when I had access to one. I went to my program manager and asked him one day if I could get one. He politely refused my request, saying that only managers with cubicles could get them. Okay, fine, no problem. Unfortunately, one day I sat there, staring at the cubicle wall and the gunmetal gray side of the file cabinet came into focus. *Hmmmm, I wonder.* I took a dry erase marker and made a small mark on the side of the cabinet. I then took an eraser and tried to remove it. Success! Well, limited success. If you looked really, really, really hard, you could see where the mark had been made. No worries. I was doing my job, sitting at my desk on time for the most part, so what could happen, right? Over the course of the next few months, I made good use of my improvised whiteboard, and used dry erasers and whiteboard spray cleaner to remove most of my writings, sketches, and football plays I'd draw up from time to time. I would not recommend that you do this, Dear Reader. I'd say save up your loot, check with your tax accountant to see if you can make a job-related tax write-off, and buy your own 2' x 3' whiteboard and supplies if you need one and your employer won't provide you one. Hopefully by now, most companies are forward-thinking and have caught up with the 21st Century as far as presentation and brainstorming materials are concerned. I digress. Back to my file cabinet/whiteboard "incident."

Everything was cool until late one afternoon, some high-up executive and his team did a walkthrough of the buildings, I guess, to see if the employees had everything they needed to do their jobs. Well, of course, they came through my area and saw my workspace and its humble accommodations. The program manager happened to be working late that day, and they called him out of his office and over to my desk. One of my coworkers, a Brother, who was a computer/IT contractor at the time, saw the whole thing and told me about it. Apparently, they inquired as to why I was writing on the sides of file cabinets and not a whiteboard. For some reason, they even had a photographer with them and they made him stand next to the file cabinet and took a very unflattering picture of him and my tasks. The executive looked at my desk, pointed his finger at it, and said, "Get this guy a whiteboard." Needless to say, I didn't win any favors from my management with that incident, but I thank God I wasn't there when it happened. Then again, who knows how I would've reacted. I may have respectfully told them why I did what I did, how I was a visual person and that I'm more focused and efficient when I see what my tasks are in large print rather than trying to keep up with everything in a binder or notebook. God only knows, but I did get a whiteboard.

3.5 THE COUP DE GRACE

It was 2003. I was approaching 10 years with Boeing and I was getting more and more frustrated with where my career was. I was doing a good job as a regular design engineer, but I felt that I could do more. At one point, I felt that if I got into a position of influence, I could effectuate some positive changes, especially for women and minorities. I still didn't have a direct mentor. I had some senior managers outside my workgroup give me pointers from time to time, but I had nobody who could really pull me along. I got a real kick in the crotch when I tried to enroll in the next level of management classes that Boeing required for its existing and potential managers. I had put in my request for a certain course and got denied by my department head. I emailed him to ask why I had been turned down, and made it a point to say that I was dying to position myself as a "valuable resource to the organization," or some politically correct bullsh*t I was trying to cook up. He only responded by saying that he had other managers who needed to take the course first. Ever since MDA was bought out by Boeing, I had an issue with this philosophy. They required all managers and executives to take these training courses that covered all kinds of leadership topics. One of the cool things that they did do was to buy this old French-style chalet that sat on a huge, multi-acre farm in St. Louis County about 10 or 15 minutes from the main Boeing complex in the suburb of Florissant, Missouri. They turned it into the Boeing Leadership Center and it was quite the spread. They had dormitory style rooms for students from across the enterprise, large and small classrooms with state-of-the-art technology, and a nice cafeteria that served up three-course meals with high-quality food, not that slop we got in the factory cafeterias. My question was what was the point of taking a manager who had been with the company for more than 20 years who had operated from the old school "No Girls or Niggers Allowed" mentality, and making them take a 1-day or 1-week course on leadership styles? Yes, they would take the course and give the appropriate answers to pass, but as soon as they got back into their environment, wasn't "a damn thang gon' change!" They were wasting their time and money on damaged goods. But it was their call and I had no advocate to vouch for me.

The denial for the executive class was but the first of a series of events that were about to rapidly bring my tenure at Boeing to a close. By this time, I was engaged, and around early October, my fiancée was in the backyard playing with our dog when she slipped awkwardly in the mud. She fell so hard that she fractured her ankle in three places. I had to pick her up, carry her into the house, and call for an ambulance. Thankfully, we lived not three minutes away from Christian Northeast Hospital and they were able to put her in a temporary cast. She was scheduled for surgery on a Wednesday or Thursday and I was the only one who could take her, so I told my group manager about it, as well as my supervisor, and followed up with an email stating that I would make up my time that following Saturday. Her surgery came and went, and she was bedridden for about three weeks until she was cleared to wear a walking boot.

Sometime in November, she was driving on the expressway when she got sideswiped by a town car, knocked into the concrete divider, bounced back into traffic, and got hit in the right rear side panel by a dump truck, which knocked her back into the dividing wall. To say that she was able to get out of the truck and walk away was nothing less than a miracle. Her Ford Explorer was totaled, but thank God she was okay. She called and told me what happened. I left work immediately and I told somebody what had happened and that I needed to leave. I think it was my supervisor, but I can't remember. The traffic was backed up because of the accident and I had to park at a gas station near one of the overpasses and climb or slip through the fence to get down onto the expressway where she was talking to the police and the dump truck driver. The driver of the town car never stopped.

Even though I had been denied the executive leadership courses, I was still trying to climb that corporate ladder. I saw a lead position for a boom operator trainer that was coming online for the KC-46 Aerial Refueling Tanker Program. At the time, the Bush administration had awarded Boeing the contract to start building the replacements for the KC-135 and KC-10 tankers the Air Force and Air National Guard forces used. The boom operator was responsible for operating the retractable arm that housed the fuel lines and connector that would mate up with helicopters and airplanes that had air-to-air refueling capabilities. Here was my chance to leap-frog the masses and make a real name for myself. Well, I got denied for that position, but here's the clincher: the position was given to this young White boy who had only been with the company no more than two or three years. He was a nice guy and I don't mean to berate him, but really!?! I had 10 years' worth of design experience and you're going to give some rookie a lead position? Really?! Yes, really fo' real. The writing on the wall was becoming more and more clear. No matter how hard I worked, or what classes I took and passed with flying colors, they "wasn't about to let no Negro" have a position of prominence in that organization. I felt like The Gap Band performing their hit single, "You Dropped A Bomb On Me," or like the Parliament lyric, "I was so low, I had to look up to see my feet." You get what I'm saying. I was "feelin' mighty low." I went to my group manager and asked why I was denied the position. Hell, I wanted to know why I wasn't even given an interview. He gave me some 'round-the-world answer, but it didn't sit right with me. Not to mention the fact that he never looked me in the eye when he was talking. It was the first time in my eight years of working for this man that I questioned his character and credibility.

The final straw came in mid-December when I was sitting at my desk and my supervisor came behind me, placed a hand on the back of my chair, and said, "Dusty, do you have a minute?" Based upon his tone, I could tell that something was amiss, but I didn't know what. We went into the conference room nearby and he closed the door behind us. *Ohhhh sh*t, now what?* He proceeded with, "——— wanted me to talk to you. You've been missing a lot of work lately." Excuse me? How so? I asked him what did he mean? He mentioned the one day I was gone in the middle of the week.

"The day I had to take my fiancée to the hospital?! I told you what was going on and sent you and ——— an email. I even made up my time by working that Saturday."

"I know, but he felt that it was necessary to talk to you about our personal time-off policy, and 'Wah, wah, wah, wah-wah'…"

I had effectively tuned him out, and sat there feeling angry and insulted. It was right there and then that I decided, "In six months, I will NOT be working here!" I had had enough. I was being held to an unreasonably high standard while the White boys could damn near get away with murder. Like I said, the rules that you are expected to follow don't apply to them. I found an opportunity with Gulfstream Aerospace Corporation (GAC) in Savannah, Georgia, in January, as a Contract Engineer. I resigned my position from Boeing with a two-week letter of resignation and left at the end of the month. I don't think they took me out to a farewell lunch. Matter of fact, I think in my twenty years, I may have been treated to lunch once. Oh well, that's the reality of being a Black man with a tenacious spirit in the White man's world.

4.0 Corporate Politics

Gosh, where do I start? I am going to try to cover a few do's and don'ts that may make the difference between a demotion, a promotion, a lateral move, or being stuck (pigeon-holed is a popular phrase) in the same damn job for the next 10–15 years, if you're not careful. Engineering is a wonderful profession. [*Profession*: A calling requiring specialized knowledge and often long and intensive academic preparation.] It has been around since the Egyptians and other ancients began their masonic crafts and built the pyramids and other majestic structures and waterways thousands of years ago. Engineering can be loosely defined as "the use of the laws of math and science for the benefit of mankind." When you have a group of skilled men and women, using science and technology, working together in harmony, great things can be accomplished. Unfortunately, as I stated earlier in the preface, in the corporate workplace, you have to deal with people. And with people, there will be differences, and there will be *conflict*.

4.1 Why You are Here

Let's talk turkey. You aren't subjecting yourself to days, weeks, months, and years of mental stress, strain, and anxiety to get a piece of parchment that states you know what the hell you are doing in a certain area to be paid peanuts. You earned that degree and now you want to see it pay dividends on your investment. I already stated earlier that the same rules that apply to them don't apply to you. Every now and then, you'll have a White manager who's fair and objective and will give you a chance to perform and rise up the corporate ladder. But if his or her superiors have subconscious biases against minorities, your manager can and will only do so much for you without damaging themselves by falling out of favor with their peers and superiors. They can't risk losing their "White Union card" as I like to put it.

You are there to do a job, get better at it, and *get paid*. Engineers can make a great living in the technology arena, but it also depends on the industry and geographic location. I will touch briefly on this when I discuss finances later. The problem is, everyone else is there to get paid, but not necessarily by doing a good job. People by their nature are lazy, and especially in large organizations, you will find people who get a paycheck every week and don't do a damn thing all week. You will find yourself wondering: How are these people on the payroll and haven't been fired *yet*? Unfortunately, that is life, and it will always be that way. It's not your problem and you don't want it to be. I'd say try to avoid these people as much as possible and interact with them only when necessary.

4.2 SOCIALIZATION

Because you are working with people and dealing with folks' livelihoods, there is going to be a good dose of cutthroat activity. I already touched on limiting your socialization and disclosing your personal business in the workplace. These people aren't your friends, and don't make the mistake of thinking as such. Unfortunately, because office success is predicated on your technical skills as well as how much you are liked and well-thought of, you have to learn to play the game. This will involve some social interaction outside of the job with your coworkers. I wish I had known this 15 years ago, but it's water under the bridge. One of the things that White folks like to do is drink, many times in excess; the consumption of alcoholic beverages is a staple in the White community. If you are not a drinker, you'll have to figure out how to interact with them while politely abstaining from drinking. But if you're a drinker, you want to enjoy a social glass of your favorite wine or spirit while keeping your wits about you. There is a Latin saying, *In Vino Veritas*, which translates into literally, "In Wine, There is Truth." You can learn a *whole* lot from folks if they get comfortable and the "licka" starts flowing.

You can learn some good and not-so-good things about the job, as well as people's personal lives and issues. Just don't you make the mistake of getting too "lit up" where you might say or do something that could put you in a bad light or worse yet, fired. The other mistake I'd avoid is trying to keep up with your coworkers as far as drinks or shots of liquor go. I made that blunder once during a business trip.

We had completed a major project milestone, so the managers took the team out to dinner. As the night wore on, after everyone had finished their meals, the waitresses started bringing shots of liquor to the table. At first I thought it was complimentary, but I noticed every few minutes, the waitresses would bring a different type of liquor or mixed drink in shot glasses for all of us. Had *no* clue that one of the managers was ordering the drinks for our table. In my naivety, I tried to keep up with my coworkers and violated one of the cardinal rules of drinking: Do *not* consume various forms of alcohol in a short period of time! I *think* as a group, the total bill was over a thousand dollars that weekend. What I *know* is that we were still working the airline project and we wrapped up dinner well after midnight.

By this time, I was drunk as a skunk, and had to report back to the hangar by 7 a.m. After catching the shuttle back to the hotel, I managed to get back to my room without stumbling or falling down. I lay down for only a few minutes before my stomach decided that eight-plus shots of strong drink was not agreeable with it. I sprang toward the toilet as my wonderful Italian meal hurled from my throat, causing me to leave the maid a very generous tip the next morning. I managed about three hours of sleep before having to get back up and make my way to work that morning. I greeted my managers and coworkers as they arrived to the hangar, and they *all* were just bright-eyed and bushy-tailed as if they had gotten a full night's sleep to my surprise. I talked to my wife about how I was dying all day to stay awake and focused through my hangover, and the others in the group were flowing like the previous night's activities had never happened. She chuckled and told me that most of them had probably been drinking since they were teenagers and had built up a tolerance for large amounts of alcohol, so they weren't as affected by the shots. My wife went to school in an affluent St. Louis neighborhood, and had plenty of opportunities to witness White high school kids, with access to their parents' liquor cabinets, consume beverages from ninth grade on. Whereas, my "non-drankin'" ass should've stopped after the second shot if I had been privy to what was happening.

"That's what you get!" she huffed as I bid her goodnight. I swore to myself I'd never allow myself to get that drunk again outside of the privacy and comfort of my own home. It was a valuable lesson learned.

I would highly recommend you use the good 'ol slave tactic when it comes to office gossip. When you are seen but not heard, you can learn truths and rumors, whereas keeping a certain degree of discretion can keep you out of the line of fire. 'Cause trust me, if they talking bad about each other, God only knows what they will be saying about you if you get caught up in folks' mess. You can participate in a conversation without ever saying a damn thing aside from neutral comments like, "Oh really?" or "You don't say?" But keep most of your opinions to yourself. Until you get a feel for who you think you can trust partially, but not totally, you might can make a comment about someone if it's based upon a general truth. But you don't want to say something about someone and it gets back to them. If you are the only Brother in the group, the last thing you need is for the whole office to gang up on you because of something you said about someone in the group. True or not, it's not worth your job and mental well-being at work. I mentioned avoiding divulging too much of your personal business to folks at work earlier, but wanted to re-emphasize that point. You don't want to gossip about anyone in your work group, not openly anyway; and you don't want to give them any ammunition to have a reason to talk about you in a negative light.

Now don't take this advice out of context. I'm not saying you can't participate in the casual conversation around the water cooler discussing sports or some world-changing event. But you need to know the boundaries and culture of the group and company you're working for. I've been in companies where the daily routine was to go to the company cafeteria at a certain time for a break between breakfast and lunch. I've been other places where the group would go to the snack bar in the late afternoon for a walk and a treat to break the stress of the day's work. You don't have to do the daily ritual 100 percent of the time, but you can be a team player and join them from time to time to show them that you're not being antisocial. That's the other edge of the sword that's swinging over your head. You can't be too social, but you don't want to be regarded as weird or sociopathic, either.

One thing I will mention is reading the signs of the group. You'll have to earn their respect by dong a great job; that goes without saying. But what if you've been there for several months, knocking the ball out of the park, and you are still getting the shunned treatment? This is the immature and rude behavior of your White coworkers that entails them purposefully leaving you out of group discussions, decisions, activities, et cetera. Even if you are in the room, they are talking around you like you're not even there. Aside from the curt greetings in the morning, they can go all day and not say another thing to you. They are basically telling you that you're not welcome there and they will do anything within legal means to force you to leave on your own accord. They did it to the African-American cadets at West Point back in the 1800s and early 1900s, and they're doing it to this day in Corporate America. You can take it and not worry about it, try to break through the walls with small talk, or make plans to bail out at the next opportune time. But like I said, you're there to do a job and make money. So as long as the money is coming, find friends in another group or outside work.

You have to also be aware of whom you are socializing with as much as how long you are socializing. Remember, if you're the only minority in the group and you're not in an open-minded organization, you're going to be held to a double standard. So aside from the group activities, you have to be measured in your social activities on the job. If folks are taking ten-minute coffee breaks, you take five or six and get back to your desk. Even if you're not extremely busy, you want to give the impression that you are. I had a situation at Boeing one time where I had come from the cafeteria for some breakfast one Monday morning. I ran into three or four Brothers whom I was friends with, but they were in different work groups. With it being a Monday in the fall, we began discussing the previous day's results of the NFL games. Now I've already told you, Dear Reader, about my insatiable appetite for the game of American football, so you can imagine my engagement in this conversation. Now truth be told, we weren't standing there for more than five minutes, but during that timeframe, my director came walking by. I saw him and didn't speak but I did attempt to make eye contact to acknowledge him. I noticed he had a blank stare on his face and he didn't look in my direction, but I figured with him being the director of a manufacturing group, he had plenty on his mind. Well, what 'choo think "happent" next? A day or so later, my program manager came to me to ask what was I working on. I proceeded to show him the various tasks I was working on and asked him what was going on. He then tells me the director, a good 'ol boy from Kentucky, came to him saying that I obviously didn't have enough to do because I had time to stand in the hallway with a group of Negroes and shoot the breeze. He didn't say the "Negroes" part (Or did he?). I threw that in for effect. Let's see, as I mentioned earlier, the White boys can stand around for fifteen or twenty minutes doing nothing, but let my Black ass be caught with a group of other people of color for more than two minutes and there's obviously trouble brewing. Some other Black co-workers I used to have would joke that the fire alarm was about to go off if we stood around for more than a minute because of the heat being generated by our "dark matter." This was in reference to a *Saturday Night Live* skit from the 80s that featured Eddie Murphy and Robin Williams discussing the "Flammability of the Black Man." That perception thing reared its ugly head again in this instance. It's petty, but you have to monitor how long you're away from your desk until you earn your coworkers' trust.

4.3 COVER YOUR ASS (CYA)

As you participate in Corporate America, you will see what my father calls, the Human Factor. On television and in other places, the false image of professional behavior is presented all the time. Some groups will have strong leadership, and others will not. Unfortunately, in engineering, the mistake is made more often than not that a good engineer makes for a good manager. The average engineer is a technical person, and doesn't always have the best people skills or leadership skills. This can be a problem because the success or failure of many a career is predicated on the blame game.

In the workforce, as well as in many pockets of society, there tends to be a pecking order. And sometimes the people with the favorable treatment aren't great workers, they just know how to manipulate situations to make themselves look better than their coworkers. This is most often done by playing the blame game. These are people who don't get something done, get it done late, or don't know what they are doing; yet, they strategically place themselves where they can tell the boss or the workgroup that they failed at their tasks because of someone else's fault. "Henry didn't give me the data in time," or "I had to make a decision without Jeff's input, even though he's the subject matter expert, because he was out on vacation…" All of these are valid, bullsh*t reasons that a boss will cut somebody some slack, while jumping on Henry's or Jeff's ass for not helping out. This is known also as "throwing someone under the bus." If you plan on becoming a good engineer, unless you are working totally alone, you will eventually face situations where you will be thrown under the bus. What you want to do is have a defense strategy, if you will, for combating this possibility.

Like in a game of chess, you have to constantly think two or three moves ahead of what you do. This is especially critical if you are working in a design group or, at present, an integrated product team or IPT. Like back in high school, you have a group project and everyone should have a role to play to ensure the success of the project. But by eleventh grade, you saw the 20/80

Rule in full effect: 20 percent of the people will do 80 percent of the work. Trust me, this will continue until your dying day unless you morph into an ant or a honeybee and everyone works the same. I'm being facetious, of course, but don't be surprised when you encounter this. You make sure you do your part, know what your part will affect when it comes to the overall project, and what the other people in the group should be delivering. This is where the CYA concept comes into play. Or in my case, CYAN, which is a handy acronym I would post in my cubicle sometimes, which stood for, Cover Yo' Ass, Nigga'!

How does one cover such said ass? First, make sure you document *everything*. When I first started working at MDA, I didn't know about documenting my assignments and work progress. It wasn't until I got burned in a meeting one time that I realized that I needed to write things down, not only for a record, but to remember what my specific tasks were, and to stay on target. This can be done by handwriting in a project notebook, spiral notebook, or binder/ledger. You can also keep an electronic document where you record your daily tasks and accomplishments. This is most helpful when you have a manager who demands daily or weekly progress reports. This can be a real joy or a real pain, but it's necessary grunt work to secure your position, especially if your manager is getting pressure from the higher-ups on how things are going. You can do like me and do both. I keep an electronic journal on what I've done on a daily basis, what issues I may be facing, and most importantly, what instructions I've been given by my supervisor(s).

Second, keep track of any electronic transmissions that can

provide a paper trail of what is going on with the project. Sometimes you can create sub-folders in your email inbox to save project-specific messages that can be readily available if something you've done is called into question.

Third, avoid verbal and unethical orders. Always record what you've been instructed to do. Sometimes you can do this by following up with your supervisor via email to make sure you are clear on your tasks. If you have a good program manager, he or she will usually give handouts or emails with task assignments and deadlines for everyone in the group. But if you are unfortunate enough to have a manager who is strictly out for his or her self-aggrandizement, you need to document everything. This is needed when you have "Do *whatever* it takes to get it done" managers who are only concerned with making themselves look good. I've seen managers like these bully people into getting some tasks done, not always the correct or *legal* way, and if it back-fired, they would conveniently blame the employee for not doing it the right way; the good old-fashioned, "I never told you to do that…" lie. This is where the need for good leadership comes in. A true leader thinks not only of themselves, but about the well-being of the group and everyone's success.

Fourth, beware of unreasonable demands. You may be a technical superstar, but employees need to know their limitations. Sometimes working a few extra hours and the occasional weekend may get you some points when you meet a critical project deadline, but you should know when a project schedule is too aggressive and beyond your capacity. You don't want to be the scapegoat, especially when it's a high-profile project. You need to also know if these tasks are a nefarious plot to get you moved out of the workgroup, as well. Remember the young Brother I mentioned earlier who got tons and tons of work dumped on him, and he ended up leaving? Now I'm not saying that every time your workload demands are increased it's a scheme to get rid of you. Cream rises to the top, and from time to time, you will be expected to give 115 percent of your efforts to make a deadline. But what I am saying is that sometimes you have to be realistic and tell them point blank that you won't be able to meet a deadline or you can't take on additional work for fear that your other tasks will suffer. Unless your supervisor clearly directs you to put the other tasks on the back burner to focus on this new or unexpected issue, you have to be able to tell them no. That way, when things go terribly awry, no one can place the blame on you, because if you don't have evidence and/or documentation of what you've done and what you were told to do, you will be the convenient scapegoat.

4.4 Communication

Earlier in the book, I mentioned keeping things professional. You're not one of the boys (or girls), and you never will be as long as racism exists in this country. You can have an issue that needs your manager's attention. When "Brett" or some other Caucasoid comes to them with an issue, they're "voicing their concerns." But when you present the same issue, you're "complaining" like some petulant child. Unless you have a supervisor who is fair and on the level, you will have to break down this racial misperception.

During your tenure in engineering school, hopefully you've taken or will take a course on technical writing as well as presentation skills. Grammar, pronunciation, vocabulary, and delivery are all valuable skills that you will need when progressing in your career. As one of my few and rare Black mentors told me, "Avoid using slang," when dealing with supervisors and co-workers. You're already having to be twice as good to get half the reward, so you don't want to give them any ammunition that can be used against you. I can recall one time I was in the main hallway outside of the company cafeteria when I was addressing some of the Brothers. I had a Freudian slip where I called them "niggas" out loud as people of all races were walking by. I was using that word as a term of endearment, but I got the shocked and dismayed looks from them as I realized my faux pas. *What we do in the hood, should stay in the hood.* Keep it professional when dealing with coworkers, all of them, until you are in private surroundings with people you *know* you can trust. This trust will only come over time as you learn your coworkers' thoughts and habits when it comes to the workplace and yourself.

As you grow in your career, you will learn how to use diplomacy and tact to maneuver through the minefield of Corporate America. You will have to keep a sharp eye and ear when going about your daily business. This will include establishing a relationship with your supervisor and coworkers, as well as knowing when you're being thrown under the bus. There are ways to communicate the facts or your thoughts on a situation without coming off as "The Angry Black Man." I'm still trying to figure out where that came from, but it boils down to not being prejudged because your supervisor or coworkers will feel threatened or intimidated by your angry and (perceived) violent outbursts if you speak louder than they or you appear to want to do physical harm to someone. As I've stated before, the White boys can get away with things that I'd never even think about doing. I've been in meetings where guys have told another person they were flat out wrong about something or they were lying. I have learned how to convey the same message without coming off as a threat or intimidating anyone.

You can politely say things like, "I'm sorry, but I disagree," or "Forgive me, but your assessment is inaccurate," rather than the good old-fashioned "That's some bullsh—!" or the ever more eloquent, "You don't know what the hell you're talking about!" You'll be quickly shut down by your coworkers mentally, even if you are correct or allowed to finish speaking. This is where diplomacy comes in. I've read where diplomacy is defined as "the ability to tell a man to go to hell, and make him happy to be on his way." You've got to know the lay of the land and be able to disagree without being disagreeable, or correct someone without making them lose face.

Sometimes you may have to be a little rough around the edges with a response to let folks know you are not a pushover or an easy mark, though. This is where the sharp eye and ear comes into play. Once at Boeing, I had a situation where I was thrown under the bus and didn't even know it. We were having daily standup meetings (which can be a real pain sometimes because you are literally standing up in a circle or around a conference table) where the leadership would give a status of the project and then go around the room for everyone to give an account of what they were working on and any problems they were having. I've learned the hard way to keep your immediate supervisor abreast of any issues you may be having so they don't get blind-sided by anything that would make them look bad. You can bring an issue up, but don't make a mountain out of a mole hill if it's not necessary. Anyway, we had this guy who was supposed to be a technician in the group. I don't think he had any formal technical background and I have no clue how he ended up in our organization, but you talk about incompetent and lazy. And whatever he put his hand to, he screwed it up royally. He was doing something in one of the support equipment cabinets on one of the simulators and blew up a power supply this particular week, and made it a point to announce that, "Well, Dusty and I were looking at such-and-such, and *we* blew out a power supply…" I'm standing right there in the circle and let that comment slide right past me, not realizing this motherf**ker was trying to deflect some of the blame onto me. That was the young, naive, submissive Dusty R. Walker, Jr. The older, mature, and grizzled Me would've chimed in with, "I'm sorry, when were *we* looking at such said cabinet? I never did any such thing, and would appreciate it if you got your story straight." You can do this once you've proven yourself in the technical arena. Meanwhile, stay alert for this type of foolishness.

Another example of standing up happened when I worked at Gulfstream Aerospace Corporation. I was placed onto a project that supported the production teams. These are the people who build the business jets on the factory floor. The electrical drawings had a series of problems that affected the completion schedule. The technical manager whom I was supporting came up to me not two days in and started chewing me out over some drawing that I hadn't even looked at yet. Now take into account this was some Old South White guy who'd been doing this for probably thirty years or more, and was used to doing things a certain way. After he pretty much insulted me and the rest of the engineering group, I looked him dead in the eye, held my hand up, and said, "Hold on a minute! I just got put on this project, and I'm here to help. Now what's the problem?" or something to that effect. He actually looked shocked because I had seen so many others cower at his insults and let him get away with it. I can't remember if he presented the problem to me on the spot, or if he had to gather himself and come back to me later with a problem to present. But in either case, he stopped me in the hallway a day or so later and gave an indirect apology for his approach to me. I took it in good stride, chose not to gloat (the prudent thing to do), and offered a retort to the effect that I understood his frustration with previous engineers, but I wasn't one of them. You can maintain your professional status while at the same time having a "I'm not gon' take dis' sh*t!" attitude. They may not always like it, but they can damn sure respect it. This also comes into play when the Freudian slip occurs and someone spouts a racial or sexist joke. You can't be too tolerant because your coworkers will get too relaxed and say what they really think about women and minorities. If they say something extremely racial, you may have to roll the dice and say something like, "I'm sorry, but that's a racist (or offensive) thing to say. I'd appreciate it if you wouldn't talk like that around me." Be polite, but firm, in letting them know you're not the one to shuck and jive with them when it comes to promoting intolerable behavior. You may have to make a case with your manager or HR if it gets out of hand. But your self-respect is worth protecting in some cases.

4.5 F**K THE RULES!

You've heard the old adage, "Rules are meant to be broken," correct? Well, I have found in my short life span that rules are a good thing, as long as everyone follows them. Unfortunately, there are caveats to any established rule system. The main issue is that everyone *doesn't follow* said rules. Other adages that come to mind pertaining to this include, "Good guys finish last" and "Laws are written to protect those who write them."

Often times, the rules of the workplace are as much of a hindrance to your professional growth as they are a help. I've been places where I was held to the "rules" to the letter while my coworkers, no smarter or harder working than I was, were propelled up the rungs of the corporate ladder with the greatest of ease. My advice to you is learn the rules, and follow them as long as they are to *your benefit*. When things don't appear to be leaning in your favor, sometimes you may have to bend the rules to get results. Now, I'm not talking about doing anything that would be unsafe or criminal that could get someone killed or get you jail time. But I am talking about being proactive in the sense that no one is going to look out for your career like you are. This includes strategically "stepping on someone's toes" while not appearing to do so. I honestly believe that I can follow the

Masonic principle based upon the Biblical scripture, "Let your light so shine before men, that they may see your good works, and glorify your Father which is in Heaven." I don't have to put someone else down to make myself look good, especially if I'm doing a good job; and neither should you if you are doing your job. But you should position yourself with strategic alliances that will help you out when things get tough. This will come together in the next section.

I don't believe in kissing butt, sucking up, or shameless groveling as a sycophant to succeed in the workplace. But you will see this on the job sooner or later. That same coworker who will stand around and talk ever so badly about the boss will do a complete 180 and be your supervisor's BFF (best friend forever) when he or she is in the room. Keep this individual at arm's length at all times. This will more than likely be one of the primary cutthroats who will try to throw you under the bus if the opportunity presents itself. And if you do happen to have a boss who seems to relish having people kiss their arse all the time, it might be time to look for a new group or job. Sooner or later, all that ass-kissing and lack of tangible results will get the attention of the boss's boss, and somebody will have to pay. Might as well *not* be you. It's a tough call because if you do submit to kowtowing, you will lose a good measure of self-respect as a professional and as a grown man. And if the boss doesn't think too highly of you from the get-go, kissing his butt may only hasten his resolve to either get rid of you, or treat you as the servile employee you are portraying yourself to be.

All in all, only break the rules when you know you won't

get caught, and the reward outweighs the risk. This shouldn't happen too frequently; you want to be known as an impact player because of your technical expertise and great work ethic. But sometimes even these fine traits will not get you your just due. That's when you may have to "make some noise" or "go around or over someone's head" to get the results you seek.

4.6 Become Invaluable

From divisional VPs to front-line supervisors, I've been told the same thing: to have career longevity, become invaluable. Become an SME in your chosen area of work. Like with most things in this world, even if the people in your work group don't like you, if you are the *best* at what you do and bring added value to the business, they have to keep you around—at least for a while. When you have a good reputation for getting the job done, word will get around, even when it appears that nothing is happening on the surface.

As with all things, this can be a double-edged sword. On one hand, you want people bringing you work to get done because it justifies keeping you on the payroll. On the other hand, depending on what kind of work group you have, they may dump everything on you to get done while everyone else takes off early for a round of golf in the afternoon. You still have to know your limits and be able to speak up when you are stretched too thin.

Oh, and my favorite one is training the dumb-ass White kid or new college graduate for the manager or department head, so he or she can take your spot and move on up. This is a constant variable in the world of Black engineers. You have to constantly "be on top of your game" just to get a decent paycheck, and then young Bob or Fred comes in (he happens to be the boss's nephew, but they don't tell you that) and they want you to get him trained up. You make the mistake of teaching him everything you know, and guess what? In three to six months, young Fred is either your new supervisor, or worse yet, you'll get fired and Fred will slide into your spot after only a year or so on the job. I've had the pleasure of teaching and training a couple of good young guys, one White and one Asian Indian, on aircraft engineering. And they both have risen to higher heights in their young careers, all thanks to me. I've also had a few situations where I helped some guys and they moved on without so much as a "thanks a lot." My suggestion to you, Dear Reader, is to follow the philosophy of the old kung fu masters: *Never* teach *all of your secrets* to your student. If you learn one secret from ten different engineers, mentors, and supervisors, guess what? You know ten secrets to add to your toolbox. If you are given the unfortunate task of training a new engineer who doesn't share your same cultural or ethnic background, be fair and kind, but only give him four or five (if that many) of your secrets. You don't want him or her using the one ace-in-the-hole you normally have to outshine you at the least opportune moment. Could mean the difference between advancement or regression.

Being the SME or go-to-guy can also afford you some leverage when it comes to salary and raise negotiations. If you have documentation of everything you have accomplished and brought to the table or sacrificed for the good of the team, you are well within your rights to demand a generous pay raise. If not, then you are either a fool or a glutton for punishment. Know your worth! Point to remember: I have on very good authority that most African-Americans are paid anywhere from *$30,000 to $60,000 LESS* than their White counterparts. Can I prove it in court? No. Have I discussed salaries with Black folks in different industries, including the technology sector, who were able to casually confirm that they were underpaid compared to their fellow Anglo employees? Yes. So if you know what you are bringing to the table, be not afraid to ask for what you think you're worth.

Unfortunately, at the end of the day, everything revolves around money. And companies are in business to make money, not create jobs, regardless of what the government leads us to believe. The reports may vary, but the largest expenses businesses have to deal with are usually taxes, materials, and labor, not necessarily in that order. Labor. Headcount. Staffing. Whatever the politically correct term is used nowadays, it all means the same thing: how many bodies are we paying to do a job? And when cash flow is tight, the first thing to get cut is either staff or working hours, or sometimes both. Why am I telling you this now? Because regardless of how good a job you are doing, if some bean-counter decides that heads have to roll to cut costs, heads are going to roll.

At the time of this writing, I had been working remotely for one client company that had some tremendous growth going. I could always be counted on to get the job done although I was literally 500 miles away working in the comfort of my home office. Anyhoo, I received an email from the engineering director that the group was "headed in another direction" and that they wanted to convert all employees to permanent status. So I was being given a heads up that my time was drawing to a close. So let this be a lesson to you, ladies and gentlemen, nothing is guaranteed. Prepare for the worst and hope for the best.

4.7 MANAGERS

I've discussed some of the types of managers you may face in your career. This section is a quick run-through of what you may encounter. I'm not saying that the following list is absolute and unwavering, but this is some of what I've faced in my life thus far.

4.7.1 WHITE MALES

The majority of your managers are going to be White guys. Plain and simple. This society is built by them for them. From time to time, they will be fairly objective and promote someone other than one of their own, but it's usually a White female and in some rare cases, someone of color. You got four kinds that I know of: the Sneaky Bastard, the Fat Bigot, the Anal Do-Right, and the Cool Liberal. I'm sure I could've chosen more tasteful words, but these cut to the chase and you won't be confused by their characteristics when you encounter them.

The Sneaky Bastard is probably the most common one that you will encounter. I mentioned earlier in the book that you will have managers who are highly ambitious and self-serving. They are usually hard driving and will do anything and everything to get ahead. These are the guys for whom you need to document everything they give you to do. They will lie, cheat, and steal, *and* sacrifice their first-born child to get a pay increase or promotion. And they will have no problems throwing you and your coworkers under the bus for their benefit. This is the guy who will ask or direct you to do something unethical, and when things go awry, they will place the blame squarely on you or your coworker who was stupid enough to do the unethical or illegal task. I can only advise that you try to do a good job for them while covering yourself (CYA), but don't expect any favors. If you can make relationships above and across from them, you might be in a position one day for a power play where you can force them to give you a good recommendation or put you in for a class or promotion. Other than that, you'll have to document your accomplishments and use them for your next work assignment or new job when you do decide to bounce.

The Fat Bigot is not always fat, but a bigot in practice, if not in principle. The late Dr. Martin Luther King, Jr., himself said in one of his writings that most White people are unconsciously racist. They may be good people, but subconsciously, they still view themselves as superior to other races. Can you blame them? What do you expect from someone who, from day one, has been bred and taught that because of their skin color, they are better than everyone else? Something to think about. The Fat Bigot is usually an overweight, mid- to late-middle-aged White man who will let you know early on that he doesn't like you; everything is going to be a problem, regardless of how well you are doing, so you're screwed anyway. I go back to my first department head who made it a point to avoid any sort of personal contact with me if it wasn't necessary. Don't take it personally; use it as motivation to show him that you are not some ignorant token who got the position purely on race. Let him know that you are worth the few pennies the company is throwing your way. If you *are* making a good salary, then give the company a good product so he or potentially sneaky coworkers can't mumble and use anything against you. But stay under the radar and only interact with this motherf**ker when absolutely necessary. If he has a lead or subordinate manager whom you can go to with progress or problems, then if he is okay with it, run your issues through the junior manager first. Ultimately, if he doesn't look like he's going to resign, retire, or die anytime soon, plan your exit strategy so you can leave on a high note before you get stuck in a dead-end job.

The Anal Do-Right is the type of manager who is a great engineer, but has the personality of a brick: very few people skills or leadership qualities. They did some great technical work over the years, so usually managers above them think this qualifies Anal Do-Rights to lead a department or project and they give them a group of engineers to manage. The other factor is that not only does this character lack people skills, he follows every rule in the book without the *thought* of wavering. Rules are good. They obstruct chaos and give a good means of keeping things balanced, but as I stated before, *life happens*, and sometimes flexibility and understanding must come into account. Unfortunately for you, this manager didn't get that memo. And if he makes life hard for the rest of the workgroup, you can damn sho' bet he ain't gonna cut you *no slack*. I've had situations where I needed to get off work early, let's say on a Friday, to take care of some personal business. Rather than burn two or three vacation or personal time off (PTO) hours, some groups will allow a worker to "bank hours" or work flex(ible) time. That is, you will work those extra three hours during the week prior to the day you need to take off, or you could come in three hours early and leave work to make your appointment. These types of arrangements happen all the time all over Corporate America. But it depends on the climate and culture of the group. And unfortunately, the Anal Do-Right isn't going to allow such flexibility. Now, in all fairness, some managers like this are brand new and may feel like if they grant too many concessions up front, they will be viewed as too weak or ineffective as managers by their superiors. But at the same time, I think the hallmark of a good manager is having a balance of rewards and punishments, like the warrior philosophy of Sun Tzu. When the Anal Do-Right is performing at his peak, even the White boys will start to grumble and word will eventually make its way up the chain of command. But until that happens, you will have to outperform and shine like the sun to get him to start softening his stance toward you. One previous coworker said he had a boss who fit the bill: "This dude was giving the White guys head colds and was giving me pneumonia!"

The Anal Do-Right is going to hold you to an even higher standard, so watch your step. As with anything, you'll have to learn how to maneuver around this guy, especially when it comes to getting the job done. Sometimes following every single rule adds unnecessary layers of bureaucracy and wastes precious time. It's a judgment call, but you may have to exercise the old adage of "Tis better to ask for forgiveness than to ask for permission." If the gamble works and you do an outstanding job, the manager can't be too upset with you, even though he'll probably still be peeved that you did something "behind his back." Learn to use phrases like, "Hey, I know you're busy, and didn't want to bother you with a trivial problem," or one of my favorites from an old gangster movie: "I thought I was doing a good thing." As long as you paint the picture that everything you're doing is for the good of the organization, you should be able to get some leeway. He won't be ready to give you the keys to the executive washroom, but he may not ride your bumper as hard in the future. If he still tries to micromanage and fuss about every little thing, then once again, look at all options on the table, including leaving or maybe even influencing one of his boys or his bosses to have a chat with him about his group's morale.

The Cool Liberal is not necessarily a liberal in the political sense, but I chose that term because this is usually a White guy who is actually a pretty good leader and fair in his dealings with all of his subordinates. The Cool Liberal is actually a leader. What do I mean? Not only is he concerned with the performance and output of his workgroup, but he is communicating consistently the status and direction of the project or the group, *and* he is genuinely concerned about the welfare of his employees. This is the type of manager for whom most folks want to work. He will tell you what your duties are, and when any deliverables are due, or project milestones. Once assignments and deadlines are doled out, he usually has other things to worry about and will let you go forth to do your job without pinging you every five minutes about your progress or ask if you are done yet. Another aspect of the Cool Liberal is that he doesn't want to be disturbed unless you *really, really* have a problem that needs his attention. That is a fair arrangement. Naturally, you should keep him apprised of what is going on as you meet or near your deadlines, and obviously, if a major challenge occurs that you can't overcome, it should be brought to his attention as soon as possible. Because this is the guy who everyone wants to work for, he is going to have the pick of the litter as far as choosing his subordinates. So if you can get into his organization, you'll still have to prove yourself and make him shine, but as long as he knows he can trust you with key projects, when it comes time for favors, he should be able to hook you up. Now once again, don't get too comfortable with this situation. He may be a cool boss, but his power and influence can only go so far, especially if he has several superiors above him *and* he doesn't have too many friends in the group. He can only push the limits of his position so far before he risks losing his Good 'Ol Boys Union card. Unless he is totally reckless, oblivious, or doesn't care about retaining his position, he can't show too much favoritism toward you. This could get him labeled as a "nigger lover," and although he is good with you, he's not going to risk his status with the rest of the Establishment for one lone Negro. They have an unwritten code that they take care of one another *first*, then White women, and finally other minorities. If the code is broken, the Cool Liberal will have more problems than you could imagine; all a conspiracy to get him to quit or get fired if he doesn't fall into line with the code. So use the Cool Liberal as much as you can, while you can, but don't kill the golden goose by asking for too much too soon. Otherwise, you'll be their next target once they are through with him. Never make the mistake of thinking that you have total protection from envious coworkers if you start climbing the ladder. One day, he is going to be mysteriously promoted or transferred right from under your nose, and then you're going to have a real dick of a boss who you'll have to adjust to all over again. Ask me how I know.

4.7.2 WHITE FEMALES

I was at GAC when I had my first female lead to whom I had to report. I told my father about the new job, and when I mentioned that I had a White lady for my immediate supervisor, the first words out of his mouth were, "A *dangerous* species." I didn't know what he meant at first, but I do now.

I don't consider myself sexist, not overall, anyway. I've met some women engineers and managers who were as sharp, if not sharper, than their male contemporaries. But the problem is that most White men are intimidated by women or "girls" who can outshine them on the drawing board or design screen, so they will take many steps to keep them from advancing in the technical arena. They work hard, but are still overworked and underpaid compared to the White boys, in most cases. Now, as unfair and as f**ked up as this is, they usually will still be doing better than you!

But this is the issue you have to watch out for: Most White

female managers are either really hard in their managerial styles, or they are treacherous and conniving in their political maneuvering. Let's face it, if you haven't noticed, engineering is still a male-dominated profession, even though there are more science, technology, engineering, and mathematics (STEM) programs out here aimed at attracting more women to the field. I applaud them. But because this is a male-dominated arena, and a lot of the women I've met and seen in technology aren't the most attractive, they have to work just as hard to get their just due, or scheme to put themselves in the most advantageous position to advance. Now, from time to time, there will be a White female manager who is good in her managerial and leadership style. She will be fair and dole out rewards and punishments adequately. She may even recognize you for your good work and give you a good raise or recommendation/"Atta Boy" award. But if she has superiors above her who she still has to appease to keep her fast track career going who don't want to see too many Negroes advancing, she's going to be hamstrung, as well. Case in point, I know a Brother who had a seemingly cool White female manager who gave him some opportunities to advance by working on some high-profile projects. However, some of his White male counterparts were dumb as bricks, and he'd have to deal with their incompetence. One day, he was in a discussion with this one guy who was a total dick. The Brother was basically telling the guy he was wrong about something, and the manager was quick to jump in and tell the Brother, "You don't have to be argumentative with him…" She basically cut him off and sent the subliminal message that "Yeah, we cool and all," but I'm going to still side with my White brethren *first* always, no matter how wrong they may be. The Brother told me that after that, he pretty much just did his job and sat back to watch the house burn down whenever this know-it-all idiot made a mistake. Like I said before, don't ever make the mistake of thinking they are going to put you on the same plane as they are on.

The attractive females will really get the sweet deals, especially when they aren't the sharpest tacks in the box when it comes to solving technical problems. If you notice "Becky" wearing the low-cut blouses with the push-up bras a lot, and all of a sudden she's now program manager of some high-profile project, there's a good chance she's done some "favors" to get ahead. Not always, but I'm being a realist. I've found out about quite a few extramarital affairs during my career between a dingy White girl and her boss(es) where she was pushed up the corporate ladder with the *greatest* of ease, while I kept getting every conceivable excuse in the book why I was passed over for an opportunity or promotion. Like I said, not always, but I'm keeping it real. If you are comfortable in this situation and aren't having too many problems, you could ride it out for a while. Hell, you may stumble across Becky and the boss in a compromising situation where you could infer the threat of "singing like a canary," and they cut you some slack to keep your mouth shut. You never know.

4.7.3 BLACK MANAGERS

Now this is a double-edged sword, to say the least. As with anything else, this can be a blessing or a curse. It all depends on what type of manager you get. I mentioned earlier a situation where I had a Black manager and had to make sure I made him look good for both of us to maintain our incomes. I won't rehash this too much, but I wanted you to be aware that depending on the company culture, you can't be too chummy with your supervisors, even if they are cool as a fan offsite.

If you have a cool manager, then don't do anything to ruin that relationship, especially if he or she has White friends in high places. They may be generous enough to bring you with them. But you'll have to really outshine your White contemporaries for them to justify doing this. Although nepotism is standard operating procedure among White folks, we as a People are never held to the same standard.

The dangerous side is if you have a manager who is the first and only one of our kind to be in that group or position and he or she is content with maintaining the status quo. In other words, he or she enjoys being the Resident Negro Company Man/Woman and doesn't need any anyone else taking away that distinction. These are the types that are *not* going to mentor you in any form or fashion. And God help you if you make even the slightest mistake; they will take every opportunity to chastise you in front of your coworkers.

Unfortunately, this can be the case with female Black managers. I've seen Sisters who got promoted, not necessarily on their technical merits, but because they satisfied the EEO requirements (minority *and* female) and the boss and HR figured this was good enough. Sad to say, but if the Sister is attractive, don't make the mistake of thinking that White guys only like to f**k White girls—you got Captain Kirks out there who endorse diversity in bed, maybe not in the workplace, but in bed for sure. You've got bosses who will promote a Black woman before a Black man because he may want some "dark meat," but he also has a better chance of controlling that woman than he does a man. And let's face it, they would rather see a Black woman advance before they will ever see a Black man advance; their egos can't take it. There have been instances where some Black women made sure they ruled with an iron fist, making it a point to keep any Brothers in line and insulting or emasculating them at every chance, much to the White male upper management's pleasure. I've seen entire work groups fall apart because of low morale and high turnover once these individuals were in place. Once again, before I'm accused of being a chauvinist, I want to say that this is not always the case. But I'd be doing you a disservice if I didn't mention the worst-case scenarios to you. When things are getting bad, find a way to jump ship before it sinks to the bottom and you're part of the blame for the group's poor performance. If that happens, the company will make sure it'll be another 10 years before they bring another person of color into the ranks. Sad, but true; I've seen it happen.

4.8 Make and Keep the Peace

I am going to summarize what I've written thus far concerning the minefield of working in Corporate America. I call it the Philosophy of the Porcupine. Why? Because you need to be like a porcupine in your dealings with White folks. Not all

White folks are bad, and I'm not advocating racism, *but* some of them can be some straight "ofays" if you're not careful. You want to go to work, take care of your business, and hang out with friends *after* work and offsite, regardless of their color or creed. You want to maintain as positive and professional an image as possible; you hear some people say "fly under the radar." Sh*t, I say stay *off* that motherf**ker as much as possible. If you can, only surface when you need to—in an emergency or when you've done something that's going to make you look good. Like a porcupine, they are pretty quiet and mind their own business; you want to be able to handle your tasks with as little drama as possible. But when a predator strikes, you want to be able to give them a mouthful of needles if they choose to f**k with you. As I mentioned earlier, you don't want to be the "Angry Black Man," but you don't want to be a pushover, either, or you'll never get ahead.

Stay out of politics, sex, and religion. Oh yeah, I failed to mention this earlier. Avoid the Child of Privilege if you can. These are the coworkers whose Mommy or Daddy is somebody in the company or their Mommy or Daddy *report* to somebody big in the company, and so they blast a clear path for Junior or Becky to make money and rise up the ranks without having to do any real damn work. I was at a company in Huntsville, AL, and one morning I got to work extra early and parked closer to the front door than usual. Later in the day, this young punk, who'd been with the outfit less than a year, comes up to me and says with the straightest face, "You parked in my spot." Huh? And he proceeded to tell me that he parked where I did every day and

I "took it" from him. I think I responded with a bland, "I didn't know we had assigned spots," and kept it moving. Turns out his uncle or father was a manager in the company somewhere so I guess he figured he had some clout in our group. As usual, he didn't know sh*t, but that didn't keep him from becoming a lead designer in the group a year or two later after I had left. Who says nepotism is dead?

Be sure to determine who is The Chosen One. The Chosen One is the guy who's already slated early on in his career to be moved up the corporate ladder fast and without many obstacles. This is the guy that if you go against his thinking, will simply "go to talk" to the manager and have your suggestion or idea overridden. Never mind the technical validity of your idea; if Timmy wants something, he will get it. I can only suggest that you try to make this guy an ally, because when he sees that you are good at what you do, he may even keep you around by putting in a good word with the boss. It doesn't always happen, but it's a possibility. You know you're doing good for him when they suddenly try to be cool with you, and try to use slang when speaking to you. It's at your discretion, but you can tell him, "Look, we're not homies. I'm here to work and help the team be successful," or something neutral along those lines. If the situation is a losing cause, get your ducks lined up where you can transfer out of the group or get another job or opportunity and get the hell out of Dodge City.

Also, my Number One Command: Don't f**k with the resident White girl! If you don't remember *anything* else I've taught you, remember this one. The resident White girl is most dangerous because she's usually the only female in the design group (God help you if she's even faintly attractive), and if she has *any* type of favor with the supervisor or group manager, she can *do no wrong*! Whether she intends to use this power or not, you be careful around her. Because remember, the boss and more than half the White boys in the group probably want to f**k her; so if she even hints at potentially giving them some pussy, she got them by the balls and can write her own destiny. Plus, even though they tend to treat their women like sh*t, when it comes to Black men, that's still their "Prize" and no one else should get it, and they will protect it at all costs. I've had situations where I've had to delicately tell a White chick she was incorrect about something without making her feel like a dumbass (even though I wanted to say that). Because if I had come at her hard (you notice I didn't say wrong), she would've run to our department head and said something and my ass would've been out the door post haste. If she is halfway attractive or drop-dead gorgeous, you're really in deep sh*t, because she may be boning the boss. You could've saved the company a zillion bucks with some innovation you come up with, but she'll get the recognition or promotion because of this.

Also, I want to make mention that even the coolest White chick will turn on you if it is to her advantage. Case in point, when I was still at Boeing, I had established a friendship with this White girl in our group. You know, the occasional conversations about relationships, personal issues, and whatnot. Nothing too deep, but more personal than what I'd ever disclose now in my later years. Well, one day when we were deep into testing one of the flight simulators, we had a hardware issue where we had to unplug a power or data cable for some troubleshooting. I don't remember who had disconnected it, but because I was part of the hardware team, I was partially responsible for making sure everything was connected back up. Because of this cable, the testing had failed several times until we discovered it. Well, let me tell you, "Becky" made sure to point a finger at me and chastise me in front of several coworkers, including my lead engineer, about how I/we didn't do our jobs and it caused them all these problems. You'd have thought we caused the project to fail ultimately by the way she was carrying on. Needless to say, I didn't appreciate that sh*t, and I quickly saw her in a different light. A few months later, I noticed she had changed her last name to the same as my lead. What the f**k?! The office administrator, who was really one of the coolest White ladies I've ever had the pleasure of working with, told me afterward, "Oh yeah, they've been dating for months now, and just got married." I missed that memo, but apparently the rest of the White people in the group knew about it. Anyway, I guess she had to let hubby know what a terrible Negro I was, as well as flex her position in the pecking order now that she was legally screwing my boss. Whatever, just don't you, Alert Reader, get caught up in this type of bullsh*t.

I don't want to hit on this one too hard, but I have to warn you (again) that some White folks can be petty and vindictive like nobody's business. We already know about having to be twice as good. But I want to also advise you to watch out for conflicting situations. I had a situation where a manager wanted me to look at a permanent position for an Army project, but I turned it down because I didn't want to be a direct employee. After that, I was *never* given another opportunity to work for this group because of that, even though there would be job requisitions right up my alley. Also, remember to be aware of how you outshine your White counterparts. Be the best at what you do, but still be low key with it. Don't get to bragging 'bout nuthin'! Else they will collectively grumble and complain to the management to have you dealt with. I "seent" it! They never forget any "offenses," be they large or small, and they are *slow* to forgive, if at all. Remember, most of these folks still have that sense of White privilege, and lose their sense of self-worth if they are slighted by a Negro.

Oh, and I'd be remiss if I didn't cover dealing with the Corporate Negro for a moment. The Corporate Negro, *Donec Aethiopissa*, is a wily creature that should be given careful scrutiny. This is a male or female who has black or brown skin, but no true consciousness of self, much less the fact that they are not (and will never be) fully accepted into the fold of their White counterparts. But they look the part, they dress the part, and they act the part of being a good employee, much to the satisfaction of their coworkers and overseers. This is the individual who will speak to every White person in the hallway, but will either look away, off into the distance, or right through you as you pass and they will never speak to you. For me, it is hurtful when "one of Our Own" doesn't acknowledge me. We don't have to be friends, but damn, it feels a little better in a hostile environment when you know there is somebody else who can relate to what you are going through. On rare occasions, they may speak if you are the only two individuals in the room or the hall, but if they look extremely uncomfortable while doing it, don't expect to be invited over for dinner. My other favorite characteristic is when no one is around and they suddenly try to be "cool" and pretend to be friends with you, but soon as other White people are around, they don't know you. If you are in the same workgroup as one of these people, keep it professional, and don't expect anything more. Matter of fact, I'd say stay away from them, too. Why? Because chances are, they will sell you out to promote themselves just as quick as the White folks will. Maybe even faster. And these are the ones who will climb the ladder, but will not try to mentor or bring any other Black folks along with them. They will attain a certain measure of success, and when you try to climb up the ladder with them, your boss or HR will tell you that that person is in an executive position, the Negro quota is full, you'll just have to wait. Not in those words, of course, but learn how to read between the lines.

5.0 Career Advancement

By now, you may be a little weary and red-eyed from reading all of this. But fear not. It is all for your benefit that I try to share with you 20 years' worth of stumbling, bumbling, foibles, trials, tribulations, and triumphs. In this chapter, I will briefly touch on my thoughts for career advancement.

Not all engineers want to be more than an engineer. We are paid to think creatively, critically, and solve problems for someone's benefit. Whether that benefit is for the good or demise of your fellow man is entirely up to someone else. That someone else is someone who signs the checks, hires or fires, promotes or demotes, or "runs sh*t" all throughout the enterprise. Some engineers want to advance to positions of greater responsibility or visibility, which would include positions of management or leadership. I was one of those engineers who wanted to eventually "run some sh*t." The problem was that I didn't really have anyone to tell me how, nor did I have anyone above me who could pull me along. So I had to look at examples outside and within my circle of influence, if you will.

Be honest with yourself and find out what it is that you'd really like to do with your career as long as you stay in the technology arena. Do you want to be a pure technologist? A "lab rat"? Or do you see yourself not only excelling in the research & design realm, but as a manager of an entire workgroup, division, or company? Either way, if you have the capacity and desire, as long as you are mentally cognizant and breathing, you can accomplish these goals. Won't be easy, though. Map out your goals in monthly and yearly segments. Make sure you make allowances for obstacles and challenges. Life can be good, but it can be a badass mutha' as well when problems crop up; and they will!

One key to advancement is to remain sharp in your chosen field of work. Required training, certifications, and documented self-study are several ways to stay up on your technical knowledge. Company-sponsored courses are another way to increase your knowledge base, whether they be directly related to your job function or not. Lastly, a graduate degree never hurts, either. Whether it be an MBA or an advanced engineering degree, that sheepskin can open doors for you within and without the company that a bachelor's degree won't. And if your company has a program to pay for continuing education, take advantage of it, especially while you are young and without the responsibility of taking care of a family. You can succeed regardless of your marital or family status, but I am suggesting that while you don't have those added responsibilities, knock out a graduate or associate degree or certification while you can fully focus. Now please remember that if you are in a very hostile environment with a non-supportive manager or inept HR department, you can have every degree in the world and still will not be allowed to advance in the company. It's time to take your skills, cash in your chips as they say, and find a place that will accept and love you for what you are bringing to the table.

The second key to advancement is movement. Remember, there is no company loyalty anymore. Yes, there are some success stories of people being in the same department for 30 years and they are doing just fine. That may be one in a hundred or a thousand. For everyone else, if you don't like where you are seated on the totem pole or spotted on the company org chart, my suggestion is to find opportunities to move. Movement can be sideways (lateral) or up & down (vertical). The lateral movement can consist of moving to a different workgroup within your present company, or a new employer. There is usually no promotion and may not entail a pay increase in the immediate future, but these types of moves are made to expose you to a new type of work or project that will enhance your skills and resume down the road. It also exposes you to new people who may be a joy to work with compared to your previous group. A vertical move is typically made to climb the corporate ladder, and one hopes that these moves will ensure career success, as well as an added measure of financial solvency. This means you take a position with an increase in salary or hourly pay, as well as more visibility and responsibility. You may take on a managerial role, where you are now responsible for the performance of a design team, or an entire group or division. Job moves like these can lead to executive positions where you might be the chief information officer, chief operating officer, or even chief executive officer (CEO) *if* it's a diverse and fair company. But in the technology realm, in most large companies, those high-visibility jobs are reserved for White and Asian men, and then White women or women of Color. I've seen very few Fortune 500 technology companies with executives who were Black men. I'm not saying you can't be one of many to accomplish this, but the deck is stacked against you and it'll be one *hell* of a fight. Oh yes, before I forget, if you do choose to climb the corporate ladder in the hopes of being a senior manager over a business enterprise, you are going to put in *work*! There will be plenty of 10- and 12-hour days, where you're only being paid for 40 hours' wages. This is the "pay your dues" phase of your career. Do a good job and *maybe* someone above you will be fair and magnanimous enough to help you climb. Remember, without a mentor or a manager with some real power or influence, your chances of moving up are going to be slim.

There are plenty of books and resources out there that give good advice and information on how to be a good engineer, a good manager or executive, or how to succeed in life in general. I've got a decent collection of some of these books myself. But I've seen very few of these items geared toward African-Americans outside of the well-established publications like the venerable *Ebony, Essence, Jet,* and *Black Enterprise* magazines. Most of the books you find are written by White folks for White folks. For example, the book *Engineer Your Way to Success,* which is sponsored by the National Society of Professional Engineers, has some good information on topics like technical skills, communication, leadership and management qualities, teamwork, integrity (*snicker*), hard work, and recipes for success. The author makes it a point to address the existing sexism in the workplace, but does so in a light and politically correct manner. Nowhere did I see an address of cultural or racial differences or issues. Maybe they are in there. I don't know because I didn't read the whole damn thing, but I had to stop and laugh several times because the same rules that are laid out in that book are the same rules myself and other Black engineers have adhered to for more than 20 years and very few of us have gotten past the senior engineer title into positions of prominence and power. So I say take these books at face value and use what you can. But at the end of the day, all of your advanced training and self-improvement courses will not guarantee you an increase in income or corporate advancement. You still will need friends in high places.

This is not a guarantee, but I did want to mention being culturally cognizant. This is especially useful if you are going to be a Global Engineer. You may have the opportunity to travel to faraway places and do business with an assortment of clients and coworkers. Knowing the local customs and social improprieties can take you a long way, especially if a project goes wrong and you have the dubious honor of being sent in for damage control. The customer may be quicker to forgive any errors if you know how to regain their favor. Note: Do not be surprised if bribery is an accepted form of coercion; not saying it's right, just saying in some parts of the world, it is a perfectly acceptable business practice.

You'll have to be technically sharp to outshine your White counterparts, that's a given. But you'll have to be able to solve people problems if you are going to have your own business enterprise one day. So be sure to develop your people and leadership skills along the way. Have a good measure of self-confidence, but protect yourself from over-confidence. You're still an employee and will have to keep your ego in check from time to time. Keep your eyes and ears open at all times, speak as little as possible, and perform like the star hopefully God meant you to be.

6.0 CONTRACTING (THE DARK SIDE)

One of my issues with many engineering schools, including Tennessee State, is that they only prepare the students to become good employees for someone else. You have to almost minor in business management or economics to get exposure to the business and managerial side of engineering before graduating. If you are at a university that has project/program management courses, then by all means, at least take an introductory course while you can. It's usually not until you've started working at a company or, if you're fortunate enough to, go straight to graduate school to work on business- or management-related coursework. These can be classes at the local college, or in some cases, the corporations will have company-sponsored courses that you can take advantage of. Completing these classes is still no guarantee of success, but it helps position you to apply for other jobs or promotions that will hopefully pay more money. Now, I've mentioned some of this before, but I'm going somewhere with this.

I got into engineering to solve problems *and* make money. When I was coming up, engineers had some of the highest starting salaries in the country. This was in the late 80s, when $40,000 was actual money. Unfortunately, a lot of companies are still offering starting salaries that, in my opinion, are glaringly low compared to today's cost of living. Anything less than $70,000 nowadays is poppycock. The annual salary reports that you sometimes see in technical publications are reflective of base salaries, but they don't always mention years' experience or geographic region. I'm sorry, but what $60,000 per year gets you in Kentucky or Mississippi ain't going to get you the same thing in California or Maryland, some of the most expensive states in the country. So you have to take these and other cost-of-living factors into account when looking at annual salary or hourly rates for a job or project.

Part of the problem is that our country talks a good game about the importance of STEM in the workforce, but in a society where you're only paying teachers $30,000 starting salary, and illiterate athletes are making *millions* of dollars for a few months' work, where's the motivation to study and work hard for four to seven years to *only* make $60,000 a year before taxes? Now within the past ten years, there have been national movements to promote more STEM education, and rightly so. The politicians haven't started crying that, "The sky is falling!" yet, but they know damn well, as well as I, that this country's global competitiveness is falling off rapidly with each passing generation that chooses not to enter the technical field. It also doesn't help that greedy US companies would rather farm out or "offshore" their work to foreign workers that they pay a third of what it'd cost them in American salaries. Never mind that these individuals can take whatever technical information these companies are giving them and use it for their own advantage or take it to their home country's state-run enterprises to compete. Our standard of living will begin to really fall off (you think it's bad now?) in a few more years if something is not done quickly.

I laugh at some of these magazines that have annual salary reports that show base salaries for different engineering positions and industries. Don't get me wrong. Compared to the average Joe, engineers are still making some serious loot. But that's just it, compared to the *average* person, where the median family income is roughly $50,000, you're doing great. But after talking to an Internal Revenue Service agent a few months back, the US Government has done a great job of pulling the wool over the peoples' eyes and making them think that middle class is anything above $50,000 to $60,000. I can tell you, on *very* good authority, that according to the IRS, if you're not making at least $400,000 per year, *you are not* middle class! Anything above $1.2 million, you're in the upper class bracket. Sooooo, how do you even get close to that number? You'd have to be a senior engineering director or VP of a company to make maybe $200,000 plus benefits per year, if you're lucky. It can be done, but out of how many employees and how many years' investment? Like I mentioned earlier, I looked around at the people who had been at Boeing/MDA for more than 20 years and decided I wanted something different.

When I was in TSS, we had a group of contractor engineers doing a lot of the design work on our flight simulators. I didn't know much about them at the time, except they had different badges, and they seemed to work a lot more hours than us permanent employees— permies or directs—did. They all worked in a closed room at the end of the hallway that was dimly lit so they could see their CAD workstation screens. It became affectionately known as "The Cave." I was eventually moved in there with some other electrical engineers when we were working on our wiring diagrams and cable assemblies. Over time, I got to know some of these guys and what they were up to.

As a direct employee, you're usually brought in on salary with benefits. What that means is that you'll be paid a fixed amount of money based upon a 40-hour work week for a year, and it should include things like health insurance and savings plans, stock purchases, etc. The caveat to this is the company's overtime policy. Many times, working extra hours is not compensated for. You're on salary now, a Company Man, so you need to do *whatever it takes* to get the job done! At least that's the argument you may be presented with by your boss or HR maggot. Some companies will pay straight time after so many hours worked to show some appreciation, or in other cases, they may give stock options or an annual "bonus" at the end of the year if profits were up. This can be taken or left behind; many times, these bonuses are a portion of your weekly or monthly salary and after taxes, you probably could've found that much in change at the vending machines or gas station parking lots. Once again, I know of some companies that paid their employees quite well, at least until the money dried up, then all hell broke loose. Also, sometimes these benefits packages aren't all that much of a benefit. If you join a large company that has an aging workforce, someone has to pay for all those retirement pensions and healthcare costs. I've seen instances where companies made employees pay weekly or monthly fees (they sometimes like to call them co-payments) for healthcare packages; and the more dependents you have, the more of your check they take. It's ridiculous as I know of people, God bless them, that are in crappy jobs making a crappy salary, but because the healthcare is deemed good for them and their families, they stay aboard, hoping they make it to retirement. Even that is no longer a guarantee of financial security. You have companies, from school systems to airlines and all points in between, which are trying to formulate schemes to pare back on what they are paying out to their retirees and their beneficiaries. Keep these things in mind when you sign up with an outfit, as Daddy would tell me.

Now, back to the contractors, or job shoppers as they are commonly called. In this day and age of quick fixes and penny-pinching, companies will bring in temporary workers to do certain jobs quickly and exceptionally well. I guess somewhere in a dark room, technical managers and executives huddle around a table and estimate how long a project will take, and how many man-hours it will burn. The permies are on board to work and live in close proximity to the job site, taking care of family or living the single life, depending on social status. If a project demands a lot of hours and there is a short duration to accomplish it from start to finish, at least for the design work, they bring in temps to work extra hours to complete the mission. They are called contractors because the company will hire a staffing firm (job shop, contract house, job pimps, etc.) to put the job requisitions out on different websites that are dedicated to temporary staffing positions, as well as have recruiters who call the names and numbers on stacks of resumes they have to fill these positions. The firms will negotiate an hourly rate that the client company is comfortable with, and this is what they will pay the employee after they get their cut. The shopper will sign an employee agreement or contract with the staffing firm that may have certain clauses in them, including nondisclosure agreements and technical property rights that usually favor the shop or the client. This is why sometimes the shops are called pimps and the engineers and designers are called whores, or road whores, because they are usually from some other place instead of the local area. The client company may also use contractors because they don't have to deal with insurance benefits or payroll taxes. The staffing firms will take care of the taxes if the contract is a W-2 employee agreement, as well as offer some sort of health insurance and disability package.

You are probably thinking, "Yeah, okay, so?" Well, Dear Reader, listen and learn. As I began to establish a rapport with the shoppers in the Cave, I began to see why many times, they would be the first ones to arrive, and the last ones to leave. Back in the early '90s, these guys were making anywhere between $35 to $50 per hour, and to top it off, they were getting one and a half times their hourly rate for any overtime (OT) worked. This is known as time and a half. If you're pulling a sixty-hour work week, that equates to $2,000 straight time (forty hours at $50) plus $1,500 OT for a total of $3,500 per week. Now this is before taxes, mind you, but remember how I mentioned a lot of these folks were not from around the local area? Well, there's a clause in the IRS codes that allows for a certain portion of someone's salary not to be taxed if they are working more than fifty miles from their permanent address and maintaining a second residence. This is known as per diem, or a daily split, which is good for one calendar year from your employment start date. Many shoppers will work a site for eleven months, then take the mandatory "time off" to avoid losing the per diem benefit. If the client and shop are good with it, they will simply renew the contract and all mandatory paperwork to stay in accordance with the IRS codes. Anyway, I don't know all the percentages, but based upon the calculations written above, a contractor could clear $2,000—$2,500 a week depending on filing status and withholdings. It also depends on if the state they reside and work in has state tax filing requirements, as well.

Regardless of the tax requirements, I would listen to these guys talk about what they were pulling in as far as hours and rates. They even began to make me privy to some of the tricks of the trade and the differences between shoppers and directs. I remember one guy who was a great mechanical designer, and he did not hide the fact that he was there strictly for the money. It was actually funny because he and the others would say little phrases that let you know they were shoppers. If a project demanded a whole lot of OT, you'd hear him say things like, "You can have the mouse when you pry it from my cold, dead fingers!" or when a permie engineer or manager asked them if they could work on the weekends, "I'll be sure to send you a fruit basket!" The point is that they may not have had the titles or glamour, but they were actually making two or three more times as the directs in a year! We had another older gentleman from Texas who told me he only took contract jobs that had a certain amount of overtime guaranteed; he would work a project really hard for six to eight months, then take the rest of the year off! I tell you what. I heard stories like that and began to really mumble to myself, "Man! I'm in the *wrong* business!"

Well, as you can imagine, this type of news is not top secret; soon I found out that there was some animosity between the shoppers and some of the permie engineers and managers. Jealousy is a mutha'. It's funny, though. You have managers and employees who don't want to work the sixty or seventy hours a week, but the work has to get done. Some directs will work themselves into the ground to accomplish the company objectives, but the home life is suffering badly and perhaps even their health. This is where the contractors come in. These are the specialists who are there strictly to work as many hours allowed, and to get the job done. Now with anything, you're going to have some bad apples who come in and give everyone else a bad name. You will have shoppers who doctor up their resumes to get into a place because with contractors, there is usually no face-to-face interview like you have with a permanent position. The hiring manager will conduct several phone interviews and if they like what they hear on the phone and see on paper, they will let the staffing firm recruiter know this and a start date is established. The bad shopper comes aboard and starts working, but after four to six weeks, the results are unacceptable and this guy is "walked out the door." So if this happens, the hiring manager and coworkers are left feeling frustrated because they spent one to two months paying this guy for nothing, and now they have to start all over again. This is the dangerous side of contracting. Unless you have some sort of agreement in writing, there is usually a clause that the contractor can be fired or "released" by the client *at any time for any reason*. I was at this one aircraft company and I think within two months, we had six or eight contractors fired. It was a real shooting gallery, and those of us who remained began to call this one desk in the corner of the room, The Chair of Death. It got that nickname because about three or four of the shoppers who'd been fired sat there. I was so superstitious that when my supervisor asked if I wanted to move there to be close to the window, I told him, "Hellll Naw!"

On my contract jobs, I always try to establish a good relationship at least with the immediate supervisor so that I can ask for a friendly warning if I'm not performing to their satisfaction, or for a one to two weeks' notice if there are plans for me to be let go. Many times, companies don't want to do this because the engineer will roll out before the job is done or a suitable replacement has been brought in and trained up to ensure a smooth transition. But with the exception of three occasions, I've always had adequate notice of an impending layoff or left jobs on my own volition.

When I saw the type of money these guys (and gals) were making, I definitely started asking more questions. The one mechanical designer I mentioned earlier would tease me and go into a Darth Vader routine where he'd mimic the *Star Wars* scene when Vader was trying coerce his son, Luke Skywalker, to come to the "Dark side of the force"; except it was regarding becoming a contractor and leaving my direct job behind.

"Dusty! Come to the Dark Side….feel the power!!" And he'd hold up his hand as if it were Vader's gloved fist.

Well, after I had been turned down for the leadership course by my department head at Boeing, I began to take on the mentality of a shopper. I had begun to be resigned to my fate of being a good employee with no hope of moving up the ranks, so I just focused on the money. I even changed my email address to reflect the acronym in military parlance: DREAD(locked) TECH(nical)MERC(enary). It wasn't until the final few incidents at Boeing that I decided to try my hand at contracting and left for the sweltering humidity of GAC down in Savannah, Georgia, in early 2004.

Now I quickly found out about some more unwritten rules in contracting once I landed at GAC. Remember how I mentioned I had my first female lead engineer, basically the supervisor of a group of engineers and designers? Well, first of all, the chick didn't have an engineering degree, she had just been a drafter/designer for so long that the group manager at the time promoted her to the position.

Second, I don't think she had ever worked at any other aviation or aerospace outfits, so her perspective was strictly that of GAC. When I got briefed on how things were done, I was given a project and set about quickly to get the work done. I came across a situation where I made a suggestion on a drawing that I thought would "help the cause" overall, so to speak. This woman looked up at me with the strangest grin and said, "Well, we don't like Yankees coming down here telling us what to do." I beg your pardon? I didn't know what to say. First of all, I'm from Tennessee, and even though I'm not down with the Confederacy and Jim Crow and whatnot, I always thought the term, Yankee, was reserved for people from the northern United States. In these parts, a Yankee was anyone from the outside. I quickly found out that Savannah was a very slow and *conservative* town, as well as Southern as far as Southern goes. Contrary to what some people think, as progressive as Atlanta (the capital city) is compared to the rest of the southeastern US, the rest of the state of Georgia is almost as backward as the farthest reaches of Old Appalachia.

Third, I was actually confused by the fact that she was not open to what I considered a good idea that would've helped the group as a whole. My father coached me on this also, that unless they ask for your input, keep your brilliant ideas to yourself. Until the upper management sees a need for a change, the company culture at the ground level is going to remain the same, and it's usually rife with inefficiencies and malfeasance. This is usually par for the course when it comes to contracting. You are the consultant or SME who is there to do a specific job, and that job only. Keep your head down and appear busy even if you complete the job way ahead of schedule. When they do ask for your input, you give them the best answer you can, but leave the door open for them to make the final decision. It's not your company and you're not holding the purse strings, so why rock the boat?

Another rule I found out the hard way is that job shoppers are looked upon as the scourge of the technical ranks. Scoundrels and miscreants we are! Only thing missing is the eye patch and a pirate flag hanging on the cubicle wall. When you have a manager who quickly displays the attitude, "I don't like contractors because they are only here for the money," you do your job and keep quiet as a church mouse around this guy. This is the motherf**ker who's itching to walk a shopper out the door on a Monday or a Tuesday rather than on a Friday when most layoffs occur just to make life hard. But once again, you have to raise an eyebrow when you see this attitude and ask yourself, "Would you do this sh*t for free?" If the answer is no, then they are there for the money, as well, with the delusion that they are more righteous than the shoppers because their badge is a different color. Remember that jealousy I mentioned earlier? I've been in situations where I was engaged in a full conversation with a supervisor or coworker as a contractor, and the group manager literally walked up and started talking to them like I wasn't even there. The first time it happened to me at GAC, I wrote a stinging email to my recruiter complaining about how I was being treated. I forgot the response, but it was basically like, "Don't sweat the small stuff, you're getting 50 hours a week!" So I learned to get thick skin and look past the small insults that come with the contracting territory.

Now with everything, you have to draw the line somewhere when your self-respect and integrity are called into question. This is my opinion only, but I've had a few instances where I went head-to-head with a supervisor who tried to insinuate that I was lying about hours worked. I was scared to death of being fired on the spot, to be honest with you, but I walked out of these people's offices with my head high, knowing that I stood up for myself as well as for the right thing. You take as much as you can, but if you see the need to bounce, find a new contract or direct job as soon as possible. With that, I will offer another caveat: An unwritten rule of contracting is to stay on a job for at least three months. That way, everyone has gotten something out of the deal, and even if you leave for a better opportunity, you can say something like you had some family matters to tend to back home for a while. If you do a good enough job, they may leave the door open for you down the road. Depending on your industry, you're going to have the opportunity to work at the same place more than once over your career if you are good at what you do and the economy has the demand for your skill set. So try to always leave on good terms.

Of course, this doesn't always work out. I worked at a place where they didn't offer per diem and I was driving from Nashville, TN, to Huntsville, AL, every day. *Big* mistake! *Never* take a contract that does not offer per diem, especially if you qualify for the 50 miles or more commute. Needless to say, after a month, I was definitely digging a hole for myself and quickly found another opportunity within a month. It just wasn't feasible with a family to feed and bills to pay, so I had to burn that bridge. You're a temporary technical worker, paid for the knowledge and experience you're bringing to the table without a long ramp-up time to get trained. It's this situation where I do like to deploy the pirate and mercenary phrases that keep me well-motivated:

- Have mouse, will travel
- Technical Mercenary – Services available to all, loyal to NONE
- Take what you can, give nothing back!

If you're not happy with a contract situation, give a one- to two-week notice once you've secured more gainful employment and get the hell out of Dodge. Prime example: I know of a few instances where the cash flow at a company was drying up, so they convinced the directs and the contractors to stick with them. Meanwhile, they started paring back on the hours until they were working a paltry 30 or 35 hours a week. Doing what it takes to help the company out, right? Everyone doing their part, being a team player, eh? Well, I can tell you on good authority that the owners and/or executive managers weren't being a Lee Iacocca and giving themselves a $1 salary until things got turned around. Meanwhile, the "loyal" employees had been duped into working fewer than 40 hours a week, which technically made them part-time employees; if they had gotten laid off, they may not have qualified for any or full unemployment benefits, and the company men would have been laughing all the way to the bank. So if you find yourself working for someone and they try to get you to keep producing a good product for little or nothing, unless you get a written agreement for partial ownership or know where to find these jackals so you can take a baseball bat to them or their prized possessions, (Not really, but it'd be nice. Get an attorney.) quickly find a new source of income!

Before you venture out into the world of job shopping, here are a few more suggestions. First, work in the industry for a few years to figure out what area(s) of engineering you really enjoy. You may have to hopscotch a few times before you find your niche and enjoy your line of work. It has to be something that you find rewarding and has a steady demand in the foreseeable future. This is especially true for my software heads. Coding is *never* going away, but don't do it if you don't love it. The software heads probably make the most money as far as hourly rates go, at least from what I've seen outside the realm of the pure consultants. The pure consultants are with firms or they operate independently, and have the reputation and clientele to demand $200–$500 per hour, depending on what their industry is. Once you know what you are good at, you need to gain anywhere from three to five years of experience before jumping into the contracting pool. That way, your resume shows that you are experienced enough to justify a decent hourly rate. Naturally, someone with five years' experience is not going to make what someone with fifteen to twenty years' experience is bringing in.

That's one thing I enjoy about contract work. You are paid for the hours you work, whether it be four, eight, ten and a half, or fourteen; if you have documentation that you've put the hours in, your paycheck should reflect that. Now, unfortunately, many times OT has to be preapproved before you can work it. Especially if you have a situation where you've worked some extra hours and the next week your manager gives you hell about it because they are budgeting for only straight time. Make sure you have an email or a definitive yes or "however long it takes you" from your senior manager so they won't have ammunition to use against you.

The other thing I appreciate about contracting is that because you are an "expendable asset," you have to stay up on your skills to be kept around. The directs can coast and spend half the day playing solitaire and dominoes, or chat on Facebook while you are busy solving problems, and being well-paid for it. Sometimes companies will send all of their employees, including contractors, to required or recommended training. If you can get some value-added training at their expense, don't be a fool. Suck up all the knowledge you can!

Second, consider how far out you are willing to travel to chase that dollar. If you live in a city that has beaucoup opportunities in your chosen field, then you are "sh*ttin' in high cotton," as my Daddy would say when things are good. Or you may find opportunities in cities, regions, or even around the world that you can travel to for a certain period of time. Most contracts are predicated on weeks, months, or sometimes years. A standard period is six to twelve months, and if the project is ongoing, the client will sometimes grant you an extension. As long as you are getting per diem and a good hourly rate, if you minimize your expenses, you can stack some serious chips if you play your cards right. You may not always get an opportunity in that glamorous cosmopolitan city, but rather an isolated town with a burgeoning plant or technology center that needs talented technocrats to get the operation up and running. You'll have to travel home or to the nearby city on the weekends, or once every few weeks, to enjoy your favorite pastime or see friends and family. I was at this one aircraft modification company in the middle of a bunch of chicken farms in Delaware back in 2006. The work and hours were great, but there wasn't much to do aside from going to the beach or driving up to Dover or Newark, which was money- and time-consuming. I was able to work out a deal with my supervisor once I had proven my worth where I would work for ten days straight, then drive over to the Baltimore airport and fly home to see my wife and kids for four days, and then I'd rotate back on the afternoon of day four to Delaware. If you are in a position to take a contract overseas, private or government, give the job shop its due diligence and make sure lodging and travel arrangements are set; but you can make some real good money if you can stand being out of the States for nine to twelve months. I stress the twelve months because there are certain IRS clauses that dictate how long a person has to be physically out of the country for the income to be nontaxable. Either way, I know some folks who routinely go abroad and come back with fattened bank accounts.

Third, don't make the same mistake that I did where I left a steady contract gig for another one that offered a slightly higher rate per hour, but was farther away from home, and I had *not* discussed the overtime situation or policy. I assumed that there was overtime and was banking on there being some. I went from St. Louis, Missouri, to San Antonio, Texas, to work for an extra $200 a week. It was a $5 hourly rate increase, *but* travel was more expensive (gas to drive or airfare), and I had to find a place to stay, which turned out to be a nightmare. Even with per diem, a decent hotel is going to cost you anywhere from $50–$100+ a night, and you haven't even eaten yet! I stayed at a hotel for a week or two, then found a place that another contractor was staying that was furnished and offered weekly and monthly rates. It boiled down to this: I was not getting any overtime and my monthly expenses at home and at the job site were more than what I was bringing in. I was losing money! Lesson learned: Overtime is the contractor's lifeblood, but it is not always guaranteed. Only take jobs where the straight time (40 hours) will cover all of your costs and have enough left over for savings, emergencies, and a little fun. If you do get OT, you squirrel that money away for investments and any toys you wish to get down the road. Like my father told me afterward, "Don't get dependent on overtime, you'll get hurt down the road."

If you are going to be an over-the-road contractor, have a dependable vehicle. I traded in my 1995 Chevy S-10 pickup truck for a 2004 Ford Sport-Trac with a hard tuneau cover on the bed. I didn't have GPS at this time, so my direction-finding and map-reading skills became second to none as I worked different contracts over a ten-year period and racked up the miles. This was mostly because I was now a family man, and so I was trying to get home as often as possible to keep my family intact. Another expense is vehicle maintenance if you're going to be doing a lot of driving like I did. At the time of this writing, my Sport Trac, "Po' Boy," had amassed more than 390,000 miles before I put him out to pasture. You take care of your vehicle, and your vehicle will take care of you! Now with contracting over the road comes an inherent amount of risk. When you are doing a lot of long-distance driving, learn your limits! Don't be too macho to pull over at a rest stop or truck park and snooze for a few hours. Your body can subsist off of so much caffeine before sleep takes over. God has woken me up from behind the wheel on more than a few occasions where I could have run off the road or been killed in a head-on accident!

Speaking of accidents, I have to mention this one incident where I was contracting for an inflight wi-fi company based in Chicago and almost got killed on I-65 South driving home one night. I had been commuting from Nashville, TN, to the Chicago suburbs for a little more than a year. Five hundred miles and eight hours one way, week in and week out. I'd leave out late Sunday night or early, early Monday morning to be in the company parking lot by 9 a.m. I had a few times where I got there closer to 10 a.m., and would try to creep into the building and to my desk without being spotted. Hard to do that though when you're the only Negro in the group. But I digress. Although it was a long drive, it had become routine, and as long as there wasn't massive construction, bad accidents (I witnessed a truck driver fatality north of Indianapolis, on the afternoon of February 22, 2013. It shut down the highway. I saw the poor guy's body in the wreckage...some sh*t you just don't forget.), or inclement weather, I could burn up the road and make the trek sometimes in just over seven hours. This particular day, a snowstorm had pushed through and was making its way southeast. For the Midwest and East Coast states, snow is a way of life and their highway departments have the means to keep the roads fairly clear with salt trucks and snow plows. But once you get to the Mason-Dixon Line, everybody south of it shuts down if a quarter-inch of snow or ice even *looks* at the ground. I had just crossed the Ohio River into Louisville, Kentucky, and was cruising through light snow into the outlying suburbs. I think I had passed the last major town when I was coming up on a tractor trailer in the right lane that was going much slower. I wasn't going that fast, either, since it was nighttime and snowy, but the truck was definitely doing under 55 miles per hour.

This section of expressway was still three lanes wide so I was going to simply get into the middle lane, get past "Big Heavy," and keep it moving. There was other highway traffic, mostly other commercial trucks since most commuters were probably already at home or taking the side roads. I put my turn signal on and began to change lanes. Then it happened. The nose of my truck turned left and then I apparently hit a decent patch of snow or ice because I went into a spin while changing lanes! Not only was I spinning, but I was sliding across three lanes of road with big trucks to the side or behind me, at night! Obviously, this occurred in mere seconds. While I was spinning, I could see the trucks and the headlights flashing past my window. I saw the entire truck and its trailer that was in the farthest left lane as it continued on. By the time I had completed the second full rotation, I was perpendicular to the highway and was headed straight for a bridge piling—not good. Instinctively, I cut the steering wheel hard right since I was still moving forward and gave a little gas to begin rotating away from the concrete structure. The truck had rotated parallel with the road by the time I had reached the median and avoided impacting the bridge, but now I was still rotating to the right and was about to head back onto the highway and possibly into traffic that was still behind me. I pulled the wheel slightly to the left to keep in the median, but if you've ever driven the highways, you know that once you pass a bridge, the landscape gives way to a grassy median until the next overpass. I drove into the grass, but instead of panicking and slamming on my brakes, I accelerated some and used my momentum to get back onto the left shoulder of the road. If I had stopped, I would have surely gotten stuck in the ice and mud on the left side of the interstate in northern Kentucky on a snowy night. Once I had control of the vehicle and felt solid pavement under my tires, I kept on the left shoulder and turned my hazard lights on. By this time, most of the traffic that was in front or to the side of me had already passed, and the traffic behind me saw what had happened and slowed down, thank God.

A tractor trailer in the left lane that was coming up on me slowed down and flashed his high beams to let me know I could get over and back on the road. I turned my right signal light on and crept back onto the highway, making my way back into the far right lane and poked along about 45 miles an hour while still processing what had just happened in the past ten to fifteen seconds. When people have a life-changing event, a brush with possible death and they say they saw their lives flash before their eyes, they ain't bullsh*tting. I didn't have time to panic, but I had a thousand thoughts and reflections when this near miss occurred. Believe it or not, physics crossed my mind! *Well, we're all moving forward, so if one of these big trucks hits me, scientifically speaking, I should bounce forward with less damage than if we were going head-to-head, and I should survive if the driver is trying to slow down when/if such said collision occurs.* I plodded along for a good five or ten minutes while I gathered myself and my hands stopped shaking. Spun out on the highway, in a snowstorm with big trucks all around me at night, and *not a scratch*! You think God wasn't with me that night? If you don't think so, you're an atheist, a fool, or both. Needless to say, I told my supervisors that following week about what happened and that this would be the *last* winter I ever drove back and forth to Chicago ever again. Haven't done it since. Back to the lesson.

Look at your lodging options and decide what's best for you. Because of the volatile contracting environment, you want to pack light, but pack what you need to *minimize your expenses*. I say this because if you do get fired or laid off unexpectedly, you want to be able to pack up and move on to the next opportunity or go home to regroup without having to deal with a lot of matters to tie up like leases, utilities, early termination fees, and whatnot. Successfully finding a decent place to stay while saving money is the trick here. Now if all of your bills are paid and you've got money to burn, you can rent a room or an apartment in a more upscale part of town if it suits your fancy. If you're like me and trying to pinch every penny you can until Lincoln's face grimaces, then you'll want to do some research on the area you'll be working in for affordable housing, if you can. Some apartment complexes will work with you if they know you are a temporary worker and they are familiar with the company you are working for. If you can negotiate a month-to-month rate, that's always a good thing; it may cost a little more, but at least if you have to go, you are free and clear to jet. If you think there is a good chance you'll be on board for at least six months, then you could sign a six- or nine-month lease and save a few dollars on rent. Because this is an apartment, you'll have to get your own furniture, cookware, bath and bed linens, and food. I invested in a cheap set of cutlery, pots and pans, dishes, bedsheets/ sleeping bag, bath cloths, air mattress & pump, and packed food and provisions for at least a week. (Another trick I learned from an old contractor is to get cheap furniture from a local Goodwill, pawn shop, or thrift store when you find a place; when your contract is up, just leave it or donate it back!) You can pick up your perishable items at a local grocery once you get settled in. As a practice, I don't eat out a lot, and try to prepare my own meals as much as possible. I recommend you monitor your fast food intake, as well as daily meals even if you are going to a three- or five-star restaurant every day. You want to eat healthy, but you don't want to use up your disposable income on food only. An even sweeter deal is finding a furnished studio, apartment, or room for rent on a monthly or weekly basis. A flat fee for all expenses is the ideal situation. If you are in a city where you know someone or have relatives, you may be able to stay rent-free or rent "couch space" for a few weeks or the duration of your contract. As with anything, be prepared for any contingencies when dealing with people. You don't want to get roped into a deal with shady roommates or landlords that have crazy rules. I remember I was looking for a place to stay when working in Delaware, and this one place offered a room, but no access to the kitchen or the laundry room. To top it off, I saw someone's clothes hanging on a line out back. How weird is that? Only share an apartment if you know and trust the person you are going to be splitting expenses with. And make sure all agreements are in writing.

If you really want to be hardcore, convert your vehicle into a camper or stay at an actual campsite. I met some contractors who had a sleeper on the back of their trucks, owned a mobile home, or pitched an actual tent behind their cars at a local campsite! When I was working at a few places, I was in situations where I was between getting an affordable place to stay and had to improvise. Although my wife begged me to get a hotel room, I was determined not to put anymore charges on our credit card than necessary. One time in Delaware I was able to work out a deal with the landlord of the place where I was waiting for a vacancy that I knew was coming (A coworker staying there was about to go out of the country for a few weeks). I paid only for access to the showers and the kitchen while this guy was wrapping things up. I would wait until the regular tenants were done and I'd creep in, fix a quick meal, and then grab a shower and sleep in my truck. I'd get up before everyone and get cleaned up for work and roll out so I wouldn't be detected. Plus the landlord asked me not to advertise this arrangement to anyone else for fear of her yard turning into a mobile home park. The other situation was being able to grab a shower at an acquaintance's place, then going back to work where I would eat at my desk (I'd pack or purchase enough food for the week and kept it in the company refrigerator), work on this book, check things on the Internet, and then sleep in the backseat of my Sport Trac in the company parking lot until morning. This one company I worked at had couches scattered around the place. I would wait until the cleaning staff was done for the night and then go up to one of the prayer/meditation rooms (they had a sizable Hindu & Muslim employee population) and sleep on the couch until about 4:30 or 5:00 a.m. I made sure not to disturb anything out of respect, but I also didn't want anyone to find out that I was damn near a vagrant sleeping on the premises. My TSU training had paid off, making good on a bad situation.

If you do decide to contract, consult, or even have your own technical company one day, you have to do your homework. Learn about all of the local laws and required paperwork and certifications from a credible source, including an accountant, government agencies, and experienced mentors, if possible. That mentoring thing will have to cross all color and gender boundaries because there's still not enough of us out there. You will have to establish a positive reputation inside and outside of your current company where you are a direct before leaving. And as you do begin to work in the contractor world, establish contacts along the way. One of my best contracts came because of a fellow contractor who knew of an opportunity that he actually turned down. Learn how to be an effective networker.

I digress (again) about one of my pet peeves: Black folks don't network with each other worth a sh*t most of the time. As I mentioned earlier about the Corporate Negro who achieves a certain measure of success but won't help anyone else of our kind along the way; this is a pervasive problem with Our People. Am I saying that you should get a job just because you're Black or of another minority ethnic group? No. But I am saying that we should be making a few more phone calls for each other to give support and open doors for the recent college graduates, potential interns, job seeker, or layoff victim. The White folks do it all the time. I've seen White boys with less than 3.0 GPAs get into an outfit just because they went to the same university as the group manager or company CEO; no further examination needed, point blank. Meanwhile, we continue to have a *handful* of success stories and are subliminally told to be happy with that. I've met my fair share of African-American executives in different companies who apparently had some power and influence (entourage of subordinates and assistants in tow). But when I reached out to them for help or any potential leads, there was usually a padded response that there were no opportunities for me at the time, or *no response* at all. Well, if you can help yourself to success and bring some Brothers and Sisters along with you, then please do it! You may have your own company one day where you can hire more than a handful of Colored folks. It can be done. I've met too many White boys making some serious money in their own businesses who were no sharper than you or I. You've got to have an entrepreneurial spirit and be willing to fail and leave it all on the table to attain that success.

Contracting has been scary at times, but it has also been good to me. As I write these lines, I can tell you that I've been blessed to not have to ask my wife to take a job so that we could make ends meet. Contracting paid for our wedding back in 2004, and my wife has been a stay-at-home mom since day one. It has not always been easy. I've had to work long hours in faraway places to keep the monies flowing, and I've missed a few life moments in my family that I wish I could get back. But I'm hoping to be able to not miss any more within the next five years, and focus on enjoying the rest of what time God has granted me. Oh, and for those kids who didn't let me "fly it," back in first grade: That's okay, I get to fly on, crawl on, walk on, and play with *REAL* airplanes now, you Suckas!

7.0 FINANCIAL COMMON SENSE

7.1 HAVE A MIND FOR MONEY

Forgive me for not knowing the exact statistics, but I do know this: African-Americans comprise the largest consumer group in the United States, and collectively, we don't own 10 percent (Hell, I've heard 1 percent) of the assets in this country. We have the lowest median incomes, and the lowest home ownership rates. We have great publications like *Ebony*, *Essence*, and *Black Enterprise* magazines, yet we still don't have sh*t to show for it overall. Once again, we have a handful of success stories with a few athletes and entertainers who enjoy extravagant lifestyles (compared to the common folks) and flash a few dollars to keep the masses subdued into thinking that they are the measuring rod to wealth and success. They made their riches from *our* dollars, especially from *our children* buying some footwear or clothing or music albums, and have done nothing to raise our people out of abject poverty. No making of public service announcements to encourage our children to read and work hard (Except Denzel and the Boys & Girls Clubs, had to give him props for that one). And just as important as reading and getting an education, the *creation* of wealth and sustaining wealth, is not readily promoted in our communities. Success starts in the mind, and wealth is a measure of success. As I write, I am busy trying to teach my children to respect the value of money, to save it, and be willing to work for it. As with anything, if it's always given to you, you won't appreciate it and you won't respect it. But once it's taken away, you won't know how to make it on your own.

When you do land that first job and start making a few dollars, try to live as frugally as possible for your first year or two. Even if you do have a roommate, save as much as you can; if you are able to live at home with your relatives, then double good for you. If you have to get a new vehicle, get one that you can afford without breaking the bank. Unless you were on full scholarship, you may have some college debt to pay off, so you have to take care of that, as well. Get a savings and investment plan going as soon as possible! Too many of us make the mistake of trying to keep up with the Joneses and getting things too early to make an impression on folks, especially young Brothers trying to date or chase women. I know of too many examples where young guys get that paycheck on Friday, and after a few days of clubbing or dinner dates, they got a few nickels and dimes to barely cover weekly expenses. You shouldn't buy what you think Puffy and Jay-Z are sipping on if it's going to take half your cash out of your pocket in one sitting. Remember, those guys are *paid* to advertise to you the product the distributors are pushing, and you helped write the check. I'm not saying to not have a good time every now and then and enjoy life; what I am doing is encouraging you, Dear Reader, to be smart with your money. Talk to folks who are at the level to which you aspire. Or learn from the mistakes and experiences of poor saps, like myself, who have blown a whole lot of money on foolishness and schemes.

Once you decide where you want to drop anchor, so to speak, look toward buying a home within three to five years. Establish your savings and investment plan like I mentioned earlier, and stick with it. This is the 5–25 percent, minimum, of your income that should not be missed if you do it correctly. Sit with a financial advisor if you can; many of your banks and financial institutions have an in-house certified financial planner whom you can consult free of charge. If you can invest in real estate or rental property, do that as well. Make sure you establish an emergency fund that can sustain you for three to six months. You never know what the future holds, and like I mentioned earlier, there is no company loyalty. The old adage concerning Colored folks is still true: LHFF—Last hired, first fired. When the finances get tight and companies start cutting overhead, don't be shocked if your manager pulls you into his office and starts with a line of bullsh*t about how they "really appreciate all you've done for the company," and whatnot. This is the prelude to them dropping the hammer and walking you out the door. That's why it's important to save; unemployment benefits are a joke nowadays. I don't see how folks live off of $300 a week or every two weeks.

We, as a people, have been conditioned to spend money over and over on things, many times on items that *we don't need*. We don't invest in ourselves or our communities, sadly. What do I mean? I'm not talking about the church or your respective place of worship, specifically. I believe in God, and I believe in giving back according to His principles, but we have plenty of churches with high-living Negro pastors who have too many congregants who are getting by paycheck-to-paycheck while the local schools can't afford soap for the bathrooms. But I am a strong proponent of education and real estate. Our neighborhoods tend to be unkempt, and that is a reflection of how we feel about ourselves. Our schools tend to be unkempt and underperforming, another reflection of ourselves. I am especially passionate about the current financial state of our HBCUs, at present. While the majority schools like Harvard, Vanderbilt, Yale, Alabama, Cal-Berkeley, and countless others enjoy endowments well into the hundreds of millions of dollars, our HBCUs are on the cusp of going bankrupt and closing their doors. These are the same institutions of higher learning that, not more than two generations ago, were the only places that African-Americans could go to further themselves in this society. They have produced countless success stories in our ethnic group, yet we have failed to give back to nurture and expand their facilities and capabilities as a whole. African, Black, Negro, Colored, or African-American should not be equated with mediocre or sub-par. This is part of the mental conditioning I have suffered from, and wish to help break. If you are an HBCU student or alumnus, please make sure to *give back regularly* to your Alma Mater. That is the only way it will continue to grow and improve and attract the best and the brightest, as well as inspire the lesser performing students to strive for excellence. If you did not attend an HBCU, then give to your university's Black Student Alliance, fraternity or sorority chapter, social or technical organization, and/or department of your choice that will help another minority student to matriculate. If you can, become a "friend" of an HBCU and provide whatever support you can as your time and resources allow. I don't think these few paragraphs are going to change our conditions overnight, but I felt the need to say something to this matter.

7.2 BEWARE OF "BUSINESS OPPORTUNITIES" (I WAS AN AMWAY PROSTITUTE)

Most young people are energetic, ambitious, and open to all kinds of possibilities that may provide success. There is nothing wrong with that. But I am writing to admonish you, Dear Reader, to temper your blissful ambition with a healthy dose of skepticism. I wrote earlier about how predators in cults prey on young, naive college student to fill their ranks. Well, the same thing applies to any opportunity that crops up dealing with making money. If someone approaches you with an idea or "business opportunity," you need to be skeptical as hell and analyze it to no end. Oftentimes, they are willing to do business with you as long as it's on *your* dime.

The summer I interned at MDA in St. Louis, I befriended an older Black lady who worked there. One afternoon, she was kind enough to give me a ride back to the apartment complex, and she casually invited me to have dinner with her and her husband one evening at their home. No big deal, right? Starving college kid being shown some love by some elders isn't unusual. So when I was hanging out at their home, the conversation eventually turned to how they had their own business and were looking to expand. To this day, being an entrepreneur and starting your own business is a big deal. The average person is trained to be an employee, per our country's "education" system. Only in the past few years have colleges and universities at the average level begun to have more programs aimed at assisting small businesses. The larger schools have had management and entrepreneurial programs in place for generations. But I digress again. I was told that they were part of a larger organization of business owners and that they had weekly meetings at one of the local hotel conference rooms. If I was interested, they'd pick me up on a Tuesday evening and take me to an information session. Okay, sounds good—who doesn't want to learn how to make some extra money? So Tuesday comes, they show up at my apartment, and I'm casually dressed. They got on full suit and business dress attire, and they ask me to go back in and put on a shirt and tie because this is a "business" meeting. O-kay, uh, sure. I run back upstairs and changed into a shirt and tie and jump in the back seat of their car and go to this meeting.

The guests of this information session were all seated on the first two rows and the business associates were seated in the remaining rows of chairs that were divided in two groups on either side of the room. I noticed that everyone was paying two or three dollars to get in. It was roughly an hour-long presentation, including a brief Q & A. The presenter on this particular evening was a Black gentleman who had achieved a good deal of success in this business, and when he was introduced, *everyone* in the room stood up and clapped and cheered as he came running to the stage. You'd have thought Frederick Douglas or Martin Luther King had come to speak based upon the ovation. Now it was a pretty mixed crowd this particular night because of who this guy was, and the numbers were strong. The business consisted of joining this organization (for a fee), which distributed different products and services to customers, as well as actively recruiting other distributors or "business owners" to join through you and you made a percentage from your sales and product usage, as well as from sales and product usage of distributors in your network. The presentation showed you how easy and simple it was based upon a pattern they called "6-4-2." You recruit six people, they recruit four people, their four recruit two people, and as long as *everyone* was using or moving at least 100 points' worth of products, which equated to roughly $200 (1:2 ratio back then, but the dollar amount was actually more), you would supposedly make an extra $2,000 per month. This level was called a direct distributor and was a big deal. But the real money was when you helped six people in your network to reach the direct level, then your title was that of a diamond distributor and you'd be making at least $100,000 per year, and you could retire from working a stupid, dumb job as they all put it. Ideally, you could be a diamond in two to five years if you just put in the work. Anyway, the parent company was the Amway Corporation based somewhere in Michigan. It was short for American Way and was all about the capitalistic and character principles that served as the foundation of this great Nation.

For the record, all Amway did and does is make household and commercial products, cleaning and laundry supplies being their backbone, followed closely by personal hygiene and health-care items. The products were actually pretty good and supposedly very eco-friendly. At the time I was about to join, Amway had started creating joint venture programs with other companies to market their products, supposedly at a discount to its distributors. So this was an added feature of joining the organization. The issue was that a lot of the stuff was highly concentrated so they lasted forever and a day, especially for a single person like myself not having a family of four or more to use the products. The distributor organizations were responsible for building the distribution networks and were granted a great deal of leeway within a supposed framework of rules. You'll hear more about this later.

At the end of the meeting that Tuesday night, everyone was excited and hyped up about become a diamond, and being free from jobs and indebtedness, and living happily ever after. Naturally, I was caught up in the mood of the room as well, and quickly bought in. Everyone was nice and friendly and encouraging with phrases like, "You can do this!" and "You're a winner!" I took some of my internship money and joined up, and "started my own business." The starter kit included paperwork for registration and a boatload of products composed of cleaning supplies, vitamins, and some personal care items, if my memory serves me correctly. The couple who recruited me were known as my sponsors, and they would begin to train me and assist me in recruiting other distributors. Part of this training involved reading a recommended list of books and listening to audio tapes of different speakers, including the man who was at the top of this particular distributor organization and who had achieved a rank of crown ambassador, which meant he had at least 18–24 diamond distributors in his network. This all made sense at the time. It was the early 90s and the age of self-help, success/prosperity thinking, and motivational programs was in full swing. So anybody and everybody was either writing, talking, attending, or reading up on how to be successful and more organized in their lives. I had just listened to a Black man who was successful in

Amway and he and the others at his level and above had fine cars and beautiful homes, and had achieved the American Dream. If he did it, so could I, right? I have an affable, outgoing personality, so talking to strangers is not a problem for me. Matter of fact, I remember my mother kept a journal about my first few years and one entry observed that I was not afraid to talk to strangers, so it was in my genetics. But there's a difference between casually talking to a stranger about where they got their shoes, and striking up a conversation to lead into going into business with someone.

When you first get into a type of networking business like Amway, your sponsor or recruiter is going to tell you to make a list of *all* your family and friends and begin to call them to tell them about a "great opportunity to make money," or something along those lines. I was able to do this without much difficulty or reservation. But I should've known something was amiss because you're calling to talk about a business, but you're not supposed to *tell* them what it is up front! Okay, what gives? Well, more people supposedly join after they see The Plan (this is that 6-4-2 I mentioned) and are more open to it after the presenter had given the "facts," and painted the "dream." That's one thing they would always push at the meetings—you can't be successful at this or anything without a dream. So I was supposed to call folks, set up meetings either at their homes or a neutral place, and show up in a shirt and tie with my sponsor, who would present the Plan and add credibility to what we were doing. I was not aware of it, but Amway had developed a reputation of being a pyramid scheme and cultish as far as the distributors were concerned. So there was all this secrecy as far as telling folks up front what we were doing.

Meanwhile, my sponsors had deluged me with a stack of tapes and some books to read while I was there in St. Louis on my internship. I also met the White couple above us, our "up-line," who were our direct distributors; they reported to our diamond distributors who were a couple over in Indianapolis, Indiana. Direct distributors at the time were classified as such because all products ordered in their networks would be delivered directly to their business address, usually a home office, and then the distributors below them would show up at prescribed times for product pickup. Our directs had product pickup on Friday evenings.

I didn't have a car, so my sponsors started picking me up for the Tuesday meetings, product pickup on Friday evenings, and then spending Sunday evenings with them for what the distributor organization called phone team. Phone team was a gathering of distributors to take turns calling people they had contacted about joining the business team, and it also served as motivation to overcoming fears of rejection as you burned through your contact list or business cards. They actually had established scripts for us to follow sometimes when making these phone calls. The script was to help you provide the invite to the meetings, as well as address any concerns or hesitations the contact person might have to close the deal and have a commitment to attend the meetings.

I exhausted my limited phone list of friends and family very quickly, but at the end of my summer internship, I had sponsored my then TSU roommate, who was from the St. Louis area, and my Haitian-American roommate at MDA. We were young and excited about all of this money we were going to make. And naive. All of the time we were being bombarded with positive affirmations and assurances that this was an easy go of it, and that in five years, all of our asses would be millionaires and laughing at our friends and classmates who chose not to join us. I think I was the most susceptible to the atmosphere because I had always been in an environment that was harsh and negative most of the time. Well, I will fast-forward to the fall semester and tell you that I lost my "downline" very quickly. My MDA roommate went back to Perdue University in Indiana, and found out that Amway distributors were already crawling all over the campus and the Midwest since it was conceived in Michigan nearby. He went through his friends and classmates and got no one to join, and soon faded away. At TSU, my roommate and I set up a meeting in one of the engineering classrooms and gave a presentation to the classmates who did show up and actually did a pretty good job, right down to having a few product samples and audio tapes to hand out. The problem that nobody told us about, though, is that most White college kids come from money and got money to burn. So the success stories we heard about with college kids going direct, or ruby, or emerald while still too young to legally drink were not too far-fetched. However, most African-American college students *did not* come from families with inordinate amounts of disposable incomes, but rather mod-est backgrounds with median family incomes usually at or below the average American family income. Plus, the other catch to

Amway distribution, at the time, was that all product orders had to come through your upline direct distributor. Unless we were going to stockpile products in our cramped dormitory room, we had to place weekly calls to my sponsors in Missouri, who would then call our directs to place our orders, and *then* once they picked them up, they would ship the order to us on campus. So what normally took five days to arrive if you lived locally, would sometimes take eight days to two weeks to arrive. It's hard to convince folks what a great deal you have going on when they need stuff in the immediate. Plus, regardless of how "enviro-friendly" and concentrated the products were, they were sometimes way more expensive than the off-the-shelf stuff you could get at the local store. Broke college students aren't concerned with changing their buying habits on your behalf, no matter how good a friend you are; and we were broke right along with them. After a couple of orders that broke the bank, my roommate and I both had to call it quits; I did for the moment, anyway. My sponsors said they understood and to focus on our degrees, and once we graduated, they would be waiting for us in the wings to get back started.

Fast forward to January of 1995, when I was headed up to Berkeley, Missouri, to begin my career at MDA. Part of the relocation package was they put you up in a hotel for two weeks until you secured permanent housing. Once you found a place, they would have your furniture and possessions transported by a moving company to your new locale. Turns out, the very hotel they put me up in was the same one that my uplink distributor organization had its weekly meetings and larger monthly/quarterly meetings. So on a Tuesday evening around 7 p.m., I went downstairs and found the conference room that they were using. I went in as a guest and found my sponsors and sat through the presentation, remembering everything that I had learned during the three months that I interned back in 1993. I told them I was interested in getting back started, with the caveat that I would give it a good year. They quickly overrode that notion with a bevy of reasons to stick with it and I "meekly" acquiesced. After the meeting, they tried to get me to stay for the distributor meetings that occurred afterwards, but I had just started my first week on the job and was actually pretty tired. My direct even tried to talk me into taking a quick shower to freshen up and go with them; I should've seen the oddity in this—explanation coming SOON.

As you can guess, I jumped back into Amway with both feet in the deep end. Part of the distributor practice was to look and feel every part of being a successful business owner as often as possible. This included wearing business attire at all meetings, whether it was a large organizational function or a one-on-one meeting with a potential distributor at their home; we were suited to the teeth in business suit or shirt and tie and dress shoes. My first few years at MDA allowed me to operate covertly as an Amway distributor without raising too much alarm because the director in the Avionics Integration Center wanted his engineers to continue to look the part of the Space Age engineers and technicians from the Glory Days, right down to the pocket protectors. Once I transferred over to TSS, this became risky business because you didn't want to get ridiculed by coworkers for being in Amway; plus, you ran the risk of being fired if you got caught trying to do Amway on company time. For a while, I stuck out like a sore thumb wearing a suit in the more relaxed confines of the training systems organization. People would be nosy and all the time ask me why was I so dressed up. I'd always have to cook up some excuse to throw them off the trail. I would go to work, then get off and go someplace public to meet people and hopefully get their contact information to discuss this great opportunity, without telling them it was Amway. There would be many a day that I was tired as all get-out from work, but because I was "serious and committed" to building my own business, I would not go to the meager comforts of my apartment, but would go to the mall to make contacts. After two or three hours of plying the Galleria or Northwest Plaza or the grocery stores for strangers to make conversations with to get their info, I would drag myself home, fix a quick meal, try to force myself to read one of the many recommended books my upline provided, and go to sleep.

One of the things they did with new distributors right away was to give you a boatload of audio tapes to listen to that contained success stories of sponsoring and organization-building techniques. They also had a huge list of recommended books for the "success mentality." Like Dean Rogers told me, you are what you read and listen to. I was becoming immersed in the "Amway mindset" with the plan and hopes of becoming the youngest, *single* African-American diamond. It practically became an obsession. Meanwhile, I was going to the regular meetings on Tuesdays, product pickup on Friday, and phone team on Sunday nights at my sponsor's home. After the Tuesday meeting presentation, the distributors would remain for a teaching session for another hour or so to listen to the speaker that evening (who was required to be a direct or above) discuss whatever they felt like; *then* the serious folks would gather at a Shoney's restaurant up the road for food or coffee in what was termed a "night owl." A night owl was supposed to be for the hard-core distributors who would listen to the directs in the room talk about their successes, and then they would go around the room and allow anyone to speak about their week's successes or epiphanies when it came to building their organizations, making a new contact, or overcoming some challenge(s) that was getting in the way of them achieving Amway success. It was always refreshing because everyone was so positive and excited, and we were almost elitist in our thinking because we were trying to be successful in life and not work a job like the average, dumb American. These meetings would wrap up around midnight or so, then I'd drive myself to the apartment half-asleep, read some, then go to sleep, and try to be back at work by 7 a.m. sharp. There was more than one occasion where I overslept and came into work late because of this, or fell asleep at my desk. But it was cool because, according to the guys on the tapes, I was "paying the price" and was bound for success!

I was aggressively doing everything that I was supposed to do to try to build an Amway network. I was reading at least one recommended book a week, and listening to an audio tape of a well-respected Amway distributor in my truck or on my cassette player several times a day. Another thing they taught was positive speaking and affirmations. You were supposed to make a list of goals and dreams and recite them aloud several times a day, to "speak them into existence." This was supposed to be in accordance with Biblical principles, namely verses like Deuteronomy 8:18, Habakkuk 2:2–4, Romans 8:28, Isaiah 55:8–11, and Proverbs 12:13–14, to name a few. You were programming yourself and bringing the "unseen into the seen.' At least that's what they told me was happening. I was brought up in church, as I mentioned earlier in the book, so these things were not unusual to me. So I made out a list of things that I wanted, including a wife, laminated it, and carried it with me all throughout the day, picking certain times to go outside or in the men's room and recite it silently or aloud.

There I was, sitting at a computer terminal for eight hours a day and a half-hour lunch, and then spending anywhere from two to eight hours trying to build my Amway business. It didn't help that I had grown accustomed to sitting on my wallet in my back pocket, which was thicker than usual, not due to the wads of money I was trying to make, but because I had my and others' business cards, and other kinds of sundry items in it that made it bulky. Sitting on my wallet, as well as long periods of inactivity, caused my back to crook over time, as well as wear down the cartilage in my lower vertebrae, which began to pinch a nerve. It also didn't help that I was naturally flat-footed, and was walking the tile and pavement trying to contact people every day in dress shoes, which had no support at all. My lower back would be in such pain when I got home that I found it difficult to sleep at times. I finally went to see a chiropractor (the White one that milked my Boeing insurance for all he could get) before I wised up and saw a Black orthopedic surgeon who told me that I needed to get on an aggressive exercise program to strengthen my lower back. The cartilage could not be replaced, but if I built up my muscle tissue, it would alleviate the pain to a noticeable degree. I had a weight set in my apartment that I had left over from my high school days, but was too busy chasing the Amway dream to put it to good use. It's a medical condition that I live with to this day.

Another thing my upline distributors had me doing was to get on a weekly tape program that required me to buy one or two new audio tapes every week during product pickup. At the time, I think the tapes cost $6, plus tax. This was to help you grow your business, because obviously the more you listened, the better motivated you were to stick with it. Also, they had a voice-messaging system from Amway called Amvox that they recommended all distributors get on so you could receive or send messages from/to your upline, downline, and other distributors across ("crossline") the whole organizational network. You'd get a daily dose of motivation from your direct or diamond distributor, which may include a voicemail from another distributor in the group that was "really tearing things up." It was all another means to keep people plugged in and motivated to build the(ir) business. And the book program was recommended, as well. If you were really serious, they said, you'd read *two* books a week, and that would almost guarantee your success. I admit that a lot of the books were excellent reads for self-improvement, organizational development, and leadership, things I probably would have read whether I was in Amway or not. And then, of course, there were books that were tailored strictly to people in the Amway business or any other type of "network or multi-level marketing" business. It was starting to boil down to leading, or "influencing" (controlling was more like it) people to do what you wanted. If I hadn't mentioned it yet, here it goes: Aside from the initial books and tapes that they *loaned* to you or another new distributor, *none* of this sh*t was free. You were a business owner, so you were expected to buy your own supply of books, tapes, and Amway support materials to use for yourself as well as new distributors whom you recruited.

Now, in the midst of all these tools (books, audio tapes, Amway information, video tapes) as they called them, the crux of the Amway matter was still about moving products. Once again, if you were to get a check, you had to at least do 100 PV, or point value of products, whether it was from customers, signing up new distributors, getting orders from your downline distributors, or self-usage. And remember, the whole selling point of the main product line was their concentration to minimize usage and save money, right? Well, being a single guy with very few married friends made it very difficult to move a lot of household cleaning products. The Amway vitamin line was supposedly organic and top-of-the line, but they were expensive, as well. So my sales skills were not the best, to say the least. What was the other option? Aside from my father buying coffee and a case of paper towels from me on a semi-regular basis, I was buying vitamins, food products, and other unnecessary items on a monthly basis just to meet my minimum quota. I didn't have any downline on a consistent basis, so I was the only horse in the race, so to speak.

The final piece of the building blocks for your Amway network was to attend large gatherings known as functions and seminars & rallies. Seminars & rallies were local or regional events (Indianapolis or Cincinnati, for example) that took place on a Saturday, once a month or every other month, where a speaker would be a couple who was usually a ruby or above from somewhere in the crown's organization who drove or flew in from out of town. The early afternoon session would be teaching the nuts-and-bolts of building a network and/or moving products and lasted about two to three hours, let's say from 2 to 5 p.m. Then everyone would disperse for dinner either at the hotel or a local restaurant. The directs and up, and sometimes special invitees, would join the guest speakers at a more elegant location for dinner. Then around 7 or 8 p.m., the evening session, known as the rally, would begin, and this is where the speakers would tell their story of how Amway changed their lives and the challenges they overcame on their way to success. And of course, afterward, there would be a night owl, either in the same conference room, or over at the Shoney's the organization had frequented. The functions were the *pièce de résistance*.

Every quarter (three months), there would be a three-day conference, if you will, at some civic center or coliseum in someplace far enough away from St. Louis that it required the people under our direct distributors to caravan in each other's cars, or rent vans, and share hotel rooms over the weekend.

The function usually started on a Friday night with some sort of rally, speakers at the emerald level and above, and a series of seminars all day Saturday. The motivational speakers were selected diamonds who would begin that evening and close usually with the crown ambassador couple talking about their story and how Amway had shaped people's lives, and in many cases, "saved" some. It was impressive to see thousands of people from all over the country, and even Canada, coming together to hear all of these successful Amway leaders talk about how to build it, and how they started with nothing and kept their dreams alive and achieved financial freedom. These trips were more costly because everyone had to buy a ticket, like with any other business meeting, to cover the cost of the venue, and the speakers' travel, hotel, and meals, I'm guessing.

At the functions, there would be entertainment, if you will. They would have some band perform and play music and sing popular tunes that were family-friendly, usually stuff from the 60s through the 80s that conservative, White people preferred. And as usual, on Friday and Saturday night, the diamond organizations would break up and have night owls at a designated hotel or restaurant that would last well past midnight. You were then expected to get up Sunday morning after only a few hours' sleep and go to either a Christian, Hindu, or Muslim church service after a hasty breakfast. Then there would be another seminar for a few hours until late afternoon. How far away we were from St. Louis determined how long we could stay on Sunday, because many of us had to be back at work on Monday morning. These were anywhere from eight- to twelve-hour drives from places in Virginia, North Carolina, Tennessee, and Alabama.

For a while, these trips were rough, because you were crammed into someone's personal vehicle that may or may not make it the whole way. As the group grew, we were able to split the costs on a rental car, and then finally graduated to renting a full-fledged coach service, which made the trip bearable. But having to share a hotel room with three to five other grown-ass men had its limits. We were "business owners" on our way to success, but we were road-tripping like sophomores in college. I'm sorry, but seeing your upline, a dude in his 50s or early 60s "in they draw[er]s" (underwear) was unappealing, to say the least. And another pet peeve of mine was we had this one dude who *always* pissed on the toilet and the floor and *never* wiped up behind himself. I had always vowed silently to myself that I would try to avoid having to room with him at all costs. To no avail, I wasn't that fortunate unless he didn't come. I lost my high school class ring on one of these trips in some roach motel we were staying at in Winston-Salem, NC, one time. It's 2015, and I still haven't replaced it nor purchased my college ring yet.

Have you noticed anything yet, Dear Reader? These people painted this rosy picture that I, and others, would be successful business owners by dedicating "only a few hours a week" to this opportunity, and in two to five years would be independently wealthy. I was spending what little disposable income I had (I did mention that I was a new-hire fresh out of college, right?) on products I didn't need—books, tapes, Amway literature, meetings, and quarterly trips after I had paid rent, truck note, utilities, and a few groceries. What vacation time I was accumulating was being burned up on functions. And after a year or so, it was pretty much the same people telling the same damn stories at the same scheduled functions; people *weren't* becoming diamonds at breakneck speed. Did I also mention that I was still trying to maintain a relationship back in Nashville with the young lady I had dated my senior year in college? So I was burning gas and money trying to maintain that love interest, too.

Meanwhile, my immediate sponsors and my direct distributors were starting to control every aspect of my life outside of my job at Boeing. If I wasn't at work, I was supposed to be "building my business." It was crazy. Sometimes I'd be at work and get a phone call at my desk from my sponsor telling me to meet him at such-and-such a place to go "contacting." Or several times I'd be awakened out of a deep slumber early in the morning to hear about how we were going to road trip over to Indy to hear our diamond or somebody downline from him speak in the middle of the week (this was a 4-hour trip, *and* Indy was an hour ahead of us).

Product pickup on Friday evenings started turning into mini rah-rah sessions with our direct distributors, and sometimes I wouldn't get home until after 10 p.m. Every now and then, I'd go fishing out at a place called Busch Wildlife, where they had a series of man-made lakes, some of which were dedicated to certain types of game fish. But other than that, as one of my fraternity Brothers put it, "With Dusty, it's Amway *always*."

You want to know how badly I had gotten inculcated by this mindset? I had an opportunity early in my technical career to go to Texas A&M for graduate school, at the invite of a young

African-American woman professor, Dr. Karen Butler, whom I had met at Howard University during an engineering conference. She had flown me down to College Station, Texas, during a busy weekend there to recruit me and several other young African-American engineers for a power systems and utilities program she was putting together. I had mentioned this to my sponsor's wife, who then told my sponsor about it. Would you believe I let this man talk me out of going to grad school, because in a few years, I'd be a diamond and wouldn't need another degree?! I couldn't give her a reason why I refused to come down, and never returned her phone calls. After many, many years of shame and embarrassment, I can finally publicly admit this and ask for her forgiveness. Dr. Butler, if you get a chance to read this, I am so sorry that I let a golden opportunity slip through my fingers. More importantly, I apologize for abusing your trust and efforts to allow me to work with you on your research.

I had a chance to go to a family reunion on my mother's father's side, the Hollowells, and let these Amway people talk me into forgoing it to attend a function somewhere. Their rationale was that once I was rich, I could see my family all of the time. Some of the Hollowells whom I had heard about but never met, have since passed on. It is one of my biggest regrets. Another one is missing my Line Brother's wedding in Atlanta, Georgia. He had asked me to be a groomsman, and I skipped out because I was on my way to a presentation. As another Line Brother addressed me one weekend, "Dog! I heard you an Amway prostitute now! *What's up with that?*"

Instead of saving up my money and vacation time to have

a solid monetary foundation, I was pouring all of my resources into being a successful Amway distributor. I was doing a mediocre job at Boeing sometimes because at one time, I thought I wouldn't need my job. Amway also offered a Visa credit card that gave distributors back a whopping 1 percent on all purchases, so you know they were trying to get everyone in the organization involved with that. I joined in and started using my card to cover more and more purchases, not realizing that the interest rate was somewhere between 14 and 18 percent. I had also switched over my phone service to MCI (some of you may be too young to remember them) because they also had a "great deal" for Amway distributors and you were supposed to get either a discount or money back on your long-distance services. What they didn't tell you was that the real money was made in having a downline to buy all of these services. The people above you were getting a cut of what you were putting in. They also didn't tell me that everyone, from my direct distributor and up, was getting a cut from all the books and tapes that I was buying on a consistent basis. My credit card bill was starting to get out of control and nobody above me was the least concerned. I think I had accumulated *over $30,000 in credit card debt* over a ten-year period. No, that's not a typo, Dear Reader. I should've known it was all a sham. I remember one night at a meeting, I was lamenting to my direct's sponsor, who had come over from the Indianapolis area, about how I was using my credit card to support my business and wasn't seeing a return and he didn't say anything. That should've been the wake-up call. But I was told to keep the faith, and "It'll happen, just keep trusting God."

I mentioned earlier the quote my father sometimes uses, "God takes care of babies and fools." Well, let me tell you, He took care of <u>this</u> fool. There was more than one occasion where I met folks of questionable character and would meet them somewhere that wasn't the safest of spots. I can remember driving over to the East St. Louis, Illinois, area to show the Plan to some people and they'd answer the door either drunk or high because they honestly forgot we had a meeting, or that we had even met and talked about a business opportunity. I recall seeing folks in some remote areas where I was conducting business or waiting for a person who "no-showed" me, having a good time with someone who *wasn't* their spouse. Because I had spoken to them about Amway in the recent past, their faces were still fresh in my mind. If they were married, I remembered this, too.

I recall how this one Brother gave me that "look" when I spoke to him in passing because I had him dead to rights as he was having dinner with one of his "freaks" while his wife was at home with the kids. I remember another case where an Amway distributor, a White guy, was found dead over in East St. Louis, the apparent victim of a robbery. This poor bastard had driven all the way from some predominately White suburb like St. Charles, or St. Peters, Missouri. The newspaper article quoted someone who knew the victim as saying that he was always "chasing a quick buck," and was willing to go anywhere if there was money involved. Luckily for me, driving around in my little Chevy S-10 did not give off the slightest hint that I was a "millionaire in the making." Au contraire, Dear Reader, I had the most unassuming appearance you could imagine. If anything, I was mistaken for a

Jehovah's Witness because I was suited up and running around a shopping plaza looking like I was trying to proselytize, or in one case, I was mistaken for the manager at a Denny's because I was sitting at the counter by myself in shirt and tie, sipping coffee, and waiting for a potential distributor to meet. Yeah, God was with me on more than one occasion as I was chasing the Amway (pipe) dream.

Rather than go out, date, hang out with my peers, and enjoy the life of a bachelor, I was hanging out with mostly older people, who were already married, and talking about Amway all the damn time. I was told to talk only to men since I was single and didn't want to give any female contacts the false impression that I was asking for a date. Because of this "organizational decree," I had one female engineering counterpart say to me one night that I was giving off the impression that I was gay because I would only talk to all of the sharp-dressed men in the room! What the hell?! I was just trying to "build my business," wasn't thinking 'bout chasin' no tail. But that's what was happening.

I failed to mention that over the course of the indoctrination, the organization would mix religion and politics into the fray. They also stressed the importance of tithing, and that God would bless me abundantly if I continued to give 10 percent above what I was bringing in. I was supposed to spend what I was earning on Amway stuff, pay my regular bills, *and* give 10 percent *before taxes* to my church and I would be alright. I don't want to offend anyone, but I had to pick and choose how much I'd give to my church at the time; I still had to eat, even if it was only ramen noodles and soup and crackers. They would convincingly announce that Amway was going to "save the country" from the sinful liberals, and all other sorts of things that appealed to conservatives. For a while, those people had me professing to be a Republican and endorsing the party and its principles. (Yes, for real, for real.) It had gotten to the point that they were telling me that I should only date women who were already in the business because I didn't need to be involved with anyone who would distract me from my goals. (Sounds like a damn cult, don't it?) And if I missed a meeting or didn't call in at a prescribed time, my sponsor would take the liberty of rolling up to my apartment or house unannounced to "check up on me." I had entrusted my entire being to these people who put on the facade that they genuinely cared about me and were in my corner. Let's see, someone is regularly putting some serious change in my pocket every month, come rain or shine? You damn right I'm going to try to keep you around for as long as possible. Wouldn't you?

But I was starting to see the inconsistencies and false fronts melting away. Even with all of the "positivity," you will eventually see people for what they truly are, even if you don't want to believe it. I had a situation where I had passed out some of the larger Amway catalogs that had high-end items that you would find in a major department store, all over-priced, of course, but there were some nice things, regardless. Someone made a credit card purchase for an expensive stereo or something, and I received a nice profit check from Amway directly for more than $100. Well, a few weeks later, I got a letter from the corporation that the credit card bounced and I owed them all this money back. Huh? When I called my direct distributor to explain what had happened and to also find out what could be done on our end, his wife, who handled the money portion of their business, lit into me on the phone about how this was my fault, and that *I cost them money.* Excuse me? I'm the one making $3 a month for 100 PV, after spending $300–$500 a month on bullsh*t I didn't need, and having to pay back Amway with money I did not have! As my father taught me, you don't really know someone until you've seen them under pressure. Once again, that should've been the wake-up call, but I think I let my sponsor convince me to forgive and forget. Another thing the top levels of the organization touted was that everyone was happy and wholesome and there was *hardly any* divorce among married couples in our distributorship. Well, let me tell you, that was a big, fat lie. Over the course of time (I did this sh*t for almost 10 years straight), you noticed that people who were once at meetings with their better halves wouldn't be wearing their wedding bands anymore, or couples would flat-out disappear and word would get back that they separated or divorced, even at the upper levels of the business. It's a sad thing, but it's the reality of life, and truth be told, as stressful as doing Amway was for me as a single person, I can only imagine the stress it caused married couples who were already thin in the pocketbook with kids to feed.

From 1995 to 2000, I was all-in with Amway, even to the point of cutting off the young lady I was dating off-and-on in Nashville. But I had not gotten completely brainwashed yet. I happened to be at least smart enough to follow the example of this one software engineer at Boeing and started putting money into my 401(k) to invest toward a house, which I purchased in

1999. I had hooked up with my financial planner at the credit union and started trying my hand at mutual funds. I also had joined some older fraternity Brothers and started an investment club, back when they were really popular and everyone was making money in the stock market before the bubble burst in 2001. When we dissolved the club, I had actually amassed a decent portfolio. I also should've listened to my father and saved up my money and bought a boat. He had warned me early on to beware of "get-rich-quick" schemes, and for whatever reason, I put these people's slick words over his. I still mustered enough strength to work on my MBA at St. Louis University part-time, even though I didn't finish it. And I also tried my hand at a few other business ventures in the entertainment promotions arena. I failed miserably, but didn't let my entrepreneurial dreams be extinguished.

The links in the Amway chain began to weaken because of two women who came into my life. One young lady was someone I befriended at a social event early on in 2000, after I had finally ended the roller coaster relationship I was trying to maintain back in Tennessee. (For the record, she was a good woman, but we could never come to an accord on a commitment, and of course, I was still chasing Amway.) This woman was slightly older and more mature, and strangely, we hit it off right away the day we met. We exchanged numbers and over the course of a few weeks, we went from being casual acquaintances to having a full love interest. At that time, we did not have the same views on religion, which I allowed to put a strain on our relationship. Outside of that, she was a much-needed change in my life. It turned out that I was able to fill a need for her, as well, so we both took the situation for what it was and enjoyed the ride as long as we could. We started hanging out discreetly because we both had ended stressful relationships and agreed that we didn't need folks all in our business. Plus, I didn't feel like having my Amway sponsors coming in and trying to evaluate and pass judgment on her; it was bad enough they were trying to control my every move. She would've told them what they could do with their Amway products, anyway. For the first time in years, I felt alive and like a real man. Spending quality time with someone of the opposite sex without a lot of confusion or unnecessary emotion was gratifying, and going to different places around St. Louis was pleasant. I had finally started taking time out for myself and enjoying life again. We were able to end the relationship amicably, and move on to seeing other people. I can't say that it was an easy thing for me to do, but it was the right thing to do.

The second woman who got me away from the Amway Dragon was none other than my wife of 11 years now, Shautel. We had known each other as casual acquaintances for a good while after we had met at a planning meeting for the Black College Expo when I first moved to St. Louis. The "BCE," as it was known, was an annual college fair hosted by a local AME Church at a venue near downtown that promoted HBCUs among inner city and suburban African-American high school students. Many times, the local alumni of various colleges would man a display table with information and paraphernalia, if available, and work in shifts throughout the course of the day. Shautel graduated from Howard University and was the BCE secretary when we met back in '95. To be honest, I don't remember how we started dating, but I remember having her and my stepson over to my house one Sunday to watch football. At that moment, it was strictly platonic. It wasn't until early 2002 that we went out on our first date. I had been in and out of a few relationships since late 2000, but I didn't think about dating seriously, or even marriage, until I had ruined a relationship with a young lady who had been friends with a close female friend of mine. I had vowed that I wouldn't get involved with anyone else until I felt like they were "wife material." Anyway, one day, Shautel and I were emailing back and forth about an upcoming BCE event or social activity, and I asked if she would be interested in going fishing with me one day. She accepted and one Saturday morning, I took her over to Spanish Lake Park to try to catch some bluegills and anything else that might bite. A cold front must've moved in because we didn't catch a single thing that morning, but it gave us an opportunity, or her rather, to discuss our views on marriage and relationships. She told me in no uncertain terms that she was looking for a long-term relationship and was beyond the girlfriend stage in her life. Sounded good to me. We started dating in June 2002, and in December, I let her and her son move in with me. Now, coming from the ultra-conservative Baptist upbringing that I did, both of my parents had a fit that I was "shacking up" with a woman. But I tried to explain to them that this was something we both agreed to do because we wanted to make sure that we could get along and live together. I had seen my mother get divorced twice, and did not want to go down that road. Likewise, my wife had been in a relationship that revealed to her quickly that she and the person she was seeing at the time were not compatible.

Now while all this was happening, I was still on the fringes of being involved with Amway, and I cannot remember if my sponsors had met Shautel yet. We got engaged in February of 2003, and starting making plans for our wedding in 2004. My wife has been the chief of finances since we hooked up; coming from her humble beginnings, she knows how to stretch every dime and prioritize bills and expenses. One day after we had begun our "merger" operation, she was looking over the cost per unit for something I had ordered that week. She did a tally and immediately quipped, "You tripping…" you can get such-and-such for much less at Wild Oats. And when she saw how much money I was bringing in, a whopping $6 or $7 and some change, after spending almost $500–$600 per month, she finally put her foot down and said, "We are done with Amway."

We were preparing for a wedding, starting a new life together, and had to watch our spending. I slowly started letting her do the shopping, and started backing off my orders. Well, you know my sponsors probably noticed the sudden drop in my orders and felt it necessary to get me back on track. One Saturday afternoon in September, they both rolled up on us at the house unannounced. I gave them a puzzled look as to why they had come, and his response was that they wanted to come over and talk to me and my wife about our relationship. Translation: We don't approve of you guys living together in sin, and you need to focus on God and Amway. Thankfully, Shautel kept right on cleaning up or cooking, because we had guests arriving for our engagement party. Some of my family had driven up from Memphis, and my wife's family had come up from the city. My sponsors suddenly realized what was happening and tactfully excused themselves. It was the last time they'd ever set foot in my house again. A few months later in December, either my sponsor called me or I called him. I cannot recall, but I know this: When I told him I was taking my leave from Amway, his immediate response was, "So you're going to quit, and go back to being average like everyone else?" All the oxygen left my body at that moment. Did my ears deceive me? The very man whom I had allowed to lead me around blindly like a father figure for almost 10 years, someone I had trusted and confided in with matters that I didn't even share with my own family, chose in an instant to intimidate me into sticking around and then verbally put me down because of my decision to leave Amway. A flood of emotions coursed through me as I tried to process what happened. I paused for a moment, took a deep breath, and then responded almost timidly, "I'm not average…and I'm going to make it. Good-bye."

After I hung up the phone, I was more crushed than when I had back-to-back "turn-downs" for the junior dance in high school. I had poured every fiber of my being into a business enterprise that left me mentally scarred and drowning in financial debt—more than $30,000 in credit card debt over a ten-year period, with nothing to show for it except a room full of unneeded cleaning supplies, vitamins, cassette tapes, and books. I would be totally wrong if I did not make mention that my mother had helped to pay off some of this debt, much to my shame. This is a matter that I have not shared with too many folks, because I was too embarrassed about it. Dusty Walker, the smart engineer from

Tennessee State, got hoodwinked into a pyramid scheme? Yup. I had been *completely* snookered.

If you are reading this and you have a successful Amway business or any sort of enterprise like it, then good on ya. I've met other distributors in different business systems that would flash their monthly checks in my face, making $10,000+ a month. I'm not saying you *can't* make money in any of these ventures, but what I am saying is that you got to be one hell of a used car salesman to build a network of people and get them to *consistently* use the product or service (they have to have money, too!). It's akin to being able to sell ice to Eskimos, wings to a fly, and stink to a skunk. You've got to be very influential and almost conniving to have a successful business venture where you constantly have to keep people motivated. It also pays to find people who are easily influenced, or manipulated, into following the business model to the letter. If you are able to do this, then you'll go far. But my main point here is to warn anyone who may be involved, or is considering getting involved, in any type of unconventional enterprise, such as the one I was in. I caution you to watch your finances and personal resources closely. If you find yourself spending your money with no kind of return, bail out early. I say don't get involved until you've got a ton of money to burn and too much time on your hands and you wish to throw some of it away. It took me 10 years to get my credit card debt to a manageable level. I dare say I do not wish for anyone else to go through what I did.

7.3 FINANCIAL DISCRETION

This section won't be too long, but I want to caution you about how you flaunt your earnings in front of your White counterparts. If you are fortunate enough to work in an environment where everyone from the janitor to the CEO are well-paid and your company is not shy about it, then it's no big deal to drive your seven-series BMW or Tesla into the main parking lot. But if you are in a hostile environment, I'd advise you to be low-key with what you drive and wear to the job site. I'm not saying you should wear rags and drive a "hoopty" to work, but if you have two vehicles, leave the better one at home. Here's why: Most White folks, be they rich or poor, still enjoy a sense of superiority and entitlement when it comes to the other races, especially Black folks. The last thing in the world they want to see is an African-American looking more prosperous than they. Two perfect examples for you: A coworker at Boeing was a computer specialist and made some real long money for the position he held. This Brother drove a nice Lexus, but I noticed he always parked toward the rear of the lot where we both worked. One day, I finally asked him why. He replied that he didn't want everyone in his group knowing what he drove because then they'd start "hating on him" and that could cause potential problems. I didn't really understand at the time what he meant.

Second example entailed a Sister who was the office administrator (they don't say "secretary" too much these days) at the company I worked at in Huntsville, Alabama. She probably made $15–20 an hour back then, if she was lucky, which is not a lot of money in the grand scheme of things. However, one day she had to drive her parent's Cadillac Escalade truck to work for whatever reason. No big deal, right? Well, let me tell you, Dear Reader, them ofays saw her in that nice, shiny, luxury SUV, and the first thing they did was cook up some excuses to cut her work hours back. Why? Because this Negro woman was obviously making too much money in order to afford to drive such a nice vehicle, and they couldn't afford to tolerate that. It might upset the balance of things in their perfect world. Now, the truth is that it wasn't her vehicle, but because of appearances, they made the assumption that she was doing pretty well and they were contributing to it.

What is the lesson here? The average person out here doesn't really care that you are doing well for yourself. In this competitive, dog-eat-dog world, misery loves company, and the last thing your average coworker wants to know is that you're making just as much or more than they. I've seen a former manager of mine get the axe because the company decided to cut 100 middle managers; but I believe he was put on the list because he hadn't been there very long and would boast on Mondays about how much he spent on landscaping his home. I could tell that the locals didn't take too kindly to his showboating, so it wouldn't surprise me if the seed had been planted by them with the powers-that-be to get his ass out!

As my Daddy says, "Sometimes you gotta scream 'Poor Mouth.'" That means you have to give the appearance that you are doing just "okay," or even not-so-well, just to keep jealous coworkers out of your business. That way, you will have one less problem in the world to deal with. The only ones who know what you are making should be God, HR, your director, anyone above your director, and your spouse or Mama. Everyone else gets ballpark figures.

8.0 CONCLUSION

As I wrap up this book, I wish to leave you with a few parting thoughts. One that I failed to mention earlier in the book concerns job interviews, especially if they are not local to you. If you receive an email or telephone call from a prospective employer for an interview, that's good news. However, if they are in another city and they want you to travel to sit with them face-to-face, but are not willing to pay for your travel, that's a bad thing. Major red flag waving.

When we lived in Nashville for the first time, I had applied for an avionics engineer position with the now defunct AirTran Airlines. The airline was based in Atlanta, and was one of the places my wife was amenable to moving to, so I figured I'd make a go of it. Well, one of the requirements for the job had a phrase along the lines of "clean cut, professional appearance, no extreme hairstyles…" Obviously, this caused me to take pause as I was filling out the application, but I applied anyway. I received a phone call from the AirTran HR lady for the position to set up an interview appointment. During this process, I told her plainly that I wore my hairstyle in dreadlocks "for personal and spiritual reasons…Is this going to be a problem?" She responded that it would not be. After setting up the interview, I paused and waited for her to tell me my travel arrangements since I lived 250 miles away. It turned out that I was responsible for getting myself to Atlanta if I wanted this job. O-kay…Not that big a deal since I was able to set up the interview on the Monday after my nephew's birthday. We were going to the metropolitan Atlanta area anyway, so why not kill two birds with one stone?

I arranged to take that Monday off and we drove to Atlanta where we stayed at my wife's godparents' house the Friday before. That Monday morning, I shaved and donned my best suit, packed copies of my resume, and drove down GA400 to the Hartsfield–Jackson airport to meet these people at their head-quarters that afternoon. I sat in a conference room with three White guys and the HR chick, and I could tell immediately by the looks on their faces they weren't too pleased with what they saw. Yes, they were pleasant and as professional as possible, but my Native-American senses can detect negativity fairly well. Now, to be fair, I can't say for sure that my dreadlocks were the "issue" any more than the fact that a Black man sat in front of them vying for a technical job in their company. But in either case, I answered their questions as best I could and left the inter-view feeling like I had just wasted my time.

I can't remember if the HR lady contacted me directly, or if I had to email her after a few days to inquire about the status of my application. I want to say that I had to chase her down, because I remember an email like, "Oh yeah, you didn't get the job, sorry." When I asked for an indication of why not, she gave me some bullsh*t about they don't disclose why candidates weren't selected. The first thing that flashed in my mind was that they had a problem with my hair. Granted, potential employers are *not* obligated to disclose why an applicant is not selected, but come on. I'm old enough and have been around long enough to have seen explanations that ranged from "they selected a more experienced candidate," to "they couldn't meet your salary expectations," and all the other fluff in between, whether it was true or not. This experience left a bad taste in my mouth, but it was ultimately a blessing in disguise. If you are halfway up on current events, AirTran was bought out by Southwest Airlines three years later so I may have dodged a serious bullet. When a company is bought out, there is usually some sort of shake-up that results in layoffs of duplicated employees and managers. I hope they asses *all* got laid off.

Interview Lesson #1: Do *not* interview for a job if it is more than 50 miles away and the prospective employer is not willing to compensate you for travel, have you flown in, or conduct a telephone/online interview. That says to me that they are too chintzy to respect your time and money, so why should you waste your time chasing an opportunity at a place that you'd probably end up hating anyway?

Interview Lesson #2: You want to conduct a successful interview, but beware of the level of details of the answers you are giving. Why? I have it on very good authority that when times are tough and companies can't afford to increase headcount, they sometimes will bring in well-qualified candidates for "interviews" with the intent of not hiring a single one! Why? Because the manager will ask how you would solve such-and-such a problem while the other person(s) in the room is sitting there fervently taking notes. Are they noting your technical ability to answer the questions? NO! They are getting *free advice* on how to solve their problems, without paying you a dime, and will cook up some excuse about how they are in a hiring freeze when you call back after a few weeks without hearing anything. It's "skanless" like a mutha', but it has happened.

Remember to take everything White folks tell you at face value. I'm sorry for being stereotypical, but White folks will lie in a New York minute! And remember how I told you they already think they are above everyone else in the world? So for them to lie to a Black person ain't much of a sin. I've seen program managers straight-face lie to military customers about the status of a project I was on when I was at Boeing. As I write these last few pages, I recently had a situation where I believe a former manager lied to me about the availability of a spot in his group. I was coming to the end of my contract with an inflight wi-fi provider and asked this guy if he had any possible openings since I had worked for him before and felt he knew my work ethic. He said that his hands were tied by the senior VP and the finance department and couldn't do anything for me. Well, not 30 days later, a mass email went out welcoming a new engineer to his group. So much for not being able to bring anyone else aboard. I didn't say anything about it, but made damn sure I printed out the emails for this book. I'm not saying he lied, but he didn't offer me a job, nor bend over backwards to help me find work.

I made slight mention of how companies will paint the rosy picture of how professional they are back in Section 4.3. Well, I want to inform you that in many cases, once you get past the pressed suits and blouses, there's a fair chance you will have to deal with some of the most *unprofessional* people in your life. White folks can be petty over insignificant matters. I want to prepare you for the surprisingly high levels of immaturity and laziness you shall see in the workplace. Not everywhere, but be prepared when you do. You know it's tight when there are signs posted up to remind people to clean up after themselves in the break room. Or some sonofabitch has a sizable bowel movement and did not bother to flush the toilet for the next man in, leaving you with an image in your memory that might make you wish you were blind. Who spills half a pot of coffee while pouring it and doesn't wipe it up? Your boss or trifling coworkers, that's who. Beware of shaking hands with the bozo who doesn't wash up after using the toilet, too. Plenty of them to go around. Be extra careful when participating in the company potluck, because some of these folks aren't too clean or thorough in their handling of food. If you have dietary restrictions, be double careful and make sure you know what the hell you are taking into your body before having that first mouthful of Peggy's "special stew." And remember, there's the potential situation where they have an issue with you, but instead of talking about it like men or adults, they take it to the boss, who then flows it down to you. You'll witness your fair share of, not disagreements, but full-scale arguments between folks, also. So be ready for minor headaches that you haven't had to deal with since eighth grade.

Not every place has a competent, fully functional security department, so keep your head on a swivel. I'd be doing you a disservice if I didn't remind you that "violence in the workplace" is real. Especially if you work in the manufacturing sector and have a sizable labor force that is composed of non-degreed tradesmen. Some of the factory floor workers can be some of those very people you see on television toting guns to protect their rights and whatnot. I'm a gun owner myself so don't go in on me about the Second Amendment, but what I am saying is that I've been places where guys have been escorted out for getting into physical altercations with a coworker or a boss. It was at some of these places where a few other cognizant coworkers and I kept a sharp eye over the next few days to make sure the fired person didn't come back to shoot the place up. This is especially true if you *know* that person was ex-military, had a personal arsenal that would make the Marines jealous, and had a propensity for violence. You keep a lookout for any trouble. Don't get lax with any of your degreed coworkers, either. There has been many a news story about that "nice, quiet" person who snapped and murdered his family, or did a violent act in a public place. Oftentimes, these nut jobs were well-educated and came from "good homes." You just be sure to look up from your monitor or peek over the cubicle wall from time to time, especially if you hear a ruckus going on.

Here's another aside: You're African, African-American, or some other minority that's held to the double standard. I can't speak for the Asian community because they usually have the stereotype of being smart, productive, but docile when it comes to disrupting the corporate caste system. They usually get moved up (in pay at least, if not in title) before the Brothers because they aren't stigmatized like Blacks and Hispanics/Latinos are. Not always, but I'm speaking in generalities. I'm leading into the whole dress code sham, so stay with me. I believe in looking professional, to a certain point. I also know that clothes don't make the person any more professional than standing in a garage makes you a car. Because I'm a freelance contractor in my own engineering company at present, when I'm at a client's worksite, it is usually in an aircraft hangar with little or no air conditioning. I like to wear safety-toed combat boots, blue jeans, a polo or tee shirt, and a bandana over my dreadlocks. It is a very unconventional appearance, to say the least, but I like it.

I started locking my hair the Saturday before Mother's Day in 2002, after I was denied progression in the Boeing premanagement program. For several years, I had female acquaintances tell me repeatedly that I should lock my hair because of its texture. I have my mother's hair, who has her grandmother's hair, who was supposedly half-Cherokee, so my hair texture is a mixed blend of curly and straight. At the time, it appeared to be a passing fad to me, and I was too busy worrying about my Corporate Negro appearance and place in the world to consider it seriously. But after my managerial ascent had been stalled, I was open to the idea and made my way to St. Louis City to a Sister whom I knew locked hair. I started the transition from close-cropped flat top to "radical Blackness" with 2-inch locks after I let my hair grow into a mini Afro to make the initial process easier for the stylist, as well as my tender-headed scalp.

Surprisingly, I had more backlash from Black folks about my locks in those first few months than from a couple of well-intended White folks. Hell, I remember this one Uncle Tom over in the Hornet Building (B270) pulling on one of my locks, talking about, "When you going to cut this? This makes you look bad." Only because I didn't want to be thrown out for fighting did I not lay into his ass. Not necessary and not any of his business, but you know when you've been programmed to think that one person speaks for the entire race, things like this happen. He wasn't anybody of importance in the company, but I had to say that.

I locked my hair for a few reasons: I wanted to try something different, and I wanted to challenge the System in my own quiet way. I can honestly say that it was for spiritual reasons, as well; not that I was converting to Judaism or Rastafarianism (no disrespect), but that it was definitely a step of faith to go against the grain at this moment in my life. I knew I was going to get raised eyebrows from some of my White coworkers, but never did I think my own people would give me flack. I basically let my work and the quality of services I provided speak for themselves. What the hell my hairstyle got to do with wiring up a plane or getting the proper documentation written up for installing an avionics package? Not a damn thing. I can say there are plenty of well-dressed charlatans out there who look good, smell good, talk good, but ain't worth a damn when it comes to real work (in some circles, they are called "consultants"). They specialize in putting on a good show while bullsh*tting and getting others to do their work for them.

I may have mentioned this earlier, but wanted to reinforce it to you, Dear Reader. Obviously, if you play the game and look the way they are comfortable with, you stand a better chance than I ever would. But let's not jump to conclusions. I tell anybody that when the time is right, I can shed the SEAL Team headscarf and don the navy blue suit and tie as necessary. My point is that regardless of what you wear, you may not get a fair chance to succeed. I can only share with you what I have experienced, and what you may encounter. I have been informed from a very trusted source that I have not been allowed back into Gulfstream because some redneck manager didn't like my hair. Never mind the work performance and technical proficiency. I never turned anything in late. The issue was with my dreadlocks. Oh well, God has blessed me not to have to grovel for a job in that place. At least not yet...

When you do start enjoying a great measure of success, don't let the "power" corrupt you. Stay humble but confident, as I mentioned earlier. When you start thinking too highly of yourself, that's when things can go awry. As the Bible reads, "Pride goeth before destruction, and an haughty spirit before a fall." (Proverbs 16:18) I've seen it, and I've been through it! Defend yourself from overconfidence. Life favors the prepared and the paranoid.

As far as spirituality goes, at least while you're in college, practice what your upbringing is. Like my Daddy says, "Dance wit' the girl that brought ya [to the party]." Once you've gotten your degree, you can seek whatever spiritual truths might be out there for you. This is my suggestion only, but I say this only to prevent you from losing sight of why you enrolled in engineering school, much less college, in the first place. Believe what you believe, question it, and *study* it. Beware the pied pipers, the roving cultists I mentioned earlier. Even Jesus used common sense! There will always be unknown variables, like Genesis 4:16–19, where Cain left Eden and "found a wife..." Where these other people come from? I don't know, but I've been of the Christian faith this far, so I figure the Lord will take me the rest of the way.

You have the power to choose your belief system. Just be secure in it while not messing up your opportunities for engineering and/or academic success.

Concerning the dating scene, that's a tough call. I was the stereotypical nerd and didn't get much action when I was in college. If you can maintain your grades and enjoy the company of ladies (or gentlemen, if that's your flavor), then full speed ahead. But there are going to come, more often than not, times where you are going to have to tell your lover or girlfriend that you can't hang out because you've got a big exam or a lab project due and you need to focus. If they are in your corner, they will understand. If they give you hell for wanting to be successful, then you might have to "redefine" your relationship with this person. Many a good Brother has fallen by the wayside because they let affections and sexual proclivities become major distractions from the Goal. Once you graduate and start making some money, even nerds look good when they have a nice ride and some pocket change. Just be careful whom you spend time with.

Concerning the distance dating thing, I tried it for several years, but it didn't work out. I have a good friend of mine who met his wife at the Black Engineer of the Year Awards Conference in Baltimore, MD, when we were still in undergraduate school. He was at TSU and she was at the University of Oklahoma. One hell of a walk or bus trip, if you ask me. But they were able to maintain contact and see each other at regular intervals, and have now been married for almost 20 years and have three children. In my case, I found myself doing all the driving, traveling, and spending time and money to be with someone for a day and a half on a weekend for months on end. Word of caution, Dear Reader, as my Daddy told me one foggy day when we went out fishing against our better judgment: "If this girl ain't making no effort to come see you like you are bending over backwards to come see her, then she ain't really in love with you… you're providing a relationship of convenience until something better comes along." Isn't that how it always is? You will go to hell and back for someone that you know you can't or shouldn't have, rather than get with the One who will love and treat you right. Expensive and painful lesson learned. Don't you be fooled, either. Exercise the practice of *quid pro quo*: Something for something. Unless she is *extremely* beautiful or *rich*, and you're willing to put up with foolishness, I'd say find someone who's bringing gifts to the table like you, or as close to it as you can find when you are ready to seriously date. My two cents.

As a People, we are the minority in the engineering ranks. It's not that we don't have heroes in the field to look up to, past or present, but I believe society has strategically set it up to keep us out of the higher paying career fields. Most inner city and rural schools don't prepare our students for the academic rigors of college life (Do they even *talk* about going to college anymore?), much less the introductory mathematics and science courses *needed* for a solid foundation in engineering. The media does a poor job of promoting the STEM fields to our youth. Another glaring disparity in our communities is that outside of President Obama and preachers, we don't have any highly visible leadership or positive images of Black men on a consistent basis outside of sports and entertainment. This is my opinion only, but

I think it has merit. I recently read a book about the Tuskegee Airmen, and about how one pilot was consistently denied being awarded the Congressional Medal of Honor by his commanders, all of whom were White. When he was finally able to ask one of them why, this is the response he received:

"I belong to a group who believe it's our responsibility to keep Negroes in their place, and the most effective way is to deny them leadership. Then there's never any threat to anyone. If the medal was posthumous, no problem. Or if you were an inarticulate enlisted man, I would have no objection. But being who you are, you'd be out encouraging Negroes to do the things you do. Without leadership, Negroes are harmless. But with leaders, they could be a threat of some kind... Our country can't afford this, and that's my considered opinion."

Do I believe that there is systematic racism to keep African-Americans subservient and powerless through educational, mental, and economic disparity? Absolutely. And part of the problem is that we have very few role models and LEADERS who are consistently shown to the masses to bring about a generational change in condition and status. I encourage you, therefore, Dear Reader, to become a leader in your community. As you achieve your career successes, make sure you try to inspire and lead several of your peers and younger mentees to aim for higher heights, as well. Obviously, this can only work with the ones who are willing to learn and be led by your positive influence. But I believe in W.E.B. DuBois' notion of the Talented Tenth reaching back and elevating the masses of Black folks to a better status in life. You are a Leader in the making. Do your part to uplift the race.

Be a professional. You earned, or are earning, that degree. Keep learning and refreshing yourself to get better at what you do. You may decide to change careers, but at least you'll be mentally sharp and the transition will not be as difficult.

Make your money and control it. Don't let the money control you. Avoid getting into a large amount of debt. Financial pressures can be debilitating and you may start to feel immense stress. Then you begin to hear the *voices:* One time I went to an acquaintance of mine who sold marijuana on the side of his day job to inquire how I could become an "investor" without actually touching the product. I just wanted to be able to double or triple my money in a short period of time. Thankfully, he had enough respect for me to not allow me into the game. Another situation is where I was working in San Antonio and losing money, as I mentioned earlier in the book, when extreme thoughts began to overtake me. One night after getting off the telephone with my wife, I was so distraught at the state of our finances that I actually considered *suicide,* but making it look like an accident so she and the kids would be able to cash in on my life insurance policy. Obviously, I was able to quash those voices, but it was something that crossed my mind at that moment in time. Real Talk. You make sure you don't get to a point where you feel so overwhelmed that you have no way out. There's always a way, and there's always someone to talk to about your problems. Find a mentor you trust and respect.

If you're going get up every day to go to work for someone else, make sure you're getting something out of it. Hopefully, you're getting good money as well as marketable skills. It's cool if you enjoy and love your job, but all bullsh*t aside, if I didn't need money, I'd go fishing more! Oh yeah, don't let your job kill you. I forgot to mention how in April, 2003, I got so stressed on the job that the company nurse thought I was having a heart attack. Remember, if you die, they *will* have your replacement in three weeks or less! I have since made it a point not to get too worked up over a job that can go as quickly as it came. You try to do the same.

Don't get trapped by a job. Be willing to move around to stay alive mentally and emotionally. Don't stay unless you really love it or have to because of some sort of obligation. I also say be wary of when you move for a job. If it's direct placement and the company is going to cover your moving expenses, as well as help you sell/find your house, then Game On. But in my case, we moved to Maryland in 2008, after I had accepted a contract position because it was supposed to be a five-year defense project. We sold our house in the St. Louis area and had made plans to become permanent Maryland residents. Well, after about a year and a half, suddenly the economy tanked and cuts were being made across the board. On my birthday, June 10, 2009, me and thirty or so other workers were terminated from this project, even though we were told our last day would be that Friday, June 12. Here we were, in one of the most expensive parts of the country, and I had no job. I was able to find something for another six months in Kentucky from a referral of a Brother I was working with, but I also had to move the family to the Atlanta area. I determined after that snafu that we would never move for a job again. When we moved again, it would be because we wanted to, not because we had to.

Make an adventure out of your career. Get some accomplishments that you can be proud of, as well as make you marketable. There's that word again. I want to see more of our engineers increase in the entrepreneurial ranks. Treat yourself as a business. If you invent something, by all means, you should reap the benefits, and not just get a meager bonus while the company is raking in thousands, millions, or billions off your brain cells!

I hope that my story inspires you to achieve success in your chosen field, Dear Reader. I want to be that voice of support as you travel through your academic or corporate wilderness. Have things gotten better since the days of segregation and Jim Crow? To a certain degree, yes, things have improved. But things have regressed to a certain degree as well, and racism and hatred for the Black man has never been higher since President Obama's first inauguration in 2009.

As I conclude, I want to ask that you become a Success to honor the memory of the Trayvon Martins, Tamir Rices, Michael Browns, and the other young Brothers (& Sisters!) whose lives have been needlessly extinguished due to violence at the hand of a hateful Caucasoid or misguided Brother or Sister. Whether they were engaged in criminal activity at this point is irrelevant to me. What is relevant is that a strong education and positive influences lead to a better chance of success in *this* society. For the last time, I am not advocating hatred toward White folks, but I am cautioning you, the Reader, to not expect a fair chance when you enter the corporate or, in some instances, the academic arena and you're the only one of our ethnic group. Hopefully, things will get better in another twenty years or so, but I'm not holding my breath. Do your best in whatever it is you choose to do. You owe it to your predecessors. Help out others when you can along the way. I have no doubt that some of you reading this will be on the cover of a prominent magazine or technical trade publication one day. God bless you.

9.0 PICTURES

My Father, Dusty R. Walker, Sr., during his days as an Avionics Electrician in the US Navy in the 60s.

My Mother, Dr. Sadie Hollowell Walker-Charlton, in her college days at LeMoyne-Owen College.

Winter break after my first semester at TSU at my best friend's house, Roderic Ross.

I wasn't kidding about the electrical symbols and major being added to my haircuts. Gung ho, to say the least. "EE" engraved on my "wig."

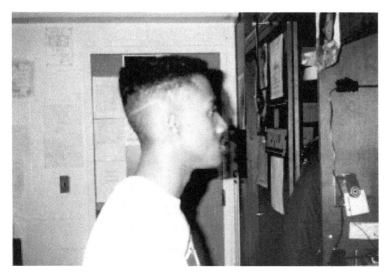

A resistor symbol etched on my right side.

One of the few "Brothers" at Exxon Pipeline Company and me, during my internship in Houston, TX, in summer of 1991. I was wearing contact lenses at the time.

At a gathering of African-American employees and interns who worked at Exxon in Houston, TX. Most of the people were HBCU students or graduates.

Engineering classmates who were going to "walk" with me during the TSU Commencement in spring 1995.

Dr. Marpaka and I after Commencement. He was my favorite instructor.

Fellow classmate, Rashara N. Givhan, now Dr. Givhan, and I.

Some of the fellas after Commencement.

A pic with the "Bros" of Omega Psi Phi.

Classmate Stephanie (Smith) Jones and me. Pay no attention to the man in the background.

The fellas showing off a little prosperity in our fledgling careers. This was back when $20 was actually a lot of money.

A copy of my face I made at MDA during my internship, summer of 1993. Shows you how bored I was.

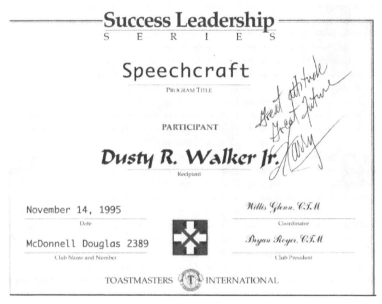

A signed copy of my Speechcraft Certificate from then CEO of MDA, Harry Stonecipher. Wonder if it's worth anything?

My clean-cut appearance at a career fair at the Black Engineer of the Year Award Conference in Baltimore, MD, with some of the other Black men representing various Boeing locations. Circa late 90s.

On the AH-64 Apache Training Program. The design group had the opportunity to see and examine a real helicopter. Here I am sitting in the cockpit, wearing a two-piece suit because I probably had an Amway meeting that night.

My medical release and diagnosis when I thought I was having a heart attack at work.

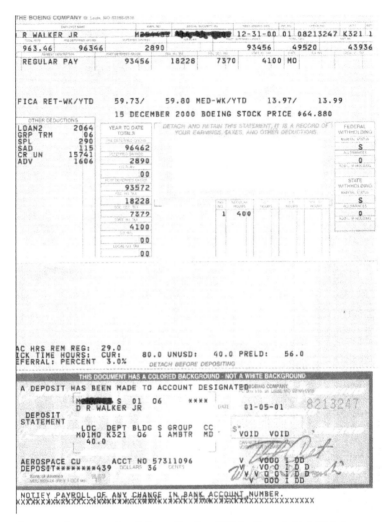

A copy of my paycheck from Boeing/MDA after eight faithful years. I wasn't making $25/hour before taxes!

I had made the "pilgrimage" to Amway "holy ground" in Ada, Michigan, with my distributor group.

A pic of me, my then fiancée, my cousin, Kathy, and one of her best friends in Washington, DC. Hard to see, but I had started locking my hair by then.

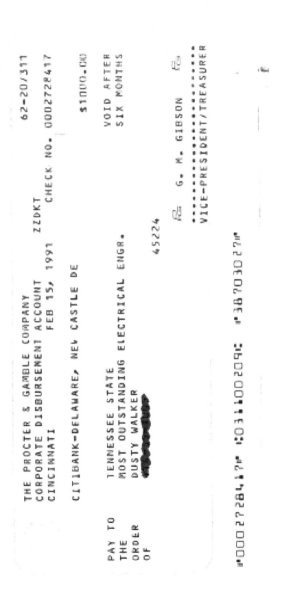

THE PROCTER & GAMBLE COMPANY
CORPORATE DISBURSEMENT ACCOUNT   ZZDKT
CINCINNATI   FEB 15, 1991   CHECK NO. 0002728417

62-20/311

CITIBANK-DELAWARE, NEW CASTLE DE

$1000.00

PAY TO
THE
ORDER
OF

TENNESSEE STATE
MOST OUTSTANDING ELECTRICAL ENGR.
DUSTY WALKER

45224

VOID AFTER
SIX MONTHS

G. M. GIBSON

VICE-PRESIDENT/TREASURER

It pays to be smart.

ENTRANCE EXAM FORMULAS

CALCULUS

1. $a^2 + b^2 = c^2$

2. $d = \sqrt{(x_2 - x_1)^2 + (y_2 - y_1)^2}$

3. $(x-h)^2 + (y-k)^2 = r^2$

4. $(y - y_1) = m(x - x_1)$

5. $(g \circ f(x)) = g(f(x))$

6. $\sin^2 x + \cos^2 x = 1$

7. $0 < |x - c| < \delta \Rightarrow |f(x) - L| < \epsilon$

8. $\lim_{t \to 0} \frac{\sin t}{t} = 1, \quad \lim_{t \to 0} \frac{1 - \cos t}{t} = 0$

9. $\frac{f(b) - f(a)}{b - a} = f'(c)$

10. $\int_a^b f(x) dx = A_{up} - A_{down}$

11. $V = \pi \int_a^b [R(x)]^2 dx$

12. $V = \pi \int_a^b [R(x)]^2 - [r(x)]^2 dx$

13. $V = 2\pi \int_a^b (r) h \, dx$

14. $(\ln x)' = \frac{1}{x} dx$

15. $\lim_{x \to \infty} \ln x = \infty$

16. $(f^{-1})'(y) = \frac{1}{f'(x)}$

17. $D_x e^u = e^u du$

18. $D_x a^x = a^x \ln a \, dx$

19. $\int a^x dx = \frac{1}{\ln a} a^x + C$

20. $D_x \log_a x = \frac{1}{x \ln a}$

21. $\int u \, dv = uv - \int v \, du$

22. $\int u e^u du = (u-1) e^u + C$

23. $\int \ln u \, du = u \ln u - u + C$

24. $\int u^n \ln u \, du = \frac{u^{n+1}}{n+1} \ln u - \frac{u^{n+1}}{(n+1)^2} + C$

6. $\beta = \cos^{-1} \frac{\Delta y}{A}$

7. $\gamma = \cos^{-1} \frac{\Delta z}{A}$

8. $\vec{A} \cdot \vec{B} = AB \cos \theta$

9. $W = \vec{F} \cdot \vec{r}$

10. $\vec{A} \cdot \vec{B} = AB \sin \theta$

11. $a_x = \frac{\Delta v_x}{\Delta t}$

12. $v = v_0 + at$

13. $d = \frac{1}{2}(v + v_0) t$

14. $d = v_0 t + \frac{1}{2} at^2$

15. $v^2 = v_0^2 + 2ad$

16. $t = \frac{2v_0 \sin \theta}{g}$

17. $h = \frac{v_0^2 \sin^2 \theta}{2g}$

18. $R = \frac{v_0^2 \sin 2\theta}{g}$

19. $y = (\tan \theta) x - \frac{g x^2}{2v_0^2 \cos^2 \theta}$

20. $s = r\theta$

21. $v = rw$

22. $a_c = \frac{v^2}{r}$

23. $a_c = r\alpha$

24. $f_k = \mu N$

25. $W = \Delta k$

26. $U = mgh$

27. $P = \frac{W}{t}$

28. $p = mv$

30. $\tau = I\alpha$

1. $1 A^\circ = 10^{-10} m$

2. $\frac{C}{F - 32} = \frac{5}{9}$

3. $E = mc^2$

4. $c = \frac{Q}{m \Delta T}$

5. Heat Loss = Heat Gain

6. $M = \frac{\text{moles solute}}{\text{liter solution}}$

7. $V_1 \times M_1 = V_2 \times M_2 = \#\text{mole solute}$

8. $S = N - A$

9. 1 atm = 760 mm Hg = 760 torr

10. 1 atm = 1.013×10^5 Pa

11. $P_1 V_1 = P_2 V_2$

12. $\frac{V_1}{T_1} = \frac{V_2}{T_2}$

13. $\frac{P_1 V_1}{T_1} = \frac{P_2 V_2}{T_2}$

14. At STP, $V = 22.4 L/\text{mole}$

15. $R = 0.0821 \frac{L \cdot \text{atm}}{\text{mol} \cdot K} = \frac{8.314 J}{\text{mol} \cdot K}$

16. $(m) = \frac{\text{moles solute}}{\text{kg solvent}}$

H = 1	F = 19	K = 39.1
He = 4	Na = 23	C = 40
Li = 6.94	Mg = 24.3	
Be = 9.01	Al = 27	
B = 10.8	Si = 28.1	
C = 12	P = 31	
N = 14	S = 32.1	
O = 16	Cl = 35.5	

PHYSICS

1. $F = m \cdot a$

2. $\rho = \frac{m}{V}$

3. $m = \frac{\text{g} \times M}{N_A}$

4. $N_A = 6.023 \times 10^{23}$

5. $\alpha = \cos^{-1} \frac{\Delta x}{A}$

29. $s = r\theta$

30. $\omega = \frac{\theta}{t}$

31. $I = \sum m_i r_i^2$

32. $k = \frac{1}{2} I \omega^2$

33. $\tau = F \cdot d$

My formula study sheet for the TSU engineering entrance examination. Yes, I still have a copy.

JOINT INTELLIGENCE AGENCY SCIENCE SYMPOSIUM
CENTRAL INTELLIGENCE AGENCY
P.O. BOX 9065
MCLEAN, VA 22102-0065

22 October 1990

Dusty R. Walker, Jr.
Watson Hall, Room 125
Nashville, TN 37209-1561

Dear Mr. Walker:

The NSA/CIA Joint Intelligence Agency Science Symposium
Selection Committee is very pleased to inform you that you have
been selected to attend the Symposium on 11-14 November 1990.

It is our desire to acquaint you more fully with the missions,
functions and organizations of our Agencies while placing an
emphasis on the application of your field of study. We look
forward to your participation in this exciting and informative
event.

Enclosed is an overview of the agenda for the Symposium. We
will be contacting you soon with details regarding your
complimentary travel and accommodations. Please be sure to bring
a picture ID with you for identification purposes.

Should circumstances prevent you from attending this
Symposium, please contact either Agency representative by calling
one of the numbers listed below as soon as possible.

I look forward to your participation in this Symposium.

Sincerely,

ROBERT Q. MUNOZ
Hispanic/Asian American Employment Program Manager
Office of Equal Employment Opportunity

Robert Munoz   Ronald Patrick
NSA EEO Office   CIA Office of EEO
(301) 688-6961   (703) 874-4461

Carole Bennett
NSA Office of Recruitment
1-800-255-8415
(301) 859-6444

**Selection Letter from the "Company" when they were making a
concerted effort to recruit more technically talented minorities.**

TENNESSEE STATE UNIVERSITY

Dusty Ryemorsyl Walker

Page 1 of 3

Official Undergraduate Academic Record

Higher Education Institutions:
Tennessee State University   Aug 1989 - Dec 1994

Degrees Awarded:
Bachelor of Science   Dec 16, 1994
  College of Engineering and Technology Cmplt/T: 941
    Major: Electrical Engineering
    Honors: CUM LAUDE
    Cum GPA: 3.277

----------Fall 1989----------

Admitted Program:
  College of Engineering and Technology
  Bachelor of Science
  Major: Electrical Engineering

AERO-151 The Us Airforce Today	B	1.00	3.00	
CHEM-121H Honors Chemistry	A	3.00	12.00	
CHEM-121L General Chemistry Lab	A	1.00	4.00	
ENG -101H Honors English	A	3.00	12.00	
ENGR-110L Freshman Forum	A	1.00	4.00	
ENGR-111A Engr Graphics I	A	2.00	8.00	
MATH-165U Cal & Analy Geom I	A	4.00	16.00	
UCOR-100U Orientation	A	1.00	4.00	

DEAN'S LIST

	AHRS	EHRS	QHRS	QPTS	GPA
Current	16.00	16.00	16.00	63.00	3.938
HE Cum	16.00	16.00	16.00	63.00	3.938

----------Spring 1990----------

ENG -102H Honors English	B	3.00	9.00	
ENGR-100L Engr Development	B	1.00	3.00	
ENGR-112L Computer Graphics	A	2.00	8.00	
MATH-166U Cal & Analy Geom II	B	4.00	12.00	
PE -011U Physical Fitness Activi	A	1.00	4.00	
PHY -221 Gen Physics I	B	3.00	9.00	
PHY -221L Gen Physics I Lab	A	1.00	4.00	

DEAN'S LIST

	AHRS	EHRS	QHRS	QPTS	GPA
Current	15.00	15.00	15.00	49.00	3.267
HE Cum	31.00	31.00	31.00	112.00	3.613

----------NO FURTHER ENTRIES THIS COLUMN----------

----------Summer 1990----------

HEA -151U Personal Hygiene	A	2.00	8.00	
HIST-202U American History	A	3.00	12.00	
PHY -222 Gen Physics II	B	3.00	9.00	
PHY -222L Gen Physics Lab	A	1.00	4.00	

	AHRS	EHRS	QHRS	QPTS	GPA
Current	9.00	9.00	9.00	33.00	3.667
HE Cum	40.00	40.00	40.00	145.00	3.625

----------Fall 1990----------

ENG -211H Honors World Literature	A	3.00	12.00	
ENGR-221 Engr Computer Programng	A	3.00	12.00	
HIST-201H Honors American History	A	3.00	12.00	
MATH-341 Calculus III	A	3.00	12.00	
PHY -223 Gen Physics III	A	3.00	12.00	

DEAN'S LIST

	AHRS	EHRS	QHRS	QPTS	GPA
Current	15.00	15.00	15.00	60.00	4.000
HE Cum	55.00	55.00	55.00	205.00	3.727

----------Spring 1991----------

ENG -212H Honors World Literature	A	3.00	12.00	
ENGR-290 Circuits I	B	3.00	9.00	
ENGR-290L Circuits I Laboratory	A	1.00	4.00	
ENGR-213 Mechanics III	B	4.00	12.00	
MATH-303 Applied Math	A	3.00	12.00	
SPCH-220 Public Speaking	A	3.00	12.00	

DEAN'S LIST

	AHRS	EHRS	QHRS	QPTS	GPA
Current	17.00	17.00	17.00	61.00	3.588
HE Cum	72.00	72.00	72.00	266.00	3.694

----------Fall 1991----------

EE -212 Circuits 11	C	3.00	6.00	
EE -310 Design Of Digit Logic Sy	C	3.00	6.00	
EE -310L Digital Logic Lab	A	1.00	4.00	
ENGR-320 Introduction To Design	B	3.00	9.00	
ENGR-330 Materials Science	A	3.00	12.00	
ENGR-340 Numerical Analysis	B	3.00	9.00	

	AHRS	EHRS	QHRS	QPTS	GPA
Current	16.00	16.00	16.00	46.00	2.875
HE Cum	88.00	88.00	88.00	312.00	3.545

COPY
ISSUED TO STUDENT

Dusty R Walker Jr
Florissant MO

05-07-07

College transcript. Observe spring 1993.

TENNESSEE STATE UNIVERSITY

Dusty Ryehorsyl Walker   Page 2   of 3

Spring 1992

EE -320	Linear Systems	D	(3.00)	
	Repeat (Excluded From GPA and EHRS)			
EE -321	Electromagnetic Theory 1	C	(3.00)	
	Repeat (Excluded From GPA and EHRS)			
EE -331	Electronics I	W	(3.00)	
EE -331L	Electronics I Lab	C	1.00	2.00
EE -341	Energy Conversion	A	3.00	12.00
HP -300H	Honors Jr College	A	3.00	12.00

	AHRS	EHRS	QHRS	QPTS	GPA
Current	16.00	7.00	7.00	26.00	3.714
HE Cum	104.00	95.00	95.00	338.00	3.558

Fall 1992

EE -320	Linear Systems	F	(3.00)	
	Repeat (Excluded From GPA and EHRS)			
EE -331	Electronics I	B	3.00	9.00
EE -491	Senior Seminar I	A	1.00	4.00
ENGR-200	Circuits I	W	(3.00)	
ENGR-225	Transport Phenomena	B	4.00	12.00
HP -400H	Honors Sr College	A	3.00	12.00

	AHRS	EHRS	QHRS	QPTS	GPA
Current	17.00	11.00	11.00	37.00	3.364
HE Cum	121.00	106.00	106.00	375.00	3.538

Spring 1993

EE -320	Linear Systems	D	(3.00)	3.00
	Repeat (Included in GPA)			
EE -321	Electromagnetic Theory 1	C	3.00	6.00
	Repeat (Included in GPA and EHRS)			
EE -342	Power Systems	C	(3.00)	
EE -490	Capstone Design I	W	(1.00)	
HP -410H	Honor Senior Thesis	W	(3.00)	

	AHRS	EHRS	QHRS	QPTS	GPA
Current	13.00	3.00	6.00	9.00	1.500
HE Cum	134.00	109.00	112.00	384.00	3.429
NO FURTHER ENTRIES THIS COLUMN

Fall 1993

EE -320	Linear Systems	C	3.00	6.00
	Repeat (Included in GPA and EHRS)			
EE -332	Electronics II	W	(3.00)	
EE -332L	Electronics II Lab	A	1.00	4.00
EE -415	Digital Vlsi Design/Test	W	(3.00)	
EE -450	Capstone Design I	A	1.00	4.00
ENG -364	Lit-Black Life In Ameri	A	3.00	12.00
ENGR-420L	Engr In Training Lab	B	1.00	3.00

	AHRS	EHRS	QHRS	QPTS	GPA
Current	15.00	9.00	9.00	29.00	3.222
HE Cum	149.00	118.00	121.00	413.00	3.413

Spring 1994

CE -460	Solid Waste Management	C	3.00	6.00
EE -342	Power Systems	A	3.00	12.00
	Repeat (Included in GPA and EHRS)			
EE -350	Communication Systems	B	3.00	9.00
EE -410L	Elec Sys Design Lab	B	1.00	3.00
EE -451	Capstone Design II	W	(1.00)	
HIST-492	Afro American History	A	3.00	12.00

DEAN'S LIST

	AHRS	EHRS	QHRS	QPTS	GPA
Current	14.00	13.00	13.00	42.00	3.231
HE Cum	163.00	131.00	134.00	455.00	3.396

Summer 1994

EE -451	Capstone Design II	A	1.00	4.00

	AHRS	EHRS	QHRS	QPTS	GPA
Current	1.00	1.00	1.00	4.00	4.000
HE Cum	164.00	132.00	135.00	459.00	3.400
NO FURTHER ENTRIES THIS COLUMN

College transcript. Observe spring 1993.

TENNESSEE STATE UNIVERSITY

Dusty Ryemoreyi Walker

```
·······················Fall 1994························
AFAS-201  Intro To Africana Studie   W  (3.00)
EE  -332  Electronics II             D   3.00   3.00
EE  -343  Electric Power Dist.        C   3.00   6.00
EE  -400  Control Systems I           D   3.00   3.00
EE  -400L Control Systems I Lab       C   1.00   2.00
HP  -410H Honor Senior Thesis         A   3.00  12.00
·················································

                AHRS    EHRS    QHRS    QPTS    GPA
Current         16.00   13.00   13.00   26.00   2.000
HE Cum          150.00  145.00  148.00  485.00  3.277

Requirements completed for Bachelor of Science
··········END Of Undergraduate Academic Record··············
```

College transcript. Observe spring 1993.

Metropolitan Nashville Public Schools
Teacher Salary Schedule
2012 - 2013 School Year
(201 Days)

Years Exp	Permit	Bachelors	Masters	Masters +	EDS	Doctorate	Years Exp
0	32,446	40,000	40,882	43,478	44,294	46,136	0
1	33,744	40,000	40,882	43,478	44,614	46,467	1
2	35,042	40,000	40,882	44,317	45,772	47,625	2
3		40,000	41,671	44,979	46,475	48,947	3
4		40,000	42,333	46,302	47,844	50,270	4
5		40,000	43,656	47,625	49,172	51,593	5
6		41,010	44,979	48,947	50,557	52,916	6
7		42,333	46,302	50,270	51,931	54,239	7
8		43,656	47,625	51,593	53,321	55,562	8
9		44,979	48,947	52,916	54,691	56,885	9
10		46,302	50,270	54,239	55,998	58,208	10
11		47,625	51,593	55,562	57,352	59,531	11
12		48,947	52,916	56,885	58,701	60,854	12
13		50,270	54,239	58,208	60,044	62,176	13
14		51,593	55,562	59,531	61,377	63,499	14
15		52,089	56,885	60,854	62,757	64,822	15
16			56,968	62,176	64,080	66,145	16
17				62,259	64,204	67,468	17
18					64,204	67,774	18
19					64,245	67,774	19
25	38,287	52,999	58,290	63,499	65,485	68,791	25

Had to show this. Even though it's three years old, it shows what a joke the pay scale for teachers is. The value of education in America has taken a turn for the worse.

Supporting a Delta Air Lines modification project through my LLC. Dreadlocks, headscarf, and a working knowledge of Boeing wiring practices! A long way from my clean-shaven days in St. Louis.

In the electronics bay of a customer's 757-200.

In the hangar at a Delta Air Lines
maintenance base.

Standing next to the jet intake of a Customer 737-500.
A meat grinder!

At a fundraiser for a Fraternity Brother's non-profit organization (EEOG). I can sport a suit and tie when the occasion calls for it!

CPSIA information can be obtained
at www.ICGtesting.com
Printed in the USA
JSHW031800190222
23006JS00002B/6